The Art of Political Control in China

When and why do people obey political authority when it runs against their own interests to do so? This book is about the channels beyond direct repression through which China's authoritarian state controls protest and implements ambitious policies from sweeping urbanization schemes that have displaced millions to family planning initiatives like the One Child Policy. Daniel C. Mattingly argues that China's remarkable state capacity is not simply a product of coercive institutions such as the secret police or the military. Instead, the state uses local civil society groups as hidden but effective tools of informal control to suppress dissent and implement far-reaching policies. Drawing on evidence from qualitative case studies, experiments, and national surveys, the book challenges the conventional wisdom that a robust civil society strengthens political responsiveness. Surprisingly, it is communities that lack strong civil society groups that find it easiest to act collectively and spontaneously resist the state.

Daniel C. Mattingly is Assistant Professor of Political Science at Yale University. He was previously a post-doctoral fellow at the Center on Democracy, Development, and the Rule of Law at Stanford University.

Cambridge Studies in Comparative Politics

General Editors
Kathleen Thelen   *Massachusetts Institute of Technology*
Erik Wibbels   *Duke University*

Associate Editors
Catherine Boone   *London School of Economics*
Thad Dunning   *University of California, Berkeley*
Anna Grzymala-Busse   *Stanford University*
Torben Iversen   *Harvard University*
Stathis Kalyvas   *University of Oxford*
Margaret Levi   *Stanford University*
Helen Milner   *Princeton University*
Frances Rosenbluth   *Yale University*
Susan Stokes   *University of Chicago*
Tariq Thachil   *Vanderbilt University*

Series Founder
Peter Lange   *Duke University*

Other Books in the Series
Christopher Adolph, *Bankers, Bureaucrats, and Central Bank Politics: The Myth of Neutrality*

Michael Albertus, *Autocracy and Redistribution: The Politics of Land Reform*

Santiago Anria, *When Movements Become Parties: The Bolivian MAS in Comparative Perspective*

Ben W. Ansell, *From the Ballot to the Blackboard: The Redistributive Political Economy of Education*

Ben W. Ansell and David J. Samuels, *Inequality and Democratization: An Elite-Competition Approach*

Adam Michael Auerbach, *Demanding Development: The Politics of Public Goods Provision in India's Urban Slums*

Ana Arjona, *Rebelocracy: Social Order in the Colombian Civil War*

Leonardo R. Arriola, *Multi-Ethnic Coalitions in Africa: Business Financing of Opposition Election Campaigns*

David Austen-Smith, Jeffry A. Frieden, Miriam A. Golden, Karl Ove Moene, and Adam Przeworski, eds., *Selected Works of Michael Wallerstein: The Political Economy of Inequality, Unions, and Social Democracy*

S. Erdem Aytaç and Susan C. Stokes *Why Bother? Rethinking Participation in Elections and Protests*

Andy Baker, *The Market and the Masses in Latin America: Policy Reform and Consumption in Liberalizing Economies*

Continued after the Index

The Art of Political Control in China

DANIEL C. MATTINGLY

Yale University

CAMBRIDGE
UNIVERSITY PRESS

CAMBRIDGE
UNIVERSITY PRESS

University Printing House, Cambridge CB2 8BS, United Kingdom

One Liberty Plaza, 20th Floor, New York, NY 10006, USA

477 Williamstown Road, Port Melbourne, VIC 3207, Australia

314–321, 3rd Floor, Plot 3, Splendor Forum, Jasola District Centre, New Delhi – 110025, India

79 Anson Road, #06–04/06, Singapore 079906

Cambridge University Press is part of the University of Cambridge.

It furthers the University's mission by disseminating knowledge in the pursuit of education, learning, and research at the highest international levels of excellence.

www.cambridge.org
Information on this title: www.cambridge.org/9781108485937
DOI: 10.1017/9781108662536

© Cambridge University Press 2020

First published 2020

A catalogue record for this publication is available from the British Library.

ISBN 978-1-108-48593-7 Hardback
ISBN 978-1-108-72536-1 Paperback

For my parents, Kevin and Kristi Mattingly

Contents

Figures

Tables

Acknowledgments

I could not have written this book without a great deal of help from colleagues, mentors, friends, family, and others – especially the people who generously consented to be interviewed for this project. Of course, I alone am responsible for the conclusions I draw.

The book started as a dissertation at the University of California, Berkeley. Kevin O'Brien chaired my committee and offered fantastically helpful advice on the project from its very start. Ruth Berins Collier, Peter Lorentzen, and Noam Yuchtman spent countless hours helping me hone and refine my arguments, gently correcting my worst mistakes, and providing encouragement and support. I owe all four of these remarkable scholars an enormous debt.

In China, I benefited from the institutional support of Sun Yat-Sen University and the advice and help of scholars including Ellen David Friedman, He Gaochao, He Shenjing, Mary Ann O'Donnell, Peter Sack, Tong Zhihui, Wu Hexian, and others. Many thanks to Huang Jialing, Huang Guanqi, Liang Bingyu, Tang Ding, Tang Xianteng, Wang Kun, Yuan Wanying, and Zhang Yong for helping me implement the survey on the ground and for providing valuable feedback on its design. Chu Xingtang and Liao Jiaxu provided superb research assistance and translated interviews from Cantonese. Thanks also to Baiyue Cao, Karina Wu, Winky Wu, Sophia (Er) Xu, and Yiwen Zhang for their excellent work through the Undergraduate Research Apprenticeship Program at Berkeley and to Josh Hochman, Liren Ma, and Kiki Zhao for research assistance at Yale. I am especially grateful to two local activists who must remain anonymous and whose help was instrumental in the project.

A postdoctoral fellowship at the Center on Democracy, Development, and Rule of Law at Stanford University provided me with a year with no other obligation than to write. Thanks to Francis Fukuyama and Stephen Stedman for sponsoring my stay in Palo Alto and for funding a book workshop. Timothy Frye, Shelby Grossman, Anna Grzymala-Busse, Edmund Malesky, Jean Oi, Ben Read, and Tongtong Zhang were generous enough to participate in the book workshop and provide helpful comments that have greatly strengthened the manuscript.

I am also grateful for support from the Department of Political Science at Yale and the many people in the department who have helped me navigate the start to my career. Special thanks to Kate Baldwin, Deborah Davis, Isabela Mares, Elizabeth Nugent, Frances Rosenbluth, James C. Scott, Susan Stokes, and Milan Svolik for reading drafts of chapters and providing extremely useful feedback on them.

I am grateful for comments and discussions with Leonardo Arriola, Lisa Blaydes, Margaret Boittin, Catherine Boone, Meina Cai, Julia Chuang, Danny Choi, Jennifer Choo, David Collier, Dan Corstange, Larry Diamond, Martin Dimitrov, Iza Ding, Greg Distelhorst, Thad Dunning, Laurel Eckhouse, Peter Evans, Miguel de Figueiredo, Natalia Forrat, Diana Fu, Mary Gallagher, Alisha Holland, Lauren Honig, Jean Hong, Yue Hou, Haifeng Huang, Kimuli Kasara, Herbert Kitschelt, James Kung, Didi Kuo, Hanzhang Liu, Kristen Looney, Xiaobo Lü, Melanie Manion, Reo Matsuzaki, Lucas Novaes, Lynette Ong, Brian Palmer-Rubin, Jennifer Pan, Elizabeth Perry, Mathias Poertner, Alison Post, Carlo Prato, Sungmin Rho, Meg Rithmire, Molly Roberts, Ken Scheve, Paul Schuler, Suzanne Scoggins, Dorothy Solinger, Weiyi Shi, Victor Shih, Graeme Smith, Stephen Stedman, Ed Steinfeld, Xin Sun, Yeling Tan, Rory Truex, Lily Tsai, Guadalupe Tuñón, Denise van der Kamp, Steve Vogel, Jeremy Wallace, Yuhua Wang, Lynn White, Susan Whiting, Erik Wibbels, Yu Xie, Yiqing Xu, Qixuan Yang, John Yasuda, Lauren Young, Amy Zhang, and Dong Zhang. Apologies to anyone accidentally left off this list!

The project was funded by a grant from the National Science Foundation (SES-1228510); by a National Science Foundation Graduate Research Fellowship; by funds from the MacMillan Center for International and Area Studies at Yale; by the Council on East Asian Studies at Yale; by the Center on Democracy, Development, and Rule of Law at Stanford; by the Center for Chinese Studies at Berkeley; and by the Institute for International Studies at Berkeley. I presented various versions of this project to audiences at Brown, Columbia, Duke, Harvard,

The Hong Kong University of Science and Technology, Penn, Princeton, Stanford, UCSD, and Zhejiang University, all of which helped sharpen my arguments. Kelley Friel provided excellent edits to the manuscript's prose and Katherine Kieva was an equally superb indexer. Portions of Chapters 3, 5, and 7 originally appeared as articles in *World Politics* and *Comparative Politics*. I thank the editors for allowing me to include excerpts from those articles here.

Special thanks to Sara Doskow for supporting and guiding the project at Cambridge; to Ursula Acton, Joshua Penney, and Sunantha Ramamoorthy for expertly shepherding the book through copy-editing and production; and to three anonymous readers for exceptionally helpful and constructive comments. I am also very grateful to Katheleen Thelen and Erik Wibbels for including the book in the Cambridge Studies in Comparative Politics Series.

I owe my greatest debt to my family. Thanks to my brother Ben sister-in-law Kelsey, and mother-in-law Yvonne for support. My wife Ming Thompson has patiently supported the writing of this book, including moving across the country (twice). She has been the best partner I could ask for through a number of happy adventures. Happiest of all has been raising our son Henry. The finishing of this book has been marked by a sadder chapter in our shared life: the loss of two immediate family members. The book is written in loving memory of Michael Campbell Thompson and Ada Thompson Mattingly.

I would not be writing this book without my parents, Kristi and Kevin Mattingly, who inspired me to learn and gave me a life full of love, humor, and fun. It's not an accident that I have followed them into a career as a teacher. This book is dedicated to them.

I

Introduction

In framing a government ... the great difficulty lies in this: you must first enable the government to control the governed; and in the next place oblige it to control itself.

James Madison, 1788

How can a government be made all-powerful? Once the government is all-powerful, how can it be made responsive to the will of the people?

Sun Yat-Sen, 1924

Governance is a problem of political control. For governments, the problem is how to control society: how to maintain order, enforce laws, collect revenue, and implement policy. For citizens, the problem is how to control their governments: how to ensure that political leaders respond to their demands and are held accountable if they do not.

This problem of political control is especially severe in autocracies like China, where the state reaches further into people's everyday lives and where citizens have fewer avenues for holding officials accountable than in most democracies. Consider, for example, the relationship between the Chinese state and a woman named Qingmei, a cheerful, energetic local rights activist in her fifties who I met in Sichuan Province.[1] The state has intervened in Qingmei's life in ways that are typical for many of the half billion people who live in rural China. When it comes to Qingmei's personal life, the state has demanded control over her reproductive choices. She is one of the hundreds of millions of women in China who have been prohibited from having a second or third child under the state's family

---

[1] The names of individuals have been changed to protect the anonymity of interviewees. Please see the Appendix for an explanation of the qualitative methodology.

planning policies. She would have liked to have had one more child, but after the birth of her first, village officials monitored her closely to make sure she did not. When it comes to Qingmei's economic life, the state has demanded control over her most valuable material asset, her land. She is one of the approximately 100 million people in China who have had their property confiscated by a local government, in her case, for no compensation. She tried petitioning the local government to return her land or pay her for it, but this failed. Finally, when it comes to Qingmei's public life, the state has demanded her political loyalty. She is a patriot and proud of China's rise, but she is also one of thousands who have been detained for protesting against local officials in an attempt to hold them accountable. For Qingmei, the dilemma of political control posed by James Madison and Sun Yat-Sen is not just abstract but deeply personal.

How do authoritarian regimes prevent protest and implement ambitious policies that intervene in citizen's everyday lives? How do autocrats control society and strengthen state capacity? How, in turn, can citizens control the state? How can citizens in non-democracies – about 40 percent of the world's population – find ways to hold their political leaders accountable?

The conventional wisdom is that a strong civil society strengthens citizen control over their governments, even in autocracies. The idea has its roots in Alexis de Tocqueville's observation that civic and religious organizations in the United States create "habits of the heart" that help maintain democratic institutions. The idea that a strong civil society strengthens government responsiveness has since been applied to a wide range of contexts. In democracies like Italy, Robert Putnam argues, civic organizations from sports clubs to bird-watching societies create "social capital," or bonds of trust, that make it easier for citizens to work together and hold officials accountable.[2] In autocracies like Poland in the 1980s or Egypt in the 2010s, groups such as unions and mosques are credited with helping citizens organize against the regime and topple dictators.[3] Even in China, where most social organizations are tightly controlled, the work of influential academics argues that grassroots groups such as lineage associations or temple groups "give

---

[2] Putnam (1994, 2000).
[3] On Poland and the Solidarity trade union movement, see, among others, Havel (1978) and Huntington (1993). On the role of mosques and other civil society organizations during the Egyptian uprisings of 2011, see Lynch (2011, p. 303) and Nugent and Berman (2017, p. 69–77).

citizens leverage over officials and a voice in the political decision-making process."[4]

My central argument in this book, by contrast, is that in autocratic states, civil society groups can give officials leverage over citizens and strengthen the state's coercive capacity. I show how local leaders in rural China cultivate and co-opt social groups such as temple organizations, lineage associations, and social clubs. As others have noted, these grassroots social groups have a beneficial side: they create bonds of trust that encourage group members to contribute to public goods like roads, schools, and charities. At the same time, however, these groups also increase the prestige and moral authority of political elites in ways that they find useful for ensuring political compliance. My core finding of this book is that the presence of civil society groups helps officials in rural China tamp down on protest, requisition land, and enforce mandatory birth quotas. In short, local civil society groups in China help strengthen state capacity and serve as hidden tools of *informal control.*[5]

A strong civil society bolsters authoritarian control not just in China but across the world. In the following pages, I show how social organizations as diverse as "Civic Circles" in Viktor Orbán's Hungary, neighborhood collectives in Nicolás Maduro's Venezuela, the Orthodox Church in Vladimir Putin's Russia, labor unions in Brazil, and even churches in one-party enclaves in the United States have all empowered autocrats and strengthened state control over society. A rich literature shows how autocracies control society through repressive institutions like the secret police, the ruling party, or the military.[6] I argue that everyday political control in autocracies relies not only on these overtly coercive institutions, but on using civil society to apply hidden forms of coercion on citizens.

---

4 Tsai (2007a, p. 16). See also Madsen (1984), Chau (2008), Padró i Miquel et al. (2015), and Xu and Yao (2015), among others, on the positive effects of lineage and temple organizations on public goods provision, governance, and social cohesion in rural China.

5 This book builds on work by Berman (1997), Jamal (2009), and Satyanath et al. (2017), who examine the link between civil society groups and support for autocratic regimes and parties. By contrast, I focus on how civil society groups can strengthen the state's coercive capacity, demobilize protest, and increase compliance. This echoes findings by Chen (2017), Ong (2018), and Matsuzaki (2019a,b), on how states use third parties and social actors for state-building.

6 On formal institutions of repression in autocracies see, among many others, Tilly (2003); Davenport (2007a); Slater (2010); Svolik (2012); Greitens (2016); Fu (2017b); Hassan (2017); Blaydes (2018); Gallagher and Miller (2018); Roberts (2018); Truex (2018).

Surprisingly, it is communities that *lack* strong civil society groups that find it easiest to act collectively and resist autocratic control. The message of this book is a hopeful one for those who might wish to fight for the weak and powerless. In a high-capacity autocratic regime, it is the seemingly disconnected and disorganized groups who tend to be most successful at organizing and ensuring the state responds to their demands.[7]

1.1 MAKING AUTOCRACY WORK

Autocrats throughout the world use grassroots social groups for building and sustaining authoritarianism. For example, when Viktor Orbán suffered defeat in the 2002 Hungarian elections, he turned to creating a movement based on building local civic organizations. "I ask you," he said in a defiant speech soon after his loss, "to form small groups of people, troupes of friends, civic circles."[8] Orbán's call to action led to the creation of a reported 16,000 organizations spread throughout Hungary that helped organize tens of thousands of events from demonstrations to concerts.[9] These "Civic Circles" helped catapult Orbán into the Prime Minister's office, where he has created an increasingly autocratic Hungarian state. In office, Orbán has ruthlessly shuttered groups that oppose him while cultivating a highly illiberal form of civil society dedicated to helping him sustain his rule.[10]

Vladimir Putin's embrace and seeming co-optation of the Russian Orthodox Church suggests another way in which non-state groups can nourish help autocrats maintain order. Putin has sought to closely identify himself with the Orthodox Church and its traditions. For instance, he makes highly publicized visits to the church on holidays like Easter and Christmas. He has even invited television cameras to follow him while he took a dip (bare-chested) into a freezing lake in January to mark the feast day of Epiphany.[11] Co-opting the church poses some risks, since Putin is

---

[7] These findings echo important work by Fu (2017a,b,c), who describes tactics used by labor activists and the way that state repression works. However, the ways in which seemingly leaderless *collective* action emerges organically in rural China are quite different, from the coached but *individual* action that Fu describes. The findings also build on work by Heurlin (2016), who shows how protests influenced policy-making at the national level. I show how, at the local level, protests can be used to hold officials accountable and prevent unwanted land takings.

[8] Greskovits (2017, p. 2).

[9] Greskovits and Wittenberg (2013, p. 22).

[10] Kingsley (2018).

[11] Henley (2018).

not always able to control what church leaders do and say, but it also seems to strengthen Putin's moral authority among the devout. As one analyst put it, Putin has a "utilitarian view of the church as a conduit of the Kremlin tasked with maintaining 'stability and unity'."[12]

Hugo Chávez and his successor, Nicolás Maduro, pursued a different strategy to consolidate their control over politics in Venezuela. Instead of building Civic Circles or co-opting church leaders, they have nurtured infiltrating organizations called *colectivos*, or neighborhood collectives, that are spread throughout the country. The members of these collectives are civilians and nominally independent of the state, but they are often armed and use violence to advance the interests of the ruling party. They rally votes for the government during elections and intimidate – and even kill – anti-government protesters.[13] Despite the brutality of these infiltrating organizations, some Venezuelans have come to accept them as an informal extension of the state. As one government supporter told a journalist: "They put order where there is disorder. It's true, they are armed civilians, but what can you do in this upside-down world of ours?"[14]

What do "Civic Circles" in Hungary, the Orthodox Church in Russia, and collectives in Venezuela have in common? They all, I argue, fall under a broad definition of *civil society*. I use the term civil society to refer to groups that are distinct from nuclear families, firms, or the state; that are bound together because of a common affinity, interest, or identity; and that are voluntary in their degree of participation. This definition encompasses a diverse array of groups, including voluntary organizations like singing groups, community orchestras, and unions, but also groups such as religious organizations, extended kinship associations, and neighborhood collectives.

This encompassing definition of civil society has a long history. It has its origins in Hegel's idea that civil society is the arena that "intervenes between the family and the state."[15] In the years since, the term has been hotly contested, but in political science it is "most commonly defined as a set of organizations that operate between the state, the family," and firms.[16] For instance, Juan Linz and Alfred Stepan describe civil society as "self-organizing movements, groups, and individuals" – a category

---

[12] Pertsev (2017).
[13] Corrales (2015); Frye et al. (2017); Corrales and Hidalgo (2017).
[14] Torres and Casey (2017).
[15] Hegel (1991, p. 220).
[16] Kopecký and Mudde (2003, p. 5).

including social actors as diverse as neighborhood associations, religions, unions, and women's groups.[17]

Civil society groups are often thought to strengthen a community's *social capital,* or the "trust, norms, and networks," that can strengthen collective action.[18] For instance, the bonds of fellowship and reciprocity created by a farmers' association might encourage neighbors to help each other during a barn raising. Robert Putnam credits a strong civil society and the social capital it creates with "making democracy work."

Some readers will be quick to note that my definition of civil society is broader than some others. Putnam, for example, argues for a distinction between civic groups characterized by "horizontal bonds of fellowship," such as social clubs, and groups with "vertical bonds of authority" such as clans.[19] Putting social organizations with vertical and horizontal ties in the same category has the analytical advantage of showing how these groups operate in broadly similar ways, especially in autocracies. Other definitions of civil society restrict the term to groups that are fully autonomous from the state or that are democratic in character. Yet assuming that civil society groups have these qualities can lead to circular reasoning about the relationship between civil society and democratic governance.[20]

An important caveat is that, in the following pages, I do *not* examine some kinds of nongovernmental organizations (NGOs) such as legal aid, charities, or workers' rights organizations. In general, officially registered NGOs in China are tightly controlled and pose little direct challenge to state authority, but they can sometimes help citizens provide input into the policy-making process.[21] NGOs often cooperate with the government and in doing so can help the state learn about and correct policy failures, or mobilize volunteers in moments of national crisis such as the 2008 Sichuan earthquake.[22] Underground NGOs often do courageous work

---

[17] Linz and Stepan (1996, p. 7). See also Stepan (1978); Migdal (1988); Acemoglu and Robinson (2017).

[18] Putnam (1994, pp. 167). Political scientists often conceive of a community's social capital as the density of civic and community organizations, though individuals can have social capital as well. The literature on social capital in sociology largely focuses on individual social capital. See Portes (1998).

[19] Putnam (1994, pp. 107; 175–176). For an overview and critique of Putnam, see Portes (1998).

[20] Kopecký and Mudde (2003).

[21] See Mertha (2008) on local NGOs and activism on large infrastructure projects like dams and Pearson (1994, 2000) and Kennedy (2009) on business associations.

[22] Teets (2014); Xu (2017).

providing legal aid and other advice for the most vulnerable, although they do so from a precarious position in which they must often disguise the work they do.[23]

Instead, the sorts of civil society groups that I focus on in this book largely belong to what Mary Gallagher has called "unofficial civil society." Gallagher defines unofficial civil society in China as "groups with common interests or attributes that remain outside the sphere of state-sanctioned organizations either because the state refuses to recognize them or because these groups themselves studiously avoid organization in order to maintain their autonomy and independence from the state."[24] Examples of unofficial civil society groups in rural China include folk religious organizations, underground churches, clubs that promote traditional Chinese dance or music, and lineage associations. The fact that unofficial civil society is not formally sanctioned and controlled by the state makes it a potential resource for citizens, and arguably the most likely place to find non-state groups that are capable of holding local officials accountable.

Recent work has argued that civil society groups in China *can* be used to apply pressure on local officials – and in doing so strengthen the supply of important public goods like roads, schools, and water. Civil society groups such as lineage and temple associations are important in rural society because they create *informal institutions* (or informal rules and norms) that obligate fellow members of the group to help each other.[25] When officials belong to these groups, the informal norms and obligations these groups create can motivate officials to respond to citizen demands. A range of work now shows that the presence of civil society groups in China is associated with more public investment and better public goods.[26] These findings complement scholarship on democracies, such as Putnam's work on Italy, which shows a link between robust civic groups and improved public service delivery.[27]

Yet what if we broaden our scope to consider more than public goods? What if we also examine state control and more coercive attempts to

---

[23] Fu (2017a,c).
[24] Gallagher (2004, p. 420).
[25] See Tsai (2007a). Helmke and Levitsky (2004, p. 727) define informal institutions as "socially shared rules, usually unwritten, that are created, communicated, and enforced outside of officially sanctioned channels."
[26] Tsai (2002, 2007a,b); Xu and Yao (2015); Padró i Miquel et al. (2015).
[27] Putnam (1994).

extract wealth or implement policy? Does civil society still look like it improves the welfare of the rural poor and other vulnerable groups?

1.2 THE OUTCOME: POLITICAL CONTROL

One way to understand governance is to examine what the state provides to citizens. Most governments are tasked with supplying the public with basic goods and services such as roads, schools, water, and electricity. Many studies of civil society focus on whether governments are responsive to citizen demands for better public goods, services, and welfare.[28] A focus on public goods also drives our understanding of distributional politics in autocracies. But providing public goods and welfare is just one aspect of what governments do.

This book examines what happens on the other side of the governance "ledger."[29] In order to function, states need to maintain order, collect revenue, enforce laws, and implement policies. Autocratic states must also limit dissent and public protest. Focusing on state-building illuminates a different dimension of governance that studies of public goods may overlook. This ability to control society can also be thought of as the state's coercive capacity, or the "ability to penetrate society and implement logistically political decisions throughout the realm."[30] Throughout this book, I use the terms state capacity and political control to refer to the power of the state to impose order and implement policy.

State capacity is widely recognized as being central to governance. Half a century ago, Samuel Huntington noted that "the most important political distinction among countries concerns not their form of government but their degree of government."[31] Yet while state capacity differs greatly between countries, the wide variation in state capacity *within* states is perhaps even more striking. As pioneering work by Catherine Boone shows, state capacity and control varies widely from community to community within the same country.[32] In China, for example, the amount of taxes the state collects per capita can vary

---

[28] Putnam (1994); Tsai (2007a); Xu and Yao (2015); Padró i Miquel et al. (2015).
[29] Classic work on state capacity and state-building in political science includes Huntington (1968); Migdal (1988); Levi (1989); Tilly (1990); Herbst (2000); Boone (2003).
[30] See Mann (2012, p. 13). Mann calls this the "infrastructural power of the state."
[31] Huntington (1968).
[32] Boone (2003).

by an order of magnitude from one county to the next.[33] How can areas of the same country, with the same national political system and similar levels of development, vary so widely in degrees of state control?

I examine the Chinese state's coercive capacity through the lens of the regime's top three policy priorities in rural areas.[34] The implementation of these policies differs substantially throughout the country.

First, I examine how the state requisitions land from farmers, which has in recent years been the main form of de facto taxation in rural China. As I show later in the book, the state may requisition large amounts of land in one village, while residents of a neighboring village with the same level of development may successfully resist plans to confiscate land. In China, land requisitions have effectively redistributed trillions of dollars of property from rural collectives to the state, in one of the larger transfers of wealth in recent history.[35]

Second, I examine how the state controls family planning and implements the so-called One Child Policy, which defined the relationship between the Chinese state and families for decades. Again, the state's ability to successfully enforce birth quotas varies substantially, even between villages with otherwise identical political institutions and levels of development.

Finally, I examine how the state controls and limits protest, which once again varies from village to village. As in most autocratic regimes, controlling protest is a top priority for the Communist Party.

The stakes for people on the ground could scarcely be higher. For the rural poor, land is often their most productive and valuable asset. Likewise, family planning choices have profound implications for their personal lives and freedom. And citizens' ability to participate in politics and press their demands against the state fundamentally shapes how the state distributes important resources from land to water to education.

---

[33] Lü and Landry (2014, p. 707).

[34] See Birney (2014, p. 56) and Wang (2014, pp. 24–25).

[35] This book contributes to an important literature on property rights. See Frye (2000, 2004, 2017); Whiting (2006); Boone (2013); Ong (2014); Albertus (2015); Markus (2015); Grossman (2019); Gans-Morse (2017); Hou (2019). It also builds on a growing literature that examines land rights in China, including books by Hsing (2010), Rithmire (2015), and Heurlin (2016).

1.3 EXISTING EXPLANATIONS FOR POLITICAL CONTROL

Scholarship on authoritarian repression and control often focuses on how states build and deploy *formal* coercive institutions such as the secret police, the military, courts, internet censorship bureaucracies, and other overtly repressive institutions.[36] If these institutions are strong and effective, states do not need to be perfect or omniscient in order to encourage compliance. If people believe there is a sufficient chance that their disobedience will be noticed and punished, they will be intimidated into obeying.

Without a doubt, overt coercion and repression are important ingredients of political control in China, especially for groups the regime views as an immediate threat, such as rights activists and ethnic minorities. Rights activists face police harassment, imprisonment, and, in some cases, torture and death. Ethnic minorities on the periphery also face systematic and sometimes brutal repression. In the western province of Xinjiang, the state has reportedly imprisoned over a million people of the Uyghur ethnic minority in concentration camps, where they are coerced into assimilating into the majority Han culture.[37] The state has also shuttered mosques, and devout Muslims face harassment from security forces.

Yet theories of repression can only partly explain how the Chinese state controls society, since relying on violence and coercion is costly and likely to make the regime unpopular. As Hannah Arendt observed, "where force is used, authority itself has failed."[38] What else motivates people in China to comply with policies that intrude heavily into their personal, political, and economic lives?

A second set of theories stress the importance of *regime legitimacy* for controlling society. Juan Linz describes regime legitimacy as "the belief that in spite of shortcomings and failures, the political institutions are better than others that might be established and therefore can

---

[36] See, among many others, work by Tilly (2003); Davenport (2007a); Slater (2010); Albertus and Menaldo (2012); Svolik (2012); Greitens (2016); Ritter and Conrad (2016); Fu (2017c); Hassan (2017); Han (2018); Gallagher and Miller (2018); Roberts (2018); Truex (2018).

[37] See Cumming-Bruce (2018) and Kuo (2018) on reports by United Nations and United Kingdom officials. See also the text of the "Uyghur Human Rights Policy Act of 2018" introduced in the United States Senate. www.congress.gov/bill/115th-congress/senate-bill/3622/text.

[38] Arendt (1961, p. 93). See also Gramsci (1971).

demand obedience."[39] In democracies, belief in the democratic process can strengthen regime legitimacy, and encourage compliance.[40] In China, many argue that the regime's spectacular record of economic growth has created "performance legitimacy" that ensures widespread political compliance, even with ambitious policies like the One Child Policy.[41]

However, theories of performance legitimacy cannot fully explain why people comply with the state in rural China. National economic performance cannot explain *local* variation in protest or in compliance with mandates like the One Child Policy. And, as later chapters in the book show, compliance with the state is not strongly correlated with the level of local economic growth.[42] In rural China, what underlies the state's coercive capacity, or its ability to control society?

1.4 A THEORY OF POLITICAL CONTROL

Most people comply even in the absence of overt threats of coercion, and even in places where the state's legitimacy is relatively weak. Why?

The answer to this puzzle becomes clearer when we turn to *informal* institutions and organizations that are not officially sanctioned by the state. Civil society, broadly conceived, can serve as a hidden mechanism of political control that can strengthen the state's coercive capacity. The definition of informal control I propose is straightforward: informal control occurs when local officials exploit the social bonds created by strong civil society groups to collect information on individual behavior and to apply social pressure on individuals to comply with the state.

I argue that states exert informal control using three main strategies: cultivating civil society, co-opting local elites, and creating infiltrating institutions. These strategies are especially likely to be used in a context like China, where a strong ruling party dominates the state and seeks to infiltrate and control society in far-reaching ways.[43] Examples drawn

---

[39] Linz (1996, p. 16).

[40] Tyler (2006). See also work by Lieberman (2003) and Singh (2015) on how inclusive identities can encourage solidarity and increase state capacity and performance.

[41] Zhao (2009). See also Perry (2002) on political legitimacy and the Mandate of Heaven. In practice, political regimes combine overt coercion with attempts to legitimate their rule. Levi (1989) shows how a mix of political legitimacy and coercion can encourage what she calls "quasi-voluntary" compliance with taxation and other policies.

[42] This is not evidence that the performance legitimacy theory is wrong, but it does call into question the theory's ability to explain local variation.

[43] In this book, I refer to the Chinese "state" rather than "Party-state." The Chinese "state" refers to both the CCP and to governmental organs.

from contexts ranging from Latin America to Europe suggest the theory may have wider applicability. In the following pages, I describe each of these mechanisms of informal control and their shortcomings, and then discuss how the state strategically deploys them.

1.4.1 Cultivating Civil Society

The first strategy of informal control available to local officials (discussed in Chapter 4) is cultivating local civil society. In rural China, cultivating civil society might mean that local officials tacitly approve the re-establishment of a lineage association, encourage the rebuilding of a temple, or help establish a traditional singing group. Elsewhere, this might include attempts to strengthen social institutions like churches, social clubs, and unions, or to create networks of grassroots social organizations, like Orbán's Civic Circles.

Cultivating civil society has two major benefits. First, these groups help make society more "legible" to the state.[44] The presence of these groups makes it easier to collect information about citizens who belong to these groups, and track their behavior and attitudes.

Second, it can increase a political leader's social standing and informal authority. For example, in rural China a village cadre might donate to the reconstruction of an ancestral hall, participate in ritual activities like tomb sweeping during Qingming, or contribute to the preparation of a group feast during the Lantern Festival. Or they might help organize a temple festival or donate to the renovation of a temple.

Officials can use the informal authority gained from cultivating non-state groups when they want to enforce costly policies. For example, if an official wants to requisition land, they can use their personal informal authority to dissuade people from protesting and persuade them that it is in their interest to accept the requisition plan. Chapter 4 presents qualitative and quantitative data demonstrating that the presence of temple and lineage associations in villages leads to more land requisitions and fewer protests.

In China, the CCP controls the government through parallel party institutions that are generally more powerful than their government counterparts. For instance, the CCP Secretary of a province has more *de facto* power than the provincial governor.

However, the Chinese "state" reaches beyond formal government and CCP bodies. It includes nominally autonomous village committees and sub-village small groups. Although these bodies are autonomous on paper, they are effectively controlled by the CCP.

[44] Scott (1998).

In order for the state to exploit norms promoted by civil society to encourage political compliance, those norms must align with state policies. Yet this is not always the case. For example, China's mandatory family planning policies conflict with the norms of ancestry promoted by the lineage groups. It is therefore difficult to use lineage organizations to promote family planning policies, particularly if there are group elites outside the state, such as clan heads, who may have incentives to encourage their group to resist the policy. Similarly, church leaders in other countries sometimes campaign against state family planning policies that encourage the use of contraception.

1.4.2 Co-optation

A second strategy of informal control (discussed in Chapter 5) is the *co-optation* of influential civil society elites. This strategy can be used where civil society is already strong. Examples include authoritarian regimes co-opting religious leaders in Southeast Asia; colonial powers ruling indirectly through traditional chiefs in sub-Saharan Africa; corporatist state–union relationships in Latin America; and the Russian state's relationship with the leaders of the Russian Orthodox Church.[45] In China, the CCP co-opts local elites by including them in political bodies including village committees, the Chinese People's Political Consultative Conference, local People's Congresses, and the party itself.

In rural China, communal elites hold important informal authority that derives from their position within traditional social hierarchies, like those created by extended lineage groups, which encourage deference to group elders. They may also accumulate moral authority through acts that benefit the group such as collecting funds for charity, helping group members find jobs, resolving disputes, and performing ritual roles in weddings, funerals, and holidays. Local officials and social elites such as lineage heads have served as key local brokers for China's national leaders since at least the Han Dynasty.[46]

Much like the strategy of cultivation, the strategy of co-optation increases the ability of the state to apply social pressure to individuals. Communal elites can help local officials understand which citizens

---

[45] Putin has included church leaders including the Patriarch in honorary orders and councils. Material from Soviet archives allegedly suggests that the current leader of the Orthodox church is a former KGB agent. However, the Russian government disputes the authenticity of the documents. See Meek (1999); Satter (2009).

[46] See Brown and Xie (2015) on brokers in the Han and Duara (1988) and Perry (1980) on the role of similar brokers in the Qing.

have grievances and are the most likely to mobilize. However, the main mechanism by which co-opted elites strengthen state control is by using their informal authority to apply direct social pressure on individuals to comply.

Other autocratic regimes have similarly relied on the co-optation of communal elites to strengthen their control over society. For example, Dan Slater notes that authoritarian states in Southeast Asia rely on communal elites – "a society's leading possessors of nationalist and religious authority,"[47] – who "[grant] authoritarian regimes a critical imprimatur of symbolic legitimacy, [mobilize] followers to help suppress regime opponents, and [allow] state institutions to insinuate themselves into doctrinal practices."[48]

What incentives do civil society elites have to help enforce laws that may harm the interests of their group? Once they join formal state institutions, they have bureaucratic incentives to do so. Pay for village cadres in China, for example, is often tied to enforcement of policies like family planning quotas. However, given their meager salaries, these bureaucratic incentives are likely to be weak. Community leaders may be more strongly motivated by rent-seeking incentives to cooperate with policies that extract and redistribute wealth. For instance, when land is requisitioned in rural China, village cadres can skim money off the top of compensation funds, receive kickbacks from land developers, and sometimes even gain ownership stakes in projects built on village land. These one-shot gains provide incentives for them to defect from the group.

A drawback for local officials pursuing this strategy is that including civil society elites in local political institutions may also lead to elite capture and erode the legitimacy of the state over the long term. For example, I document a number of cases in which lineage elites take office, help expropriate land, and abscond with the benefits. Not surprisingly, this can erode popular satisfaction with the local government and can, in the long run, lead to increases in political protest.

1.4.3   Infiltration

A third strategy of informal control available to local officials (discussed in Chapter 6) is *infiltrating* local civil society. This strategy is used where

---

[47] Slater (2009, p. 209).
[48] Slater (2010, p.16). This strategy is analogous to colonial-era practices of indirect rule. See, among others, Posner (2005); Lee et al. (2012).

building other types of civil society organizations (and co-opting local elites) is impractical. This strategy involves local officials setting up networks of street-level agents who spy, snitch, coax, cajole, pressure, and persuade others on behalf of the regime. Autocratic regimes across a wide variety of contexts create nominally autonomous grassroots organizations that help the state infiltrate local society. For example, the Cuban Communist Party has long used neighborhood organizations called Committees for the Defense of the Revolution (CDRs) to surveil residents and enforce the law.[49] Similarly, in Rwanda, the autocratic state governed by Juvenal Habyarimana from 1973 to 1994 created clusters of around ten households called *nyumba kumi*, the leaders of which helped the regime spy on neighbors and elicit popular compliance with state policies.[50] In Venezuela, neighborhood groups called *colectivos* help the state repress protest and dissent.[51] In China, the CCP has created a vast network of block captains (居民小组长),[52] villager small groups (村民小组), autonomous redevelopment committees (自治改造委员会),[53] party cells (党小组),[54] and grid management systems (网格化管理), to help maintain order.

In practice, infiltration is among the least subtle methods of informal control. In rural China, villager small group heads serve as the equivalent of neighborhood leaders, ward leaders or block captains. They generally have a few dozen households under their "jurisdiction," and their primary duties include helping enforce birth quotas as well as assigning and reallocating land (often in conjunction with the village committee). They are readily identifiable as serving a state-sanctioned role in local politics, not unlike CDRs in Cuba or *nyumba kumi* in Rwanda. These tactics are not new in China, where the state has long sought to create infiltrating organizations that harness the "cellular" or "honeycomb" nature of rural Chinese society.[55]

---

[49] Levi (1989, p. 65).

[50] See Straus (2013, pp. 203–206). While the *nyumba kumi* have formally been abolished, in some areas they remain active on an informal basis (Chakravarty, 2015, p. 217).

[51] Torres and Casey (2017).

[52] Read (2012).

[53] Deng (2017).

[54] Koss (2015).

[55] Hsiao (1960); Schurmann (1966); Shue (1988); Siu (1989); Oi (1991); Read (2000, 2012); Koss (2015); Koss and Sato (2016); Pan (2018). See also Matsuzaki (2019a,b) on how the Japanese state re-purposed the *baojia* system for the purpose of "cellularization" and control through local intermediaries.

Infiltration has clear benefits to the local state. Unlike a local official who governs a town, village, or city of thousands, these agents are deeply embedded in local social networks, and are close to the people being governed. They can serve as the state's eyes and ears on the street, collecting gossip and intimate information on individual behavior. They further state interests by spreading news about new policies and persuading their neighbors and acquaintances to comply. In addition, they outsource work that might otherwise fall to higher-level agents, thus reducing the cost of implementing policies.

Like the two other methods discussed, the strategy of infiltrating civil society also has drawbacks: chief among them, as the most heavy-handed of the soft strategies of repression, it decreases the legitimacy of the state. When states make obvious attempts to control and manipulate society, it makes obeying state policies seem less like a choice and more like an unwelcome imposition. I draw on survey and qualitative evidence to show that where there are dense networks of street-level agents, there is also less satisfaction with the impartiality and performance of the local state.

1.4.4 How Autocrats Chose Strategies of Control

Local leaders in autocratic regimes strategically deploy the main three main mechanisms of informal control: building civil society, co-opting civil society elites, and building infiltrating organizations. (This strategic choice is discussed in more detail in Chapter 2.) Officials in autocracies cultivate a regime-friendly civil society where they have the resources and ideological latitude to do so, but cultural practices can constrain officials from pursuing this strategy. For example, when officials seek to use religious groups like churches or temples to strengthen order and control, their ability to do so depends on a large existing pool of believers. These cultural limitations are often regional. In China, this means that the strategy of using folk religious groups may be especially salient in places like Fujian, Shaanxi, or Guangdong, where these groups are plentiful. Ideology can also constrain regimes from using this strategy. In China under Mao, for example, using this strategy of political control would have been incompatible with the Communist state Mao sought to build.

Officials are most likely to co-opt communal and social elites during critical junctures. Co-optation is costly, since pre-existing political elites must share power with local notables and may find these local notables occasionally difficult to control. However, the payoff of greater control can be worth it during moments of major economic and political transition. For example, in Latin America, regimes co-opted labor movement leaders into the state in order to control the working class during periods of political reform or regime change.[56] In rural China, villages tend to co-opt communal elites like the leaders of lineage groups when they are about to urbanize or industrialize, so that these leaders can help ensure widespread acquiescence with policies that expropriate land and other property.

Building infiltrating organizations is generally a *substitute* for building civil society organizations and co-opting their leaders. Where it is difficult to build local civil society, or where regimes oppose doing so for ideological reasons, leaders turn instead to creating dense networks of grassroots informants and enforcers. In rural China, villages that lack lineage and temple associations rely instead on large numbers of small-group leaders to collect information on citizen behavior and encourage citizens to comply with the state. This strategy was also used heavily by some totalitarian and quasi-totalitarian states that opposed the existence of any civil society whatsoever. In China under Mao, Rwanda under Habyarimana, and Cuba under Casto, states invested heavily in creating infiltrating organizations like neighborhood committees to monitor and observe the population.[57] In Chapter 2, I also discuss how the United Front Work Department of the CCP guides officials on the use each of cultivation, co-optation, and infiltration in China.

1.5 CHALLENGES TO CONVENTIONAL WISDOM

The conventional wisdom is that a strong civil society makes governments more responsive to the interests of citizens. This theory has its roots in work by Tocqueville, Putnam, and others that largely focuses on democracies like the United States or Italy. The idea has gained currency well beyond academia: international agencies have spent billions of dollars to strengthen civil society, with the aim of promoting responsive, democratic government.[58]

---

[56] Collier and Collier (1991).

[57] See Read (2012); Tomba (2014).

[58] For example, between 2001 and 2017, the United States Agency for International Development spent $52 billion dollars in its "Governance and Civil Society" program, a substantial portion of which went toward supporting grassroots civil society groups. See Bush (2015), on democracy promotion and aid to civil society.

More recently, scholars have extended the theory to autocratic settings like China. Lily Tsai shows how the presence of lineage and temple organizations in rural China provides social incentives for officials to supply their communities with public goods like roads, schools, and water.[59] Other work by political scientists and economists has provided additional evidence that shows that temple and lineage organizations are associated with increased spending on village public goods in China.[60] Ethnographers have also illustrated how grassroots social organizations such as temple groups can be political and moral resources for citizens, in ways that sometimes allow them to challenge the state.[61]

This book, by contrast, belongs to a growing body of work that cuts against this conventional wisdom, and highlights the *autocratic* side of civil society. Amaney Jamal has shown that in the Middle East, civic associations tend to weaken democratic civic engagement. Jamal notes that civil society organizations "will reproduce elements of the political context in which they exist ... Where associational contexts are dominated by state-centralized, patron-client tendencies, then associations, too, become sites for the potential replication of these vertical ties."[62] I build on Jamal's findings by showing how social organizations not only erode democratic attitudes and civic participation, they strengthen political compliance and authoritarian state capacity.

In addition to strengthening autocrats' hold on power, a strong civil society can weaken democracy. Sheri Berman writes of how, in Weimar Germany, Nazi Party leaders infiltrated local social organizations such as sports clubs, student fraternities, and local associations; they used their membership in these organizations to help gain moral authority and learn about how to craft propaganda that would appeal to a wider audience.[63] This suggests that the dense ties created by civil society groups make them useful for would-be autocrats in democracies. Yet if we compare Weimer Germany to China today, there are clearly important distinctions, beyond obvious differences in political ideology. In Weimar Germany, local associations filled a vacuum created by the weakness of the Weimer state; as Berman writes, when "national political institutions and structures proved either unwilling or unable to address their citizens' needs, many

---

[59] Tsai (2007a).
[60] Padró i Miquel et al. (2015); Xu and Yao (2015).
[61] Madsen (1984); Siu (1989); Jing (1998); Feuchtwang (2003).
[62] Jamal (2009, p. 20).
[63] Berman (1997, pp. 20–22). See also Satyanath et al. (2017).

Germans turned away from them and found succor and support in the institutions of civil society instead."[64] In China, on the other hand, these groups do not undermine the state in any meaningful way. Instead, they are part of a larger state-building effort.[65]

I do not wish to paint a bleak picture of civil society groups. Civil society groups in China and other autocratic regimes can serve a dual role: they can strengthen social trust in ways that facilitate group collective action *and* help autocratic regimes infiltrate and control society. Previous work in China has sometimes noted the dual role of these groups. For example, Tsai notes that village cadres in rural China have self-interested reasons to supply public goods in villages with strong lineage and temple institutions: these institutions can provide them with social esteem and moral authority that they find useful for implementing policy. Tsai notes how officials use their moral authority to collect taxes, requisition land, and enforce birth control quotas; however these outcomes are not the focus of the analysis or theory.[66] Likewise, work by anthropologists often acknowledges the dual nature of these institutions. Adam Yuet Chau notes that in Shaanxi, "many temple leaders are current or former village Party secretaries" and that local elites help construct temples in order to "build or augment their basis of local influence or authority"[67] Similarly, Stephan Feuchtwang argues that religious groups "are at once a resource of local politicians and a basis for autonomous moral judgement."[68]

While civil society groups have a positive side, I argue their more significant role in autocracies like China is top-down political control. If we examine a broad range of outcomes, including both public goods provision and efforts to extract from society, the impact of local civil society on community welfare is at best ambiguous. Yet the neo-Tocquevilleian idea that these groups make government more accountable retains real power among both scholars and policy-makers.

---

[64] Berman (1997, p. 411).
[65] Some forms of civil society are inimical to democracy. Simone Chambers and Jeffrey Kopstein, for example, argue for the existence of what they term "bad civil society," such as hate groups or violent fringe political organizations (Chambers and Kopstein, 2001).These groups, Chambers and Kopstein argue, tend to become stronger in periods where economic inequality and deprivation are high. The types of groups that I discuss here, however, do not belong to "bad civil society."
[66] Tsai (2007a, p. 175).
[67] Chau (2008, pp. 12–13).
[68] Feuchtwang (2003).

In addition to challenging the accepted wisdom about the role of civil society, I also theorize the importance of *nonviolent* forms of political repression and control. In a review article on the repression literature, Christian Davenport notes that repression goes "beyond sticks, stones, and severing limbs" and yet nonviolent forms of coercion have received relatively little attention.[69] Recent pathbreaking work focuses largely on overt coercion. Sheena Chestnut Greitens, for example, explains variation in how autocratic regimes set up their internal security forces.[70] Greitens highlights a dilemma: dictators can either prioritize reducing the risk of a coup or deterring popular protest, but they cannot effectively do both. Using non-state groups for social and political control suggests an important alternative to investing in highly coercive institutions like the secret police.[71]

Other work suggests that both democracies and autocracies use the strategies of informal control I examine in this book. Davenport shows how the United States government used a mix of violent and nonviolent tactics to repress social movements in the 1960s and 70s. The US government infiltrated social movements not only to collect information but to sow distrust and fractionalization.[72] The way that law enforcement agencies in the United States used infiltration to demobilize activists is on the surface similar to infiltration strategies used by autocracies.[73]

Not surprisingly, strategies of informal control are widespread in autocracies. For instance, Reo Matsuzaki shows how the imperial Japanese state used local intermediaries to rule.[74] And Lisa Blaydes shows how in Iraq, Saddam Hussein sought to co-opt religious elites and replace clergy who did not cooperate; by the end of his rule, he had "successfully cultivated a 'critical mass' of religious leaders who worked in the interests of the Ba'th Party."[75]

---

[69] Davenport (2007a, p. 9). The same arguably remains true more than a decade after Davenport's article.

[70] Greitens (2016).

[71] This book's research design does not give me leverage on whether the use of informal control might help resolve the dilemma that Greitens highlights. Anecdotally, however, the strategy of informal control is used both by regimes that invest in coup-proofing (e.g., Indonesia, see Greitens p. 26, or Iraq, see Greitens pp. 282–291) and regimes that invest in intelligence collection (e.g., China, pp. 302–303).

[72] Davenport (2015, pp. 49–50). As an example, see Davenport (2015, p. 255).

[73] However, the Chinese government does not allow for the existence of social movements that challenge government authority, and a movement similar to the Republic of New Africa would be immediately and coercively shut down.

[74] Matsuzaki (2019a,b).

[75] Blaydes (2018, p. 252). See Blaydes (2018, pp. 246–252).

The Chinese state's use of informal control as a central part of its governing strategy provides a new window into how autocratic regimes rule. It also helps explain China's comparatively high levels of state capacity. Where, for example, the Iraqi government struggled to gather information on society and control it, the Chinese state's co-optation of local social groups allows it to excel at the task of intelligence collection (at least in relative terms). And where the Iraqi state's lack of information pushed it toward violent and indiscriminate repression, the Chinese state – outside important exceptions such as Xinjiang – has, in the reform era, relied less on outright coercion and more on the informal methods of control I examine in this book.

1.6 RESEARCH DESIGN

To trace the dynamics of political control in China, I triangulate between difference sources of data. I draw on evidence from structured case studies, from experiments embedded in face-to-face surveys, and from rich observational data that provides a picture of China as a whole.

At the heart of this book are comparative case studies of villages in rural China. These cases draw on fieldwork I conducted in China between 2012 and 2018, during which I interviewed over 100 people and conducted a year of on-the-ground research in villages.

To understand the consequences of different strategies of informal control, I created paired case studies of villages in Guangdong, Henan, Hunan, and Jiangsu Provinces. For instance, to understand how the presence of lineage groups influences local state capacity, I examined a pair of villages in Guangdong; one had strong lineage institutions and the other did not. Likewise, to examine the consequences of associations promoting traditional Buddhist culture, I conducted research in two villages in Jiangsu province, one with a robust network of organizations promoting traditional culture and the other without. This comparative strategy helped me uncover the causal process at work in these villages. Appendix C details the qualitative research design and case selection.

I complement these qualitative case studies with a wealth of quantitative data, including experiments. With a talented team of student enumerators, I conducted an original micro-level survey that includes the first experimental test of how villagers vote in village elections. The results of this experiment (presented in Chapter 3) helped me understand how civil society and the ruling party influence political mobilization in rural China.

I also created a national dataset of villages, which I used to determine whether the patterns I observed in my qualitative field research and in my micro-level survey apply to the rest of China. This novel dataset builds on the China Family Panel Studies and the Chinese General Social Survey, and I collected additional data using remote sensing imagery. These surveys randomly sampled villages while excluding some ethnic minority regions such as Xinjiang and Tibet. Chapter 4 provides more detail on this dataset.

1.7 OVERVIEW OF THE BOOK

Chapter 2 develops a theory of informal political control. The chapter examines the underlying logic, strengths and weaknesses of the three mechanisms of informal control – cultivation, co-optation, and infiltration.

Understanding the logic of political control in rural China requires an appreciation of rural China's politics and society. Chapter 3 introduces the dilemmas faced by the country's local political leaders. Rural cadres must provide public goods to their villages as well as help the state implement key policies, chief among them land requisitions, family planning quotas, and maintaining stability. Yet cadres face a problem: drawing on evidence from an original experiment, I show that villagers distrust CCP members and trust members of their lineage and neighborhood groups. This suggests that local CCP cadres might be able to draw on these other ties to help them control local society.

In Chapter 4, I examine how officials cultivate local civil society with the intent of exerting political control. Evidence from extensive fieldwork in rural China shows how cultivating lineage associations and religious societies helps local officials accumulate informal authority within the village and collect information on citizen behavior. Personal moral authority and knowledge of local society is then used to prevent resistance, especially to policies such as land requisitions. I draw on data from national surveys to corroborate this qualitative evidence.

Chapter 5 explores co-optation. Local notables, like clan leaders, draw on a mix of traditional authority (for example, by virtue of their position in the lineage's hierarchy) and moral authority (which they gain by taking actions that benefit the group). By incorporating these leaders into formal councils and party organizations, officials can gain powerful allies. Structured case studies show how including local notables in formal political institutions helps officials requisition land, reduce over-quota births, and discourage protest. Yet these communal elites can also capture local government for themselves.

A final strategy, discussed in Chapter 6, is to create institutions that help the state infiltrate local society. I primarily focus on the role of village "small-group" leaders, who serve as the equivalent of block captains or ward leaders. These grassroots informants monitor their neighbors and pressure them to comply with the law.

In the concluding chapter, I briefly recap the main findings and then examine their broader implications. In rural China, reliance on informal control has contributed to a fraying of social relations. In the long run, it seems that informal forms of political control may be nearly as corrosive as more coercive forms of repression. The most effective check on autocratic state power is unlikely to come from the state itself, but from an adversarial relationship between local civil society and the state. Independent community leaders and activists who can mobilize their groups and threaten officials with broad-based political mobilization can even the balance of power between the state and society, and create meaningful incentives for responsiveness.

2

A Theory of Political Control

People who have little experience with power, those who have been far away from it, tend to regard these things as mysterious and novel. But I look past the superficial things: the power and the flowers and the glory and the applause. I see the detention houses, the fickleness of human relationships.

Xi Jinping, 2000[1]

Xi Jinping would eventually reach the pinnacle of Chinese politics, but his political career started in a small village in rural Shaanxi. During the Cultural Revolution, party officials sent a teenaged Xi to live and work in a hamlet called Liangjiahe. According to the official mythology that has grown up around Xi's time in Liangjiahe, he slept in cave homes and labored in the fields alongside the rest of the village's farmers, until eventually he was made the head of the village party branch, his first position of real political authority.[2]

After becoming the village leader, Xi decided that his signature project would be to build a new dam.[3] It was an ambitious project for a young cadre with little connection to the village, and it quickly ran into a major

---

[1] Osnos (2015, p. 47).

[2] That is, he was made the party branch secretary for what was then called a "production brigade" (大队党支部书记).

[3] The details in this account are from official books on Xi's time in Liangjiahe. See Shaanxi People's Publishing House (2018) and Central Party School Editorial Office (2017). Liangjiahe has since become a central part of Xi's political myth, so in general we should be skeptical of these accounts, which tend to glorify Xi. However, the description of how he carried out the dam-building project by calling on kin ties does not show him in an especially heroic light, and it closely matches the dynamics of political control in other villages, making it plausible but hard to verify.

problem: constructing the dam would require seizing land that included a family cemetery used by members of the Wang clan. Lineage politics in Liangjiahe ran strong, and the Wang family's opposition seemed likely to scuttle Xi's plan.

To persuade the lineage to give up their land, Xi reportedly relied on a tactic of political control familiar to rural cadres throughout China: applying coercion through kin group ties. An influential member of the Wang lineage happened to be a government cadre. According to a widely circulated official account of Xi's time in Liangjiahe, Xi called on this lineage leader, and urged him to go twist arms among his family. "Everyone relies on you for big social events like weddings and funerals," Xi is said to have told him. "Help me convince everyone to do this project."[4]

The lineage leader went to his kinsfolk to plead the government's case. At first, they rebuffed him – so he went back to the homes of key lineage elders for three days running, pleading with them: "You're the village elders, you have prestige in the village, you must support [Xi Jinping's] plan!"[5] Eventually, thanks to this sustained campaign by a trusted lineage insider, they relented. The lineage fell in line, allowed Xi to confiscate their land, and supported the Liangjiahe dam project. Xi Jinping's first real political accomplishment relied on tactics of informal control I describe in more detail in this chapter.

Scholars of authoritarian regimes like China have often focused on formal coercive institutions that strengthen state capacity. Party organizations, secret police, detention houses, the military, labor "re-education" camps, censors, electronic eavesdropping, extrajudicial tribunals, and party-controlled courts can be used to coerce people to obey the state and its mandates. Yet most political compliance is achieved without resorting to formal institutions of coercion. Indeed, where these institutions are used it is most often because the state has *failed* at its core task of control.

In this book, by contrast, I focus on everyday methods of coercion and control, the sort of tactics Xi Jinping used in his first political posting. Informal institutions of control encourage obedience by calling on the obligations, allegiances, and bonds that non-state groups create. These social ties and obligations can be powerful tools of control.

In this chapter, I present my theory of informal control and illustrate the three mechanisms through which it is implemented: cultivating civil

---

4 See Shaanxi People's Publishing House (2018).
5 Shaanxi People's Publishing House (2018).

society, co-opting local notables, and infiltrating society. I explain how informal control leads to compliance with the state, but also how it can backfire in the long run by creating grievances and linking activists to each other. Finally, I explain how the state strategically deploys each of these strategies.

2.1 THE LIMITS OF FORMAL INSTITUTIONS

One of Mao Zedong's best-known sayings is that "political power grows out of the barrel of a gun."[6] As Mao suggests, authoritarian regimes *do* use coercion against their citizens, particularly outspoken activists and dissidents. For example, when I first met Ailian, an activist from Guangzhou, in 2012, she was fighting the local government's plan to seize and demolish her home. Not long after she started lodging complaints against the local government, she told me, men dressed in black started to follow her whenever she left the house. She showed me several photos she snapped of them as they followed her; she suspected they were either hired thugs or plainclothes officers.[7] When being tailed did not intimidate Ailian into silence, she started to get blunter messages. "One evening," she told me, the local authorities "placed some rotting pig heads and pig bones [on my doorstep]."[8] She described it as a chilling episode that hinted at the possibility of escalating violence.

Much of the literature on authoritarian control focuses on repression using the police and the military, and the morally urgent question of what autocratic states do with activists like Ailian.[9] In autocracies, the police play a central role in violent repression, since they are dispersed throughout the country and have specialized training and equipment, such as riot gear and eavesdropping tools, to deal with small-scale disturbances or individual dissidents. The security forces are also adept at more subtly weakening dissident groups – for example, pressuring unruly labor rights activists by shutting off the electricity to their NGO's office.[10] However,

---

[6] 枪杆子里面出政权.

[7] See also Ong (2018) and Chen (2017) on the use thugs for hire as a form of "outsourced" repression. This practice was common across many of the cases I studied.

[8] Author interview, Guangdong Province, Summer 2012.

[9] See for example Davenport (2007a,b); Pierskalla (2010); Earl (2011); Svolik (2012); Wang and Minzner (2015); Greitens (2016); Scoggins and O'Brien (2016); Greitens (2017).

[10] Fu (2017c).

when disturbances turn into full-blown revolutions, autocrats typically deploy the military: the Chinese Communist Party (CCP) leadership sent the People's Liberation Army to clear Tiananmen Square in 1989, and during the 2011 uprisings in Cairo the Egyptian Army ordered tanks into Tahrir Square.

Yet relying heavily on violent repression has limits. First, as work by Sheena Greitens and Milan Svolik shows, the security forces or military may become strong enough to threaten the regime's hold on power.[11] After all, why would "men with guns obey men without guns"?[12] In Egypt, for example, the military did not carry out the order to storm Tahrir Square; instead, Mubarak was pressured to resign and the military later overthrew his successor in a coup.

Second, violent repression can trigger a popular backlash. When the police lob canisters of teargas at peaceful protesters or soldiers use live ammunition to clear a public square, it can awaken a sense of indignity and bring more people onto the streets. As Lisa Blaydes' work shows, Saddam Hussein's reliance on violent repression in Iraq helped reinforce identities in ways that ultimately undermined state authority. Similarly, during the Umbrella Movement in Hong Kong, police attempts to disperse the crowd using pepper spray, truncheons, and tear gas led more protesters to take to the streets. Heavy-handed attempts to end protests by force in Ukraine, Brazil, and Turkey in 2013 also fueled popular anger.[13] Similarly, heavy repression of small-scale protests in rural China can lead to tactical escalation by protesters. Kevin O'Brien and Yanhua Deng describe a case in which "after a harsh repression produced hundreds of injuries" among protesters, the protesters "switched to more aggressive tactics, including denouncing local leaders, carrying out mock funerals, interrogating factory owners and ransacking the homes of 'traitors.'"[14]

Finally, violent repression is inefficient. A state that tried to compel people to comply with taxation through coercion alone would need a tremendous number of police officers, auditors, and tax collectors to ensure that the chances of getting caught and sent to jail outweighed the benefits of cheating on taxes. It would be far less costly to find some other way to motivate obedience.

---

[11] For further discussion, see among others Svolik (2012, pp. 123–161) and Greitens (2016)
[12] Svolik (2012, p. 123).
[13] Aytaç et al. (2017a,b).
[14] O'Brien and Deng (2015b, p. 457).

Given the costs and inefficiencies of repression, authoritarian regimes must rely on other institutions to encourage compliance. In the next section, I discuss how states use non-state groups to engage hidden forms of political control.

2.2 INFORMAL INSTITUTIONS OF CONTROL

Informal control relies on non-state groups to indirectly enforce political order. The state harnesses these community ties to both apply pressure on the noncompliant and to gather information on their attitudes and behavior. This focus on the repressive, controlling side of non-state groups and the social norms they propagate goes against the grain of a large body of work in social science that focuses on how social groups encourage cooperation for the public good.

Of course, cooperative norms can also strengthen public welfare. All small societies – including villages, slums, fisheries, clans, and congregations – face challenges that require groups to work together to fix them. Social groups must cooperate to maintain natural resources, provide aid to group members who have fallen on hard times, and supply public goods such as sanitation or security. For example, Elinor Ostrom found that groups from alpine herding associations in Switzerland to *zanjera* irrigation communities in Indonesia found creative ways to ensure that their members did not over-use resources, such as advocating norms that encouraged cooperation.[15] A sense of obligation to a group can exert a powerful pull on people. When "an individual has strongly internalized a norm related to keeping promises," Ostrom concluded, "the individual suffers shame and guilt when a personal promise is broken [and] if the norm is shared by others, the individual is also subject to considerable social censure for taking an action considered to be wrong."[16]

The logic in which tightly bound social groups create cooperative norms that help them solve collective action problems clearly applies to a wide variety of settings. For example, in *The Moral Economy of the Peasant*, James C. Scott shows how peasant communities foster collective welfare by creating informal norms that encourage better-off villagers to help those who have had a bad harvest or are otherwise struggling.

A strong civil society can smooth out the rough edges of politics by fostering what Alexis de Tocqueville called "habits of the heart." Civil

---

[15] Ostrom (1990).
[16] Ostrom (1990, p. 35).

society groups create dense social bonds and a sense of community solidarity that can grease the wheels of collective action. As discussed in the previous chapter, Lily Tsai has shown how in China, non-state groups can create norm-based incentives that encourage officials to serve their social group while in office. When officials perform well in office by supplying the group with public goods like roads, schools, and wells, they fulfill a social obligation and earn moral authority within the group.[17] Ethnographic work on lineage and temple institutions in rural China has shown how membership in these groups gives rise to moral obligations to help group members.[18]

Yet the social norms that sustain cooperation and strengthen order also tend to benefit the powerful. As the historian Yuval Noah Harari writes: "'Cooperation' sounds very altruistic but is not always voluntary and seldom egalitarian. Most human cooperation networks have been geared towards oppression and exploitation."[19] Hariri notes that in societies like imperial China, "peasants paid for the burgeoning cooperation networks with their precious food surpluses, despairing when the tax collector wiped out an entire year of hard labor with a single stroke of his imperial pen."[20]

The content of group social institutions – the rites, rituals, legends, oral traditions, and holy texts passed from generation to generation – often helps elites maintain control. The imaginary social orders that groups create, in China and in much of the rest of the world, tend to be aggressively pro-authority and pro-state.[21]

The remainder of the chapter explores how informal control works, drawing on a number of case studies to illustrate the process.

2.3 CULTIVATING CIVIL SOCIETY

One mechanism of informal control is to *cultivate civil society groups*, such as religious organizations, with norms that encourage deference to the state. The norms promoted by communal groups are often useful

---

[17] Tsai (2007a).
[18] See, for example, Madsen (1984); Siu (1989); Jing (1998); Feuchtwang (2003); Chau (2008).
[19] Harari (2014, p. 104).
[20] Harari (2014, p. 104).
[21] This is partly due to a natural selection process in which only groups that develop pro-state norms survive. Political elites will to co-opt, repress, or destroy groups that go too far in challenging their power.

for officials who want to encourage compliance with the state. Yet such norms do not always align with those of the state and its mandates. When they do not, cultivating these civil society groups can be ineffective or even backfire.

The holy texts and ritual performances developed by communal groups tend to reinforce norms of compliance with authority. While obligations to comply with authority can sometimes conflict with other duties, such as duties to help the weak and poor in times of need, elites often tend to emphasize norms of compliance.

Religious texts, including those produced by Judeo-Christian religions, are often strongly pro-authority and pro-state. Consider the following passage from Romans 13 in the New Testament:

> Let everyone be subject to the governing authorities, for there is no authority except that which God has established. The authorities that exist have been established by God. Consequently, whoever rebels against the authority is rebelling against what God has instituted . . . [22]

> This is also why you pay taxes, for the authorities are God's servants, who give their full time to governing. Give to everyone what you owe them: If you owe taxes, pay taxes; if revenue, then revenue; if respect, then respect; if honor, then honor.[23]

Although Romans is just one book of the New Testament, it was central to the writing and thinking of key figures including Martin Luther and John Calvin and has informed how many Christians understand their relationship with the state.[24]

Ministers who want to encourage the faithful to be compliant citizens often cite Bible passages that encourage obedience. During the late 1960s, for example, Billy Graham cited Romans 13 in a radio address in which he encouraged his listeners to focus less on advancing social justice through politics. "We in church today are in danger of becoming blundering social physicians, giving medicine here and putting ointment there on the sores of the world," he said in his popular radio program *The Hour of Decision*.[25] In the address, Graham noted his concern with

---

[22] Romans 13:1–2 in the New International Version.
[23] Romans 13:6–7.
[24] See (Collinson, 1994; Oates, 2012; Starr, 2016). During the Protestant Reformation, the passage was also an inconvenient obstacle for Protestant theologians attempting to develop a "resistance theory" to justify acts of noncompliance against Catholic states.
[25] Text available at Graham (1967).

racism and the plight of the poor while encouraging individuals to refrain from the most contentious and "revolutionary" politics of the era.

In contemporary China, the pro-authority passages of the Bible shape how unsanctioned "house churches" minister to their flocks and how they understand their relationship with the state. Since these underground churches are not officially recognized, they have a fraught relationship with the CCP, which closely monitors them and frequently shutters them and jails their leaders. To survive, the pastors of many such churches encourage their congregations to comply with state demands in nonreligious matters, and emphasize Bible passages that underscore the ways in which Christian faith does not conflict with the CCP's authority. For example, the well-known pastor Wang Yi of the Early Rain Reform Church (秋雨之福归正教会) posted his own reimagining of Luther's 95 Theses. Wang Yi's 95 Theses state that God is the highest authority, but draw on Romans 13 to emphasize that this does not represent a challenge to the state.[26] Citing Romans, Wang writes, "this means that all the authorities that exist in Chinese society, no matter if it is within a family, social institution, or government, ultimately originated from God ... all government officials, including the ones on the lowest levels, in their nature are all God's 'appointees.'"[27] Wang was arrested in December 2018 and his church effectively shuttered.[28]

Of course, Christianity is not the only faith or creed to encourage obedience to the state. In China, the Confucian norms reinforced by lineage and folk religious groups tend to reinforce state authority as well. The opening passage of the Confucian *Analects* begins by encouraging respect for authority and discouraging revolution:

Master You said: "A man who respects his parents and his elders would hardly be inclined to defy his superiors. A man who is not inclined to defy his superiors will never foment a rebellion. A gentleman works at the root. Once the root is secured, the Way unfolds. To respect parents and elders is the root of humanity!"[29]

[26] See Johnson (2018b) and Starr (2016) for a broader discussion of Wang Yi.
[27] While the original Weibo post has been taken down, a translated English version was found at `www.chinapartnership.org/blog/2015/08/95-theses-the-re affirmation-of-our-stance-on-the-house-church`, last accessed May 23, 2018.
[28] Johnson (2018a).
[29] The original text is: 有子曰：'其为人也孝弟，而好犯上者，鲜矣；不好犯上，而好作乱者，未之有也。君子务本，本立而道生。孝弟也者，其为仁之本与！The translation here is from Nylan (2014).

Here, Master You argues that obedience to one's parents, elders, and rulers is core to the ethos of Confucianism.[30] This passage, and others like it urging filial piety and obedience to family and the state, have been critical to the variant of Neo-Confucianism promoted by the state from the Song Dynasty to the present day.[31] According to the historian Prasenjit Duara, political elites in the imperial era viewed Confucianism and the ideology of descent as essential "for regulating behavior and social order."[32]

Chinese folk religion also reinforces the legitimacy of the state and local elites.[33] In the Qing Dynasty and earlier, many gods were thought to hold office in a celestial bureaucracy that mirrored and was interwoven with the actual Imperial bureaucracy. Remarkably, living flesh-and-blood officials were sometimes seen as having authority over gods, provided the gods had a lower bureaucratic rank in the celestial bureaucracy.[34] Positions on village temple councils often mixed some degree of practical authority – such as duties to collect funds for the temple and even organize collective village defenses – with moral authority. In one village in Northern China, for example, the village headman led prayers for rain and ritually delivered a petition for rain to the head of the heavenly bureaucracy, the Jade Emperor.[35] This arrangement strengthened the informal authority of local political elites and the legitimacy of the political system more generally. As Duara writes, "by co-opting the hierarchical symbolism of the supernatural, the imperial state extended its authority through the ritual medium into village society."[36]

Like Confucianism and indigenous folk religion, Buddhism encourages obedience to secular authority in China, if perhaps to a lesser extent. The popular Buddhist tale *Mulian Rescues His Mother from Hell* was historically one of the most popular pieces of entertainment in China (called by some "the greatest of all Chinese religious operas").[37] In the imperial era, the opera often played to large crowds of people who were often

---

[30] Master You was one of Confucius' disciples, and one of the two Masters whose own followers most likely compiled the Analects.

[31] Nylan (2014, p. 64).

[32] Duara (1988, p. 92).

[33] For classic accounts, see Yang (1961, pp. 180–218) and Freedman (1979, pp. 351–369).

[34] Duara (1988, p. 134)

[35] Duara (1988, p. 136).

[36] Duara (1988, p. 34).

[37] De Bary and Lufrano (2010, p. 95). See also Siu (1989) and Chapter 3 of this book for a discussion of religious festivals, temple fairs, and operas, and their role in reinforcing authority.

deeply unsettled by the play and its vivid depiction of hell.[38] The opera had a distinctly pro-state message. At one point in Mulian's tour of hell on his way to rescue his mother, he witnesses the following scene:

He next saw a large farmstead. Inside the farmyard were many grated pens, and the chilly air made one shiver. Countless souls had been transformed into donkeys and mules and other animals, and demon-soldiers stood guard all around. Mulian asked them: "What kind of place is this?" the demon-soldiers replied: "This place is called the Turning-into-Beasts Depot. All those people in the world ... who as common citizens did not pay their taxes in full ... they come to this place upon their deaths and are turned into animals so as to pay back their debts."[39]

The message is not terribly subtle: obey the state and pay your taxes or be turned into a donkey!

The Case of Yang Village

The case of Yang Village, in Guangdong Province, illustrates the usefulness to state actors of communal groups and the norms they create. The key figure in Yang Village's social and political life is its long-standing political leader, Secretary Liu, who served for three decades as the head of the Communist Party branch, the top position in the village political hierarchy. Liu dominated village life through its kinship and civic associations. During his time as Secretary of the Communist Party branch, he oversaw the large-scale revival of its lineage associations. Such associations in China are organized around the principle of descent, and are broadly similar to the clans and other extended kin groups found from Egypt to Zambia to Afghanistan.[40] Starting in the 1980s, with Liu's blessing, the main lineage halls were refurbished after vandalism by the Red Guards and years of neglect during the Mao era (see Figure 2.1). The lineage associations also revived the custom of holding lavish feasts during the annual Lantern Festival (see Figure 2.2). During these feasts, hundreds of lineage members, some of whom had migrated elsewhere, flocked back to Yang Village and crammed into their ancestral halls in celebrations that often spilled out into the streets.

Liu and the rest of the village leadership also promoted cultural associations including ping pong clubs, singing troupes, traditional music groups, and a dragon boat racing team. Under Liu, according to the village gazetteer, spending on these associations grew tenfold from 1990

[38] See De Bary and Lufrano (2010, p. 94).
[39] Grant and Idema (2011, pp. 74–75).
[40] See, for example, Murtazashvili (2016) on clans in Afghanistan, Baldwin (2016) on kin groups in sub-Saharan Africa, or Blaydes (2010) on tribes in Egypt.

FIGURE 2.1 A lineage's ancestral hall
in Guangdong.

FIGURE 2.2 A lineage association
feast.

to 2006. Together with the lineage associations, these civic organizations created social bonds that increased villagers' general sense of pride in their village.

Liu exploited these bonds when the village government attempted to expropriate the village's collectively owned agricultural land, on which an informal settlement had been built. The government offered a compensation plan that fell far short of what had been offered in a nearby village facing a similar situation. Some agreed to the compensation, but hundreds did not. Liu then used every means at his disposal to persuade residents of the informal settlement to accept the relocation deal.

For instance, Liu used the networks created by the lineage association to foster compliance with the land requisition. He encouraged influential members of the clan to call on their family members to sign over their land and homes to the village government. This type of "relational repression" would not have been as effective if the village did not have such high levels of social capital, generated by its kin and civic institutions.[41]

Liu also launched a propaganda campaign that called on the informal norms propagated by lineage associations – associations he had helped nurture and revive – in order to pressure holdouts to sign over their land. Liu and the village leadership plastered posters around the village encouraging community members to agree to the compensation plan out of respect for clan elders (see Figures 2.3–2.5).[42] Each poster shows a

---

[41] Deng (2017); Deng and O'Brien (2013).

[42] The eminent Chinese sociologist Fei Xiaotong discusses the general deference to elders and other powerful local authorities in rural China. Fei (1992, p. 100). See also Hsiao (1960); Watson (1982); Faure (1986, 2007).

FIGURE 2.3 "Fighting the relocation compensation shows a lack of filial piety and a hard heart."

FIGURE 2.4 "Refuse relocation and be censured by the elders; shirk responsibility and people point."

FIGURE 2.5 "Show respect and filial piety; move early for a better environment and peaceful late years."

younger villager considering whether to accept the compensation plan or fight for more, while a clan elder suffers passively because she is not living in the promised compensation housing. It is not difficult to imagine why officials thought this tactic might be effective. Over the years, most villagers would have participated in rituals that reinforced a sense of filial piety, such as Tomb Sweeping Day and the feast held during the Lantern Festival. In these rituals, lineage elders generally hold special positions of respect. In short, strong norms of solidarity and robust social networks can make communal groups a potentially powerful medium of social control.

The Case of Xiaogang Village

In the early 2000s, Xiaogang Village needed to upgrade its electrical power system. The jury-rigged wiring installed in the Maoist era could not handle the demands of a rapidly modernizing village where every home had a television set and electric lighting. Upgrading the electrical network was important to many in the village, but doing so would require compliance and cooperation from citizens. In Xiaogang, tapping into the county grid involved running power lines through farmers' fields. One farmer whose field the line would have crossed, named Wu, refused on the grounds that installing the utility pole would require digging up his crops and losing the small patch of land around the utility pole.

The village chief considered going to the township government to resolve the dispute, but he worried that course of action was too unpredictable. He thought Farmer Wu, a volatile personality, might accuse the village committee of corruption; if that happened, it was unclear whose side township and county officials might take.

The informal authority provided by traditional kinship institutions, however, can give local bureaucrats a crucial advantage. A powerful member of Wu's clan was a member of the village committee. As the leading member of his lineage, norms that encourage deference to elders and to the state gave this cadre significant leverage over his kin. This cadre told Wu the electrical upgrading project would benefit the entire village, and that the decision to run the lines through his field was fair and just. Wu felt obliged to listen to the elder, in part because of the norms propagated by kinship institutions in rural China. Wu stood down and accepted the decision. As the official told me: "Because of my position in the clan (辈分) he *had* to listen to me."[43]

In rural China, a mark of the importance of social institutions such as religious and kinship groups is that local officials cultivate them in order to govern their villages. Officials support a number of traditional activities – such as organizing lineage banquets and elaborate religious festivals, refurbishing ancestral halls, building temples, and holding dragon boat races[44] – because strengthening ties to these communal institutions helps them govern. Tsai explains that cultivating these institutions can be "invaluable for implementing state tasks such as birth control and tax collection."[45] She reports a case study very similar to Xiaogang Village. In her example, residents of West Gate Village refused to acquiesce to the digging of a drainage ditch until members of a community council went door to door to persuade them.[46]

2.3.1 The Limits of Cultivating Civil Society

The strategy of cultivating civil society has its limits. In particular, it fails to strengthen state control when group norms conflict with state mandates. An important example of this limitation is the enforcement of birth control policy in China. Lineage and folk religious groups help propagate the spread of a Confucian ideology that stresses the importance of patrilineal descent. A state policy that restricts the number of children

---

[43] Author interview, Spring 2013, Henan Province.
[44] See also Eng and Lin (2002) and Tsai (2007a).
[45] Tsai (2007a, p. 175).
[46] See Tsai (2007a, p. 112).

in families runs counter to this ideology. In Chapter 4, I find some qualitative evidence that officials call on clan and religious allegiances to encourage people to comply with the One Child Policy (which reinforces Tsai's findings), but the quantitative evidence is ambiguous. The misalignment between the policy and the norms espoused by these groups likely makes collaboration with non-state groups like clans less effective at encouraging compliance with this policy compared to other state mandates.

Exploiting civil society to exert control over local community actions can also fail, at least in the long run, if these social bonds inspire group collective action. Drawing on evidence from Italy, Robert Putnam argues that civic groups and associations create horizontal bonds between citizens that lead to the formation of social capital, which is useful for resolving group collective action problems.[47] This is the case in China as well. These groups enmesh members in vertical relationships of patronage and social obligation that make them useful to officials *and* horizontal relationships that help maintain the group. When grievances bubble to the surface, these well-organized groups can erupt in protest. The upside of control is offset by a nontrivial long-run downside of potential instability, as the case of Wukan suggests.

The Case of Wukan Village

The case of Wukan Village shows how autonomous grassroots groups can sometimes become powerful adversaries of the local state. Wukan lies on China's subtropical southern coast, a long afternoon's bus ride from the economic powerhouses of Hong Kong, Shenzhen, and Guangzhou. In December 2012, thousands of farmers gathered in Wukan's main square and major thoroughfares to protest the confiscation of their land by village and township cadres; the demonstration received global news coverage.

Officials in Wukan had been confiscating land for years. In the 1990s, its Communist Party secretary created a corporation dedicated to promoting local "industrial development," and installed himself as the company's vice-CEO. He appointed the village committee head general manager, and a developer from Hong Kong was named CEO. Over the years, the company sold off hundreds of acres of village land, reaping a reported 700 million *yuan* in revenue (roughly USD 100 million). These profits were shared between the company's owners and managers, many

[47] Putnam (1994, 163–185).

of whom were village cadres.[48] Villagers were told nothing about the details of these land transactions, and were paid only about 500 *yuan* (USD 75) per household in compensation, which represented less than 1 percent of the value.[49] Meanwhile, village officials routinely rejected villagers' applications for permits to use village land to expand their houses.[50]

Anger over the land expropriations grew slowly over time, and culminated in September 2011 when villagers discovered that much of the village's remaining land had been sold. The issue galvanized local residents. Protest leaders told me that young villagers tried to organize a protest using social media, but this proved ineffective since most older villagers did not use social media.

The village's lineage group heads instead organized the protests. Wukan has forty-seven separate lineage groups, each of which has an acknowledged lineage head (族长). These figures are generally men in their fifties or older who have proven themselves to be capable leaders. According to the villagers I spoke with, the heads are normally not elected but emerge by consensus. Before the protests (and indeed after them), these leaders often resolved disputes within the group and served as representatives of their lineage in dealings with the village government.

The protesters created a lineage council that represented each of the village's lineage groups in dealings with the local government. With the backing of lineage leaders, protesters took to the streets. The police restored order after an initial protest in September 2011, but the death of one of the protest leaders while in police custody sparked an even larger uprising that December. Protesters stormed the police station and village committee offices, forcing the police and party members to flee the village. The police then cordoned off the village to prevent residents from entering or leaving. Once it became apparent that the standoff would not be quickly resolved, both sides acknowledged that a third-party actor would need to step in to impose order. Interestingly, protest leaders and the state both turned to lineage groups.

With the party and police expelled from the village, the lineage council became the *de facto* government of Wukan. Lineage leaders helped

---

[48] See He and Xue (2014, p. 129).
[49] He and Xue (2014, p. 129).
[50] He and Xue (2014, p. 129). My interviews with village cadres and villagers in Wukan confirmed this.

enforce order and ensure that sanitation, water, and other basic services continued uninterrupted (even though the government applied pressure on protesters by cutting off shipments of rice and other basic staples into the village). According to a village committee member I interviewed, they also created a representative assembly with one to five members from each clan, proportional to the size of the group. This assembly also represented the village in negotiations with the government.

The protest leaders, outside academics, and rights activists I spoke to portrayed the role of the lineage leaders and the lineage assembly as an essential part of the movement's success. (Some thought the party pushed for the creation of this assembly, since the assembly imposed order on the village and gave the party a single institution to bargain with and resolve the crisis.) For local officials, these autonomous lineage elites have been formidable forces. As one village official in Wukan told me about his tenure governing the village, "The web of relationships here is so complex, it is essential to have these lineage leaders to coordinate (协调) with me."[51]

How, then, can officials enjoy the benefits of strong non-state groups, which help the state structure its relationship with society and channel its demands, while experiencing fewer downsides? The next section discusses an alternative strategy – co-opting powerful intermediaries like heads of lineage groups.

2.4 CO-OPTATION

Civil society elites – such as traditional leaders of clan and groups, church pastors, clergy, and well-respected labor organizers – enjoy traditional and moral authority within a community. Co-opting civil society elites can be an especially effective strategy of political control.

Imagine, for example, the mayor of an American city about to undertake a large-scale program of urban renewal.[52] The project requires requisitioning large swaths of urban land in order to build new public buildings and a network of highways and roads that connect the downtown to the suburbs. The project will involve tearing down a neighborhood; its residents will need to move elsewhere.

---

[51] Author interview, Summer 2013, Guangdong Province.
[52] The description roughly parallels the politics of urban renewal in New Haven, Connecticut, in the 1960s, as described by Dahl (2005) and Rae (2008). I revisit the case of urban redevelopment in the United States in Chapter 5.

Anticipating the possibility of resistance, the mayor creates a quasi-democratic body called the Citizens Action Committee that includes notables drawn from the city's important civil society groups, including local churches and synagogues, which represent well-organized constituencies that might mobilize against the development project.[53]

Rather than checking the power of the mayor, the body serves to co-opt key local notables. For example, the leader of the Italian-American community also happens to own a construction company, and as a member of the Citizens Action Committee he receives assurances that lucrative contracts will flow his way from the redevelopment project.[54] The committee never rejects any of the mayor's key proposals for the development project.[55] Instead, the community leaders lend their support to the plan and their moral authority helps forestall mobilization among the affected residents. The president of a local labor union rebukes the young organizers who are drawing up plans to mobilize against the project and they sheepishly agree to stop. The pillars of local religious communities tell their friends they support the mayor's redevelopment project, and the activists trying to organize a petition against the project in these communities find their neighbors reluctant to sign. The fact that the city's elders have lent their moral authority to the project gives many people pause.

The way in which seemingly inclusive political bodies can be used to exercise control in a democracy like the United States broadly parallels their use in a nondemocratic context like China. Instead of churches, synagogues, and neighborhoods, political mobilization in rural China often occurs through lineage groups, villages, and (more rarely) temples. By co-opting the leaders of these communal groups, political leaders can strengthen their control over society. Officials are motivated to overlook the potential costs and risks associated with forging alliances with local notables, which are discussed in more detail later in this chapter, because their informal authority is useful for encouraging compliance with the state and implementing policy, and because their knowledge of local society helps make it more "legible" to political leaders.

Survey work by Tom Tyler and Peter Degoey on US institutions, such as the Supreme Court and the police, has shown that "trust [in authorities] consistently influences feelings of obligation to obey

---

53 See Dahl (2005, p. 131).
54 Dahl (2005, p. 131).
55 Dahl (2005, pp. 124–125).

organizational rules and laws."[56] As Tyler notes, when a trusted authority figure encourages compliance, it can induce both a willingness to accept a decision as fair and in the best interests of the group, and a "feeling of obligation to obey the rules."[57] Lily Tsai notes that "in places such as China, where citizen distrust of the state is high and officials either cannot or do not want to use coercion ... moral standing can be an invaluable political resource that helps [officials] to implement difficult state policies such as tax collection and birth control."[58]

Individuals earn moral authority by taking actions that benefit group members.[59] Local notables might raise funds for charity, volunteer on a council, provide helpful advice, take in refugees or the needy, or more generally behave in ways that others perceive as moral, even when it is personally costly, unpleasant, risky, or dangerous to do so. Taking these actions convinces the public that the person cares about the interests of the broader community and even represents it in some way.[60]

Individuals have incentives to acquire moral authority in part because it benefits them. A city leader who helps organize Rotary Club or Chamber of Commerce events may find that the additional social status this confers makes it easier to earn the support of the business community for a city redevelopment project. A wealthy entrepreneur who funds scholarships for high school students may find that this generosity helps win votes when she runs for office. Or when a village official in rural China enjoys an elevated moral standing within her lineage group, she may find it easier to elicit compliance when seeking to raise levies, requisition land, or enforce birth quotas.

Moral authority is different from traditional authority, which is bestowed on an individual not because of *actions they have taken to benefit the group* (although they often do take such actions), but because

---

[56] Tyler and Degoey (1996, p. 336).

[57] Tyler (1998, p. 283).

[58] Tsai (2007a, pp. 89–90).

[59] When some scholars discuss moral authority, they have in mind the symbolic power wielded by large organizations such as churches or national political elites. For example, Anna Grzymała-Busse writes about how the Catholic churches in Ireland and Poland defended their countries against, respectively, the British and the Soviets, which garnered them significant moral authority (and policy influence). See Grzymala-Busse (2015, 2016).

[60] Anna Grzymała-Busse provides a similar definition, referring to the moral authority of churches as "the popular perception that churches are not only religious authorities but also representatives of the national interest and the common good," Grzymala-Busse (2016, p. 13).

of their *position within the group's status hierarchy*. For example, chiefs in sub-Saharan Africa wield significant traditional authority.[61] Similar figures include village elders, clan and lineage heads, temple leaders, and other religious figures.

More generally, the trust that many have in civil society elites makes them essential to resolving collective action dilemmas within the group. Community notables often have the most accurate knowledge about local officials' attitudes and behavior. They may also have personal relationships with village officials, with whom they may frequently consult as an informal representative of their group. For instance, the head of a lineage group may ask a village official to help fix a leaking water main or arbitrate a dispute. Officials may share information about local politics along the way.

While there are parallels to democratic settings, the role that information plays in resolving (or worsening) collective action problems is especially important in authoritarian regimes. Such regimes expend significant resources to prevent horizontal citizen-to-citizen flows of information, which leads to widespread preference falsification, or the misrepresentation of sincere beliefs.[62] China's regime attempts to control the transmission of information among citizens by using a "porous" system of censorship that allows for limited information revelation.[63]

Civil society elites are also often the most knowledgeable about the attitudes and behavior of other group members. For example, they know who has been grumbling about village officials' plans to reallocate land for a new road or which families are having children in excess of the local birth quota. This inside information makes these local notables valuable to both their group and to officials. Officials consult with communal elites to determine which houses might cause trouble and which may be valuable allies. They may ask the influential leader of a natural village or member of a temple committee how their group will react, for example, to a campaign to crack down on illegal firecracker use. Villagers may in turn ask communal elites about the attitudes of other villagers. If they hear that many other villagers will be lighting firecrackers during the

---

[61] Baldwin (2016, p. 21) defines traditional chiefs as "rulers who have power by virtue of their association with the customary mode of governing a place-based community."

[62] Kuran (1991); Wintrobe (1998); Jiang and Yang (2016).

[63] See Roberts (2018) on porous censorship in contemporary China and Lorentzen (2013, 2014, 2017) on efforts to regulate the horizontal flow of information.

Spring Festival in defiance of the ban, they may be more likely to do so themselves. However, if they hear that few will be, they may be unwilling to risk a fine.

Communities can sometimes find themselves at the mercy of badly behaved group leaders. In a field experiment in Ethiopia, for example, Michael Kosfeld and Devesh Rustagi found that community leaders with anti-social personalities tend to punish indiscriminately and mismanage common-pool resources like forests.[64] How does this dynamic perpetuate itself? Group members may rationally feel they have no alternative to their communal elites – indeed, the potential alternatives are unknown and quite possibly worse. Kevin O'Brien and Lianjiang Li write about Mr. Wang, a village official whose social authority within his lineage group helps him ensure political quiescence:

When asked why they had failed to press their complaints [against officials] ... several villagers had said it was pointless. [It was] commonly assumed that Wang had bought off the township officials, since they frequently drank and gambled together. To cap it all, nearly two-thirds of the villagers shared one surname and Wang was one of the highest-ranking clan elders; even the most disgruntled [villagers] were far from confident they could successfully challenge Wang, particularly since he was the sort of man who would certainly attempt to settle scores if he was not removed from power. "Why risk so much to remove one corrupt cadre," asked a villager, "when it's better to be governed by a full tiger than a hungry wolf?"[65]

It may seem counterintuitive that communal group elites would appropriate more from their own group. Yet as Kimuli Kasara shows, leaders in Africa tax their co-ethnics more than other groups in part because members of their own group have "fewer alternatives" – that is, no one else to turn to in elections.[66] Along similar lines, Daron Acemoglu, Tristan Reed, and James Robinson show that chiefdoms in Sierra Leone with fewer competing ruling families provide poorer-quality governance.[67] These findings may also be consistent with results from other studies that slums in India that have strong leaders (who are outside the formal state) enjoy strong property rights in part because they can help coordinate their group to gain official state recognition.[68]

---

[64] Kosfeld and Rustagi (2015).
[65] O'Brien and Li (1995, p. 757).
[66] Kasara (2007, p. 160).
[67] Acemoglu et al. (2014).
[68] Wibbels et al. (2016).

The Case of Beiyan Village

Beiyan Village, which is located in Henan Province, illustrates the ways in which communal elites with high levels of moral authority and social prestige can exploit the trust placed in them. Beiyan has a democratically elected village committee that holds elections every three years as required by law. Local residents can cast their ballots freely and can stand for elections themselves. Villagers are united by their membership in a large lineage group. According to the group's written history, the majority of villagers can trace their lineage to a single common ancestor. Lineage group norms encourage group members to cooperate with each other, for example by contributing their money, food, and labor to communal events. For instance, during funerals, members of the lineage group will often band together to provide rice and other staples to the mourning family. In theory, this would seem to be a virtuous combination: the village's social institutions encourage villagers to interact with each other and cooperate, while regular elections provide a mechanism for Beiyan's residents to hold their leaders accountable.

Yet in one recent election, a wealthy entrepreneur stood for the post of village chief at the encouragement of local government officials. He had created jobs for locals, and was a spirited, and often funny, presence on the village's social scene. His willingness to help members of his group find jobs had bestowed an important measure of moral authority upon him within his lineage group.

Once in office, however, he betrayed the trust of his lineage and village. He used his authority over land allocations to illegally requisition over a dozen acres of collectively owned village land; with the protection and cooperation of township officials, he built a factory on it. Why did villagers fail to organize against him right away?

The lineage leader's position as one of the village's key social brokers helps explain villagers' compliance. As a successful entrepreneur, he had proven himself a capable individual with connections to local officials. Villagers would approach him for information on local policies or to ask a favor. For example, when a member of his lineage wanted to set up a small hog farm, he helped negotiate with the village committee for approval.

When he used his informal authority as village leader to take land, villagers' lack of information left them divided over what to do. Some members of the community wanted to go to the village chief to ask for compensation. "But we did not know what the compensation standard was," one villager told me.[69] The chief maintained that he had near-total authority over land allocations, and cited provisions in China's rural land laws that give village political institutions authority over land contracting decisions,[70] but neglected to mention that this type of expropriation is likely illegal.

In addition to their confusion over the law, he exploited villagers' uncertainty about the intricacies of who would benefit from the project. The official claimed that he would not personally benefit from the land taking. According to villagers, it later emerged that he had an ownership stake in the factory, in which few locals received jobs. "We did not think he would betray us," one former village committee member told me.[71]

A group of villagers eventually organized a collective petition, but they did so much too late: ground had already broken on the factory project, and higher-ups in the township and county had evidently given their blessing to the project. Several years later, when I was conducting my fieldwork, the factory was running, the clan leader had stepped down to tend to his businesses, and the villagers whose land had been taken were still unsuccessfully seeking some kind of restitution.

When the social elites who customarily solve group collective action problems are on the sidelines, it makes it difficult to mobilize against land takings with the speed and scale needed to derail them. A clan leader may well lose his moral authority while in office if the group decides that his actions are unjust. But a leaderless group is still faced with a severe collective action problem, especially in an authoritarian state where collective action is dangerous.

2.4.1 The Limits of Co-optation

The outcome of co-optation depends on the incentives for the co-opted elites. When the stakes are low, co-optation tends to serve the interests of high-level government officials. Co-opted local officials help the state control their groups, collect taxes and revenue, and strengthen the political order. In return, their groups receive public goods and services. The iterative nature of everyday politics ensures that co-opted elites behave

---

[69] Author interview, Spring 2013, Henan Province.
[70] See Article 12, "Law of the People's Republic of China on Land Contracts in Rural Areas." www.npc.gov.cn/englishnpc/Law/2007-12/06/content_1382125.htm, last accessed on July 10, 2016.
[71] Author interview, Spring 2013, Henan Province.

in ways that benefit the state *and* their group. The threat of social sanctions can prevent them from extracting too much from their group, and the threat of bureaucratic sanctions helps keep them in line with state mandates.

However, rapid urban and industrial development can change the incentives for local elites. During periods of rapid growth, the benefits of extracting from their group – especially by reallocating land and property rights – can increase dramatically. For example, when a local entrepreneur wants to build a factory on town land, they can take tens or hundreds of thousands of dollars in kickbacks. Or they can receive an ownership stake in the company in return for approving a development deal. The complexity of land and development deals makes them an attractive avenue for corruption not just in China, but in much of the developing world.

The one-shot nature of development changes the dynamics of co-optation in ways that backfire for the authoritarian governments in the long run. The high stakes involved give elites incentives to behave in ways that erode trust in the state and lead to a decline in social bonds within the group. In one-shot interactions, elections are not effective tools of accountability. In the example of Beiyan Village, the local official only spent one three-year term in office, but was able to benefit from a local land deal. Had he stood for another election he would have lost, so he simply chose not to run again.

Nor are social sanctions like group ostracism effective tools of accountability if the material payoff for cheating the group is high. For instance, in Peng Village, discussed in Section 5.2.1, a village official who used his authority to expropriate from his lineage group moved to the nearby township, and rarely visited Peng, where he would have faced daily harassment from aggrieved residents. In other cases, such as Beiyan, cadres and former cadres withdraw to social circles outside the village.

In extreme cases, officials may flee the country to avoid political and social accountability. For instance, Li Fangrong, the former party secretary of Liede Village in Guangzhou, was one of the most respected members of his lineage group. He oversaw the renovation of his lineage's ancestral hall and the revival of lineage traditions like a yearly dragon boat race and a Lantern Festival feast. Yet Li, who earned a meager salary serving as the village's party secretary for decades, fled to Canada after the village redevelopment project was complete, having evidently benefited handsomely. Afterwards, the city of Guangzhou confiscated all the passports of cadres in the surrounding villages to prevent others from fleeing.

2.5 INFILTRATION

Much like the other mechanisms of informal control, *infiltration* relies on the influence of groups that are not officially part of the state but are allies of it. To infiltrate society, authoritarian regimes create para-state grass-roots organizations – such as neighborhood groups – that are designed to increase the state's reach into local society. These groups are quasi-autonomous and nominally self-governing, but are in fact controlled by the regime and serve its interests.

A key feature of these organizations of infiltration is the way in which they are layered on top of existing social networks. The more that authoritarian states infiltrate and penetrate local society, the more control they have. However, relying on infiltration involves an important trade-off between achieving control and decreasing peoples' perceptions of state legitimacy due to the use of coercive and heavy-handed tactics.

Authoritarian regimes around the world rely on institutions of infiltration for control and repression. In Venezuela, for instance, Nicolas Maduro and the United Socialist Party have relied on neighborhood-based organizations to repress anti-regime protest. These organizations include loosely organized bands of pro-regime supporters colloquially referred to as *colectivos* that intimidate protesters and use tear gas and guns to break up demonstrations.[72] The regime also relies on local party cells called "Unidades de Batalla Hugo Chávez" (UBCh) to rapidly respond to protests and repress them. During anti-regime rallies in early 2014, one ruling party official used Twitter to direct the UBCh cells to "prepare for a counterattack" against protesters.[73] These local cells were a key element of the regime's strategy for controlling social unrest.[74]

Most organizations of infiltration are more likely to use quiet information-gathering techniques and persuasion to help control populations. In Cuba, the Communist Party relies on Committees for the

---

[72] See, for example Torres and Casey (2017).
[73] "UBCH a prepararse para el contra ataque fulminante. Diosdado dará la orden." https://twitter.com/ameliachpsuv/status/435247376723615744?lang=en, last accessed May 29, 2018. Originally referred to in Handlin (2016, p. 24).
[74] Handlin (2016, pp. 22–26).

Defense of the Revolution (CDR) to monitor local populations. There are some 133,000 CDRs spread across the country to help the state implement policies and monitor the populace.[75] Fidel Castro described their purpose as helping people monitor each other and collect information on "what they do ... what they believe in, what people they meet, what activities they participate in."[76]

Institutions of infiltration can create highly personal dilemmas for the individuals involved. Should the leader of a local party cell attempt to coerce her neighbors, friends, and even her family? Where does she draw the line between loyalty to the state and loyalty to the people she knows?

It might be reasonable to suppose that a high degree of state penetration – for example, creating small party cells so people are tasked with monitoring a relatively small group – might backfire for an authoritarian regime. This approach might create *too much* familiarity between state agents and the people they are supposed to monitor. The movie *The Lives of Others* (Das Leben der Anderen) provides a vivid (if fictional) example. It depicts an East German Stasi agent who is tasked with intensively surveilling a playwright. The agent gradually becomes more sympathetic to the target, and ultimately protects him by covering up the fact that he has anonymously written a piece criticizing the regime.

Consistent with this perspective, a rich literature on "embeddedness" suggests a potential link between bureaucrats' social ties to local society and increased responsiveness to local interests. A growing number of studies find "that street-level bureaucrats who are embedded in the communities in which they serve produce better policy outcomes."[77] For example, bureaucrats in India who belong to local communities provide better public goods, so long as there are effective channels with which to hold them accountable.[78] And in Brazil, informed citizens and bureaucrats embedded in local communities have been found to improve the enforcement of innovative health programs.[79]

However, frontline bureaucrats who are involved in their communities can also help the state extend its reach. As Benjamin Read shows in his nuanced account of micro-level politics in urban China, embeddedness often cuts both ways, allowing residents to make demands on officials

[75] Read (2012, p. 251).
[76] Fagen (1969, p. 69) cited in Read (2012, p. 250).
[77] Pepinsky et al. (2017, p. 17).
[78] Bhavnani and Lee (2016).
[79] Tendler and Freedheim (1994).

but also making local society more "legible" for local officials.[80] Read observes how neighborhood personnel could draw "on the kind of micro-level detail that only someone deeply embedded in the local milieu would possess" in order to enforce the law.[81]

Historically, the Chinese state has long created deeply embedded networks of informants to help maintain order in the countryside. These networks of informants mimic the "cellular" or "honeycomb" nature of rural Chinese society.[82] Under the Song (960–1279), Ming (1368–1644), and Qing (1644–1912) Dynasties, China's emperors controlled rural society through a decentralized administrative system called the *baojia* (保甲).[83] This system required the leaders of each *bao* and *jia* to monitor their neighbors, report on their movements, inform on dissidents and traitors, encourage compliance with the law, and collect taxes. Across emperors and dynasties, the Imperial state frequently reorganized rural administration, creating smaller units when it required more control over society.[84]

Today, the CCP relies on similar institutions of control that deeply penetrate local society. In this book, I focus on neighborhood leaders of "villager small groups" (村民小组), which are nominally autonomous groupings of a few dozen to a hundred or so households. These neighborhood leaders, although not formally part of the state, are critical to the party's control over rural society in a way that is roughly equivalent to how Maduro uses UBCh cells in Venezuela or the Communist Party in Cuba uses CDRs. These infiltration networks are used to collect information on citizen behavior and pressure the noncompliant into obeying the state and its mandates.

The more that these institutions penetrate society – for example, the smaller each small group or each party cell is – the more effective they are as tools of control, because group leaders can more easily monitor noncompliers and pressure the noncompliant.[85]

---

[80] Read (2012).
[81] Read (2012, p. 108).
[82] Siu (1989); Shue (1988).
[83] Hsiao (1960); Schurmann (1966).
[84] Schurmann (1966, p. 410).
[85] Another source of leverage that I do not discuss here is violence. Armed groups like *colectivos* help the state repress protest at the end of the barrel of a gun. See also Lynette Ong's work on thugs-for-hire in China (Ong, 2018).

There are two key situations in which infiltration is an effective tool of control. First, it works when information is a key obstacle to control. One example of this in rural China is enforcing family planning policies, which requires gathering information on who is pregnant, who has given birth, who has undergone sterilization procedures, and who has paid fines for over quota births and who has not. The creation of nominally autonomous neighborhood-level leaders helps the state gather information effectively. Information on grievances and family financial situations provided by these neighborhood leaders also helps the state forestall protest and requisition land.

Second, infiltration is an effective tool of control when it empowers local agents who can persuade individuals to comply with the law. When enforcing family planning policies, a neighbor who has a personal relationship with a woman may be more likely to persuade her to go for a mandatory check-in at a local clinic. Likewise, someone who has farmed alongside her neighbors for decades may be more able to persuade them to give up a portion of their land during a state requisition.

2.5.1   The Limits of Infiltration

A major drawback of infiltration is that it relies less on persuasion and more on pressure than the other methods of informal control. The leaders of village neighborhood groups in China (or CDRs in Cuba or *nyumbakumi* in Rwanda) are not necessarily the most influential members of their village. They do not necessarily have high degrees of moral authority within their group, and are thus more likely to rely on heavy-handed tactics than, say, a clan leader.

The comparatively high degree of pressure that this strategy entails can erode regime legitimacy. The leaders of neighborhood groups in China are not formally part of the state; nor are the heads of nominally autonomous CDRs in Cuba or *colectivos* in Venezuela. As one activist told a reporter about the *colectivos*: "They attack your neighbors when they are in food lines and are identified as opposition members, they attack store owners by making them pay extortions, they attack bakers by taking away part of their production which they later sell on the black market. They are not true collectives, or political actors – they are criminals."[86] Yet the fiction of autonomy is thin. When the local government

---

[86] Torres and Casey (2017).

leans on these organizations to help implement the law, it is not hard to see who has pulled the strings. In the long run, this strategy chips away at people's sense that the state and its laws are just and fair.

2.6 HOW AUTOCRATS CHOSE STRATEGIES OF INFORMAL CONTROL

How do autocrats chose between these three different mechanisms of informal control? Consider first the situation of a community where civil society organizations are nonexistent. In these places, officials have incentives to try to cultivate social organizations that strengthen their informal authority – but in practice they face limitations. Path-dependent cultural traditions often prevent communities from building non-state groups. For example, Vladimir Putin's attempts to strengthen Russian nationalism through the Orthodox Church relies, naturally enough, on the existence of the Church in the first place and its role in Russian social life. His ability to appropriate some of the Church's moral authority is also limited by the rituals, practices, and norms that the Church has developed over centuries.

Similarly, variation in the presence or absence of grassroots non-state groups in China is often driven by factors outside of local official's control. Revival of lineage and temple institutions depends in part on path-dependent regional differences in culture, and the often arbitrary presence of entrepreneurial residents interested in maintaining social institutions. For instance, while folk religion has a long history in the coastal province of Fujian (making it easier for village elites to rebuild temples in the aftermath of the Cultural Revolution) these traditions are weaker in Hebei. Within regions with these traditions, cultivating and maintaining social institutions is "to a large extent contingent on whether social entrepreneurs happened to emerge in the village – people who were interested in reviving the group and skilled and respected enough to mobilize an initial project."[87] Detailed quantitative evidence supporting these patterns is provided in Chapters 4 and 5.

Political ideologies also limit the ability of officials to cultivate certain types of civil society groups. In principle, the CCP opposes the creation of grassroots groups like lineages and temple organizations, and it even casts a wary eye toward grassroots civic groups like village orchestras or

---

[87] See also Tsai (2007a, p. 104).

traditional dance troupes. The CCP's United Front Work Department, the organization in charge of the party's relationship with grassroots groups, generally paints clans and religious groups as "feudal" (封建) and "evil forces" (恶势力) that distort local politics. At the same time, the United Front and the party more generally recognizes that religion is an important force in the country's social life.[88]

In practice, even when it runs counter the CCP's official ideology, local officials and the United Front recognize the utility of these groups where they are present. Even official material distributed by the CCP acknowledges the usefulness of doing so. United Front documents sometimes weigh against the malign influence of lineage groups with one breath while acknowledging their usefulness with the next. For example, a document entitled "Recommendations for Striking Hard Against Unlawful Clan Activity" concludes with the acknowledgment that clans have "deep roots" in rural China and that in practice, "encouraging clans may in fact lead to more social unity and help build the New Socialist Countryside."[89] Local government documents also highlight the usefulness of civil society organizations and their networks for government "thought work." The Chengdu government, for example, issued a notice that "when it comes to promoting the demolition and relocation work, party cadres should take the lead and set an example by doing propaganda work among their kin, clan, and friends."[90] The Nanjing government similarly noted how exploiting "kinship affection (家族情) can be useful for handling problems" and implementing policy.[91]

Where strong community organizations exist, officials then face the choice of whether or not to co-opt local notables. Again, while the CCP in principle may oppose grassroots social organization, in reality it often condones co-optation. The United Front's public materials suggest that striking alliances with lineage group heads can help local cadres govern the countryside, especially in ethnic minority areas. "Village party secretaries and clan heads can govern together," writes one post on the United Front website, to create an "amalgam" (融合) of party and clan power.[92] Local governments likewise communicate the usefulness of co-optation to lower-level officials. One local government in Hunan, for example, circulated a notice about how it resolved protests over a land dispute by

---

[88] See especially Xi Jinping's 2017 speech to the National Religion Working Group Meeting (Liu, 2017).

[89] Xie (2015).

[90] See Chengdu Government (2016).

[91] Li and Zhao (2018).

[92] United Front Work Department and Xinhua News Agency (2011).

TABLE 2.1 *Interaction between different strategies of control*

Primary Strategy	Civil society groups	Co-opted civic elites	Infiltration	Critical juncture
Infiltration	No		High	
Cultivating Civil	Yes	No	Medium	No
Society Co-optation	Yes	Yes	Low	Yes

applying pressure on a lineage group head who also happened to be a villager small group head.[93]

Co-optation is powerful but costly. In order to co-opt these leaders, local officials may need to cut them in on the rents from office and must also share power with them. These elites may have their own agenda and can be difficult to control once in office. For these reasons, co-optation is not used indiscriminately.

Co-optation occurs mostly during critical junctures when the payoffs to political control are the highest. In rural China, these critical junctures are generally economic. When rapid urban or industrial development sweeps across a region, officials have more to gain financially from expropriating land and building factories on it, or confiscating levies meant for local development projects like roads. Data presented in Chapter 5 shows that lineage elites are incorporated into village political bodies when there is rapid development and when villages are urbanizing. Outside China, the critical junctures that drive co-optation can also be political. In Latin America, for instance, the co-optation of labor movements – for the purposes of political control of the working class – occurred during periods of "political reform and expansion of the state."[94]

Table 2.1 provides an overview of the different strategies. The final column notes that co-optation is most likely to occur during critical junctures.

Building organizations of infiltration is largely a *substitute* for building and co-opting civil society. Regimes that invest the most in these institutions, such as Rwanda under Habyarimana or Indonesia under Suharto, tend to be highly autocratic regimes where other civil society groups have been largely pushed underground. In rural China, leaders invest in high levels of infiltration where civil society is absent or its leaders not co-opted. Data from the Chinese General Social Survey, introduced later in the book, shows that in villages with weak social organizations,

---

93 Zhou (2018).
94 Collier and Collier (1991, p. 8).

each "informant" (that is, each villager small group leader) is in charge of only sixty-two households. In villages with strong civil society groups (specifically, lineage associations) each small-group leader has eighty-six households in their charge. Where villages have strong lineage institutions *and* the leaders of these lineage associations belong to the village committee or CCP branch, that number grows to 111 people per small-group leader, a very low level of infiltration. In short, there are dense networks of informants in villages with weak social organizations, and looser networks in villages with strong organizations.

Even though infiltrating organizations like neighborhood small groups are on paper autonomous from the party and government, in reality the CCP sees them as instruments of party control. United Front organizations emphasize that the leaders of villager small groups are "the first to know" (第一时间掌握) the situation on the ground, and are "responsible for reporting information upwards" (负责上报相关情况).[95] These institutions are an integral part of the "networks" (工作网络) that the United Front expects CCP cadres to cultivate.[96] One way in which local cadres can increase "supervision" (监督) is through adjustment of the size of villager small groups.[97] Some places have begun to experiment with reviving elements of the Imperial *baojia* system (described in more detail in Chapter 6), taking infiltration to a new level. For instance, one county in Guangxi has created a system where every fifteen households are organized into a *jia* (甲), and every ten *jia* make up one villager small group.[98]

In summary, local officials will cultivate civil society where they have the material and cultural resources to do so, but this is sometimes beyond their immediate control. Where civil society is strong, they will seek to co-opt local notables, mostly during critical junctures such as moments of rapid economic development. Finally, the strategy of infiltration is a substitute for building other types of non-state groups.

2.7 CONCLUSION

This chapter described my theory of informal control, which relies on three main mechanisms to encourage compliance. First, political leaders

---

[95] See for instance United Front Work Department of Yunnan Province (2018).
[96] United Front Work Department of Yunnan Province (2018).
[97] Wang (2018).
[98] Liu et al. (2018).

can cultivate civil society groups to increase their prestige and moral authority, which can help directly encourage individuals to obey the state. Second, leaders can co-opt local notables, who can then help the state encourage popular compliance. Finally, political leaders can infiltrate local society through para-state organizations that serve as the state's eyes, ears, and mouthpiece.

In the next chapter, I outline the problem of control in rural China. I draw on evidence from an original experiment to show that the CCP faces a dilemma: local party cadres are seen as untrustworthy, while the leaders of civil society groups enjoy high levels of trust.

3

The Communist Party's Governance Challenge

This chapter introduces the challenge of political control that faces the Chinese Communist Party (CCP). I begin the chapter by examining the key social groups that structure everyday life in rural China, including kinship and religious groups.

Next, I outline the basic governance structures of rural China and the core obligations of local officials: generating revenue by confiscating land, enforcing family planning quotas, and discouraging protest. Drawing on data from national surveys, I show some surprising patterns. For example, anecdotal evidence has led some scholars to conclude that land requisitions in China benefit villagers. I use systematic data from national surveys to show that on average, land "conversions" lead to lower incomes.

Evidence from an original survey experiment shows that lineage groups and networks are key reservoirs of social trust, while party cadres suffer from low levels of trust. The CCP therefore faces a governance challenge: controlling rural society despite low trust in its local agents.

3.1 KEY SOCIAL INSTITUTIONS IN RURAL CHINA

Two of the most common non-state social institutions in rural China are lineage and (folk) religious organizations. This section discusses each in turn. Both types of institutions have features that make them somewhat unique to China, yet they also have a great deal in common with social institutions in other contexts. Lineage groups in China are similar to descent-based kinship groups in other places, including clans in Central Asia and lineage groups in sub-Saharan Africa. Folk religious institutions in rural China share several traits with other indigenous and polytheistic religions.

3.1.1 Lineage Groups

Lineages – extended kinship networks in which group members trace their ancestry to a single male ancestor – are similar to kin groups elsewhere.[1] In China, "[a] lineage is a *corporate group* which celebrates *ritual unity* and is based on *demonstrated descent* from a common ancestor."[2] "Ritual unity" comes from specific rituals of ancestor worship, and often entails the construction of ancestral halls and shrines. Lineage groups in China are generally based on demonstrated descent from a known ancestor rather than fictive kinship. The "remarkably closed"[3] nature of Chinese lineages, in which groups very rarely absorb outsiders, arguably sets them apart from more open segmentary lineages or clans in Africa or the Middle East. However, as Watson notes, lineages vary considerably and do not necessarily meet all criteria of this definition.[4]

In the imperial era, lineage groups in China helped the state enforce local order and repress dissent. In a classic account of rural China under the Qing, Kung-chuan Hsiao writes that clan organizations were sometimes "made to help in keeping records of the inhabitants, watching their daily doings, reporting suspicious characters and offensive deeds, and apprehending characters wanted by the government."[5] Hsiao argues that "in employing the clan to help strengthen its control over the countryside, the Imperial government treated the kinship group more as a supplementary police organ than as a social body."[6] Lineage group norms also encouraged compliance with lineage elders and other authority figures – making these groups useful channels of political control. Prasenjit Duara notes that officials in imperial China promoted lineage institutions for this very reason:

---

[1] For lineages in Africa, see Evans-Pritchard (1940, ch. 5). For Central Asia, see, among others, Collins (2004, 2006).

[2] This definition is from anthropologist James L. Watson, drawing in part on Maurice Freedman's classic work *Lineage Organization in Southeastern China* Freedman (1965). Emphasis in original. Watson (1982, p. 594).

[3] Watson (1982, p. 597).

[4] Watson (1982, p. 606).

[5] Hsiao (1960, p. 7).

[6] Hsiao (1960, p. 350).

The presence of lineage groups and patrilineal ideology in northern villages was in no small measure a result of their vigorous propagation by scholars, officials, and the imperial center from the Song through the Qing. Regarded as embodying the principles of classical antiquity, the ideology of descent was seen as an ideal moral and ritual medium for regulating behavior and social order.[7]

In the years following the Communist takeover in 1949, official ideology discouraged lineage activity and to some degree lineages went underground, but they never went away entirely. Land reform and collectivization (1950–1953) stripped landlords and corporate lineages of their land holdings.[8] The party labeled traditional village elites, including lineage heads, class enemies. During the Cultural Revolution (1966–1976), the party undertook a campaign to destroy the "Four Olds" (四旧) of "Old Customs, Old Culture, Old Habits, and Old Ideas." Leaders urged Red Guards (groups of militant students) to smash ancestral halls and tablets, and to destroy lineage histories. However, in some areas, lineage identities and long-held clan feuds continued to organize village politics, albeit with a rhetorical veneer of Maoism.[9]

Since the economic reforms that began in 1978, lineages have experienced a revival in rural political and social life. Starting in the 1990s, many lineage groups rebuilt their ancestral halls.[10] Lineage groups sometimes provide private governance by, for example, helping resolve disputes between members and providing welfare for the poor and elderly. Lineage and surname groups also often serve as the basis for political competition in many villages.[11] Lineage elites, broadly construed, help protect the group's property, mobilize the group in protests, and structure village politics more generally.[12]

3.1.2   Folk Religious Organizations

There are dozens of folk religious deities in China. Some are local protectors of a specific village, while others have wide regional appeal. For example, the God of the South Seas (洪) is popular across much

---

[7] Duara (1988, p. 92). See also Watson (1982, pp. 616–617) for an interesting discussion of the degree to which state ideology played a role in creating lineage groups, especially in the Tang-Song transition.

[8] For an account of lineage institutions in the Maoist era, see Chan et al. (2009).

[9] See Unger (1998, pp. 90–94) on inter-clan conflict and Potter and Potter (1990, pp. 251–270) on collective farming and lineage identity.

[10] For a discussion of the lineage revival (复兴) see Wang (1991); Tang (1996); Yang and Liu (2000). See also Tsai (2007a, pp. 154–157).

[11] O'Brien (1994); Kelliher (1997); Manion (2006); Xu and Yao (2015).

[12] Perry (1980); He and Tong (2002); Li and O'Brien (2008).

of southern China.[13] Others, such as the Queen Mother of the West (西王母) and the Lord of the Soil (土地公), are venerated throughout the country. Historical figures, especially Imperial bureaucrats and generals, also sometimes become deities. Small village temples in China often honor these sorts of folk religious deities.[14]

Folk religious temples in China lack clergy, and before the Communist era were often run by wealthy local elites who served on temple councils.[15] These elites organized and raised funds for temple reconstruction efforts and temple fairs – major events that often lasted several days and involved processions, opera performances, music, feasts, dancing, and other pageantry. Some fairs limited participation to those born in the village, especially if they honored local gods, but many temple fairs drew hundreds or even thousands of pilgrims from nearby villages.

Buddhism and Buddhist figures also influenced Chinese folk religion and are important in their own right. Figure 3.1 maps the distribution of Buddhist temples across China in 1820, plotted against contemporary prefectural borders.[16] The map shows that Buddhist temples appeared throughout the Han areas of China, not merely along the coast or in a few major urban centers connected to the outside world through trade. Many villages had (and continue to have) temples, shrines, and fairs that honor Guanyin, a bodhisattva who is a figure of compassion and mercy, and is venerated by Buddhists across East Asia.

Under Mao, religious life in rural China effectively disappeared from the public sphere, although not for good. The CCP branded practicing religion a "feudal" and "superstitious" activity and promoted comradeship based on class solidarity and party ties. During the Cultural Revolution (1966–1976), villagers smashed statues, relics, and ancestral tablets and defaced religious iconography. Local cadres converted village temple buildings into offices, mess halls, dormitories, schools, and even, in one village I visited, a trash dump.[17] The campaigns were

---

[13] Siu (1989, pp. 79–85).

[14] For overviews, see Duara (1988, pp. 118–158), Smith (2004, pp. 136–151), and Tsai (2007a, p. 99).

[15] See Duara (1988, pp. 118–158) for a discussion of temple structure in northern China and Siu (1989, pp. 79–85) for southern China.

[16] The source for the underlying data is the *Da Qing Yitong Zhi* (大清一统志) via the China Historical GIS project. The data on 1820 temple locations www.fas.harvard .edu/chgis/, last accessed on February 14, 2019.

[17] For descriptions of campaigns against religion and other local customs, see Chan et al. (2009, pp. 87–90) and Siu (1989, pp. 125–135).

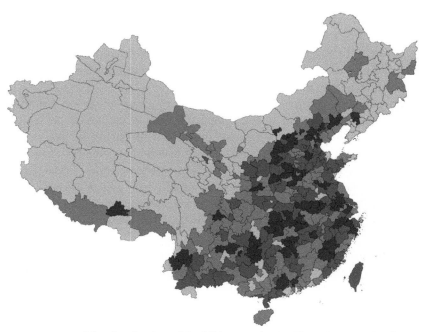

FIGURE 3.1 The distribution of Buddhist temples in China in 1820. Darker
shading indicates a higher concentration of temples.

effective, at least in changing peasants' public habits until Mao's death.
One classic account of rural life during the revolution quotes a peasant declaring: "Did the gods ever protect us? No! But since the party
came, after Chairman Mao came, we have things to eat, we have clothing, life is better. So we shouldn't believe in the gods. We should believe in
Chairman Mao!"[18]

Folk religious groups in rural China have thrived since Mao's death
in 1976. Villagers have rebuilt temples and once again observe temple rites and hold temple fairs (even if urbanization has dimmed their
importance for the younger generation). The form and ritual practice
of these groups is not always the same as in the past. First, these
groups have not reemerged in all areas; where they have reemerged
seems highly contingent and nearly random, depending, according to
some observers, on the presence of entrepreneurial residents.[19] Second,

[18] Chan et al. (2009, p. 89).
[19] Tsai (2007a, p. 104).

these groups no longer have the large collective property holdings that they did in the pre-Communist era, or the connection to local landholding elites, since that class has been destroyed. Finally, Communist Party ideology and policy has broken the direct link between religious practice and the state, and has circumscribed official participation in temple activities.

The degree to which village officials participate in religious institutions varies. Drawing on fieldwork in Hebei, Jiangxi, and Fujian, Tsai notes that "[t]emple groups rarely had village officials among their leadership since the state continues to discourage active promotion of 'feudal superstitious activities,' although village officials almost always participated in the group's activities as ordinary members. Lineage groups were more likely to have village officials as leaders since lineage activity is not considered religious."[20] By contrast, Adam Yuet Chau notes that in Shaanxi, "many temple leaders are current or former village Party secretaries" and that local elites help construct temples in order to "build or augment their basis of local influence or authority"[21]

3.2 KEY POLITICAL INSTITUTIONS IN RURAL CHINA

What political institutions govern rural China? The two key political bodies in rural Chinese villages are an elected village committee and an unelected village party branch. While village elections are now practically universal and are increasingly procedurally fair, elected village committees wield less authority than the CCP branch and the township government.

3.2.1 Village Committees

Following the dissolution of the collective agriculture system in the 1980s, and the commune and brigade system that governed it, villages lacked meaningful governments. In the early 1980s, a scattering of villages began to experiment with informal self-governing committees that governed village affairs.[22] The number of villages experimenting with self-government gradually grew, but it was not until 1987, after years of protracted bargaining and fierce opposition, that the National

[20] Tsai (2007a, p. 106).
[21] Chau (2008, pp. 12–13).
[22] O'Brien and Li (2000, pp. 465–466).

TABLE 3.1 *Key village institutions of self-government in China. Data on leader tenure and institution size from Martinez-Bravo et al. (2011)*

	Communist Party Branch	Village Committee
Leader	Party Secretary	Village Chief
Average tenure	10 years	7 years
Average size	7 Party Cadres	4 Members
Selectorate	Communist Party	Villagers

Peoples' Congress passed the "Organic Law of Villagers' Committees,"[23] which codified the responsibilities of these committees and mandated elections.[24] A 1998 revision to the law required the establishment of village committees throughout the country.[25]

Village committees consist of three to seven popularly elected members who serve three-year terms. They generally include a village committee director (often referred to as a village chief or *cunzhang*) and a vice director. On average, village committees have four to five members and their chiefs serve for seven years. (See Table 3.1.)[26]

Practically all villages now hold elections for village committees.[27] In 1983, there were around 300,000 village committees across China, which at the time were not required to be elected and had ill-defined responsibilities; by 2008, that number had swelled to over 600,000 committees, which by law are elected.[28] Figure 3.2 shows the cumulative percentage of villages that have introduced elections from 1982 to 2005.

Election procedures, including nomination, balloting, and ballot security, remain imperfect and unevenly implemented, but have become more democratic over time. For instance, the Organic Law mandates the use of voting booths to ensure the privacy of ballots, yet some villages continue to employ practices like "roving ballot boxes," where village officials go

---

[23] For more information, see www.npc.gov.cn/englishnpc/Law/2007-12/11/content_1383542.htm.

[24] See Kelliher (1997) for a discussion of the debate surrounding the law.

[25] O'Brien and Li (2000).

[26] Oi and Rozelle (2000); Martinez-Bravo et al. (2011).

[27] O'Brien and Han (2009).

[28] See National Bureau of Statistics of the People's Republic of China (2009). The high-water mark for the number of village committees was in 1991, when there were over a million. However, the consolidation of natural villages into larger administrative villages has led to a reduction in the number of village committees even as the percentage of the rural population living with elected village committees has increased over time.

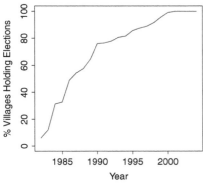

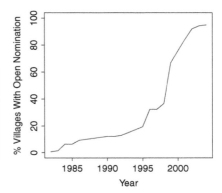

FIGURE 3.2 Villages holding elections

FIGURE 3.3 Elections with open nominations

door to door to collect ballots, eliminating the pretense of anonymity.[29] By law, anyone over the age of eighteen can vote and stand for election in their village of legal residence. In most provinces, any villager can nominate candidates for primaries (in a process known as "sea elections" or *haixuan*); Figure 3.3 shows the cumulative percentage of villages that have moved toward open nominations. Key positions such as the village directorship must have multiple candidates for office.

The Organic Law gives village committees broad authority. It declares that "villagers committees shall manage the public affairs and public welfare undertakings of the village, mediate disputes among the villagers, help maintain public order, and convey the villagers' opinions and demands and make suggestions to the people's government." Yet it also stipulates that local CCP branches, which serve "as a leading nucleus," will "support the villagers and ensure that they carry out self-government activities and exercise their democratic rights directly."

Village committees usually have discretion over the day-to-day operation of village affairs, but the CCP branch has the final say. There is, however, significant variation across issue areas and across villages.[30] In practice, the party tends to exert more control the higher the economic stakes. Quantifying the relative power of village committees and party

---

[29] O'Brien and Han (2009).
[30] For example, in the 1990s, interest in village politics was low in industrialized villages, where villagers had significant economic ties outside the village, which weakened the influence of elected village committees. Conversely, interest in village elections ran high in agricultural villages, which had few links to the outside world. See Oi and Rozelle (2000, p. 529).

TABLE 3.2 *Powers of different village officials. Table from Martinez-Bravo et al. (2011, p. 40). Village-year observations from a panel of 211 villages from 1980 to 2005. Because of rounding, percentages may not add to 100.*

Signature Required in Order To ...	Percent of Villages
Pay Reimbursement:	
Village Chief	56%
Party Secretary	25%
Village Chief & Party Secretary	19%
Hire Employees:	
Village Chief	27%
Party Secretary	30%
Village Chief & Party Secretary	44%
Redistribute Land:	
Village Chief	33%
Party Secretary	14%
Village Chief & Party Secretary	53%
Undertake Major Public Investment:	
Village Chief	18%
Party Secretary	15%
Village Chief & Party Secretary	67%

branches in different issue areas is challenging, since the party can (and does) exert control informally. Table 3.2 compares the formal powers of village chiefs and party secretaries. It shows that in each area, the village chief's signature is required for most decisions, suggesting significant practical authority. However, the party secretary must generally assent to decisions on the most economically costly issues, including major public investments, land reallocation, and hiring village government employees. In general, there has been a trend toward increasing authority for the village committee, even though the CCP branch still dominates in a majority of villages.[31]

3.2.2 Village-Level CCP Bodies

The party typically uses two mechanisms to exert control over elected village governments. First, townships can use their fiscal and administrative authority to pressure villages to bend to their will. Since the

[31] Sun et al. (2013, p. 21). However, as this book has gone to press, there have been moves to circumscribe the power of village committee heads.

1990s, governments have recentralized fiscal authority in a manner that has effectively diminished the clout of elected village leaders.[32] One survey of five provinces found that, from 1995 to 2005, the proportion of villages whose financial accounts were managed by the township increased from 8 percent to 39 percent, while the proportion of villages with a township "cadre in residence" (*zhu cun ganbu*) increased from 28 percent to 71 percent.[33] Townships also have the authority to alter the structure of village governments and to demote village cadres and dock their pay.[34]

Second, every village has an (unelected) CCP branch headed by a party secretary. Their membership and leaders are generally controlled by higher-level party cadres, especially in townships. Village committee members are also often members of the CCP, which makes them subject to party discipline and control. Candidates may already belong to the party (in some regions, township leaders urge village party secretaries to run for village chief) or the party may seek to draw them into its ranks after they join.[35] In 2015, of the 2.3 million people serving on village committees across the country, 1.4 million (59 percent) were party members; yet less than 7 percent of the total population are party members.[36]

The bottom line is that elected village committees are important actors in village politics, but their power is circumscribed in important ways. Their leaders must assent to important political decisions, but the party and township have tools to bend village directors to their will.

3.2.3 How Village Elections Strengthen Authoritarian Control

The debate over the introduction of the Organic Law suggests that the CCP introduced local elections in part to strengthen its control over the countryside. In the wake of collectivization in the 1980s, the party had great difficulty eliciting compliance in villages with the core rural policies of the time: grain procurement, the One Child Policy, and tax collection.[37] Coercion was proving to be a counter-productive strategy

---

[32] Luo et al. (2007); Oi et al. (2012); Kennedy (2013); Newland (2016).

[33] Oi et al. (2012).

[34] Alpermann (2001, p. 56).

[35] Alpermann (2001), Zhenglin and Bernstein (2004), and Landry (2008).

[36] Ministry of Civil Affairs, *Statistical Yearbook of Chinese Civil Affairs, 2015* (中国民政统计年鉴 2015).

[37] Kelliher (1997); O'Brien and Li (2000).

for eliciting compliance. Daniel Kelliher notes that many proponents of introducing elections argued as follows:

How can the state get villagers to meet the duties for grain, taxes and curtailed births? Bullying and violence have proven counter-productive. It would be better to entice villagers to take over the job of coercion on their own. How? By letting them rule themselves ... In effect, proponents say, self-government is a system for getting villagers to enforce unpopular policy upon themselves ... Proponents also say that state exactions will go more smoothly because elected cadres are more powerful than appointed ones.[38]

The law's proponents argued that ideally, "strengthened villagers' committees were to help maintain public order and assist government bodies in their work, and this, it was anticipated, would improve realization of township targets and prevent village cadres or defiant villagers from changing birth control allocations, funeral regulations, tax quotas, and so on."[39]

The introduction of elections smoothed implementation in some places but not others. Even afterwards, many villagers "continue[d] to resist state extraction and unpopular social and cultural reforms, while local cadres remain[ed] wedged between demanding superiors and reluctant or apathetic villagers – with some cadres either actively frustrating electoral reforms or forsaking their responsibilities to the state."[40] One important factor that explains the success or failure of these reforms in strengthening state control over rural areas is whether these institutions incorporated influential local notables.

The use of formal institutions to co-opt social elites is important because it helps resolve a commitment problem. It might seem as though local officials might prefer to informally co-opt social elites by buying their favor and influence on the side. However, this type of arrangement is dangerous for all sides. For officials, loyalty is best ensured by integrating local elites into formal state and party networks, where they participate in bonding rituals like banquets with heavy drinking, and where trust can be built over time. This helps reassure local officials that these communal elites will not accuse them of corruption.

The incentives to join formal institutions are perhaps even stronger for communal elites, since otherwise they have no formal authority and thus no leverage over local officials who might renege on their promises

---

[38] Kelliher (1997, pp. 73–74).
[39] O'Brien (1994, p. 40).
[40] O'Brien (1994, p. 49). See also O'Brien and Li (2000); Oi and Rozelle (2000); Zhenglin and Bernstein (2004); O'Brien and Han (2009).

and confiscate their property anyway. For these local elites, a formal position is a credible guarantee of their political safety. As one notable told me about the local government: "How else could I trust their promises?"[41]

In addition, elections are an effective way to determine which villagers have the most social authority, and therefore help local officials project state power. Competing to mobilize voters is a test of an individual's authority over their fellow villagers. Once they have proven themselves capable, these village elites are often drawn into the party.[42]

3.3 KEY GOVERNMENT MANDATES IN RURAL CHINA

The three most critical key policy mandates for village leaders in China are land expropriation and development, enforcement of family planning quotas, and protest management.[43] Yuhua Wang reports that an official told him that "only four ... indicators are critical: GDP growth rate, growth rate of per capita fiscal revenue [which is tightly linked to land conversion], social stability index, and fertility rate."[44] Each of these indicators are often veto items in the cadre evaluation system: failing to meet the targets can automatically scuttle a township or county official's promotion.

3.3.1 Land Expropriation and Development

Land is absolutely central to Chinese politics and the Chinese economy. The struggle over land ownership has in many ways defined the country's recent history: land redistribution determines its political winners and losers.[45] Mao Zedong noted that the "primary task" of the Communist Revolution was "the readjustment of the land problem," by which he meant the redistribution of land from landlords to peasants.[46] "Whoever wins the peasants will win China," Mao said. "Whoever solves the land problem will win the peasants."[47] In the decade following

---

[41] Author interview, Autumn 2012, Guangdong Province. This echoes the argument made by Gehlbach and Keefer (2011) that formal positions within authoritarian institutions help leaders credibly commit to avoid confiscation.
[42] Oi and Rozelle (2000); Zhenglin and Bernstein (2004).
[43] Birney (2014, p. 56).
[44] Wang (2014, p. 24).
[45] Rithmire (2015).
[46] Snow (1961, 444).
[47] Snow (1961, 70).

the Communist takeover in 1949, the Party kept its promise, and redistributed land from the country's landholding elite to farmers.

The winners of the first wave of land redistribution under CCP rule were hundreds of millions of peasants who before the Revolution had no land and little prospect of economic mobility; the losers were the landlords who lost their property and in many cases their lives.[48] Throughout the 1960s and much of the 1970s, China's peasants collectively farmed the land under a system of brigades and work teams. Under collectivization, agricultural productivity stagnated.[49] The late 1970s and early 1980s marked the end of collective cultivation of the land and the beginning of China's reform era.[50] Households were given rights over particular plots of soil, and in time farmers could sell the food they produced on a market that was much freer than before. Landholding remained egalitarian, with each household receiving approximately the same amount of land.

China's second great land redistribution has occurred during the 2000s and 2010s. In this regressive land redistribution, the losers have been smallholding farmers and the winners a new class of landholding elite. Tens of millions have had their land confiscated by the state. County and higher levels of government monopolize the authority to convert land's legal status from agricultural use (农用地) to construction use (建设用地).

Governments then auction the land use rights, typically for an order of magnitude more than they compensate farmers. The profits from land expropriation and conversion account for 30–70 percent of government revenue.[51]

Local governments in rural China confiscate a staggering amount of arable land (耕地) each year (see Table 3.3).[52] The official figures

---

[48] On the experience of China's peasants under Mao see, among many others, Chan et al. (1984); Shue (1988); Unger (1989); Oi (1991); Yang (1998).

[49] See Oi (1991, p. 32) for a discussion of grain consumption and productivity during this period.

[50] Kelliher (1992); Zhou et al. (1996) discuss whether peasant or elite initiative drove the reform process.

[51] See Cai (2003). More recent estimates are similar in magnitude, though there is significant uncertainty. As Rithmire (2015) notes, officials treat data on revenue generated from land as extremely sensitive.

[52] The data on hectares of land expropriated is from National Bureau of Statistics of the People's Republic of China (2016). The data on cultivated land, in this case cereal production, is from the World Bank. See http://data.worldbank.org/indicator/AG.LND.CREL.HA?year_high_desc=true.

TABLE 3.3 *Amount of farmland expropriated each year in China, and approximate equivalents.*

Year	Cultivated land seized (hectares):	Roughly equivalent to *all* farmland in:
2004	109,688	Slovenia
2005	161,315	Macedonia
2006	169,706	Botswana
2007	148,241	Albania
2008	149,112	Panama
2009	216,763	Georgia
2010	228,662	Liberia
2011	261,757	Norway
2012	246,283	Gambia
2013	206,906	Armenia
2014	181,206	Dominican Republic
2015	177,663	Netherlands
2016	155,511	Guyana

show that each year the government expropriates an area of cultivated land that is equivalent to *all* of the cultivated grain-producing land in a country the size of Norway, the Netherlands, or Botswana. These officially generated statistics most likely *underestimate* the amount of cultivated land that is confiscated. The central government places strict limits on the amount of cultivated land that can be converted to construction use. (Intriguingly, satellite monitoring to enforce these rules has led some local governments to disguise land conversion by planting vegetation on top of construction sites.)

In many ways, land markets drive local politics in China. Local government officials forge ties with local business elites and, in return for healthy kickbacks, give them preferential access to land. Susan Whiting's important work shows that property rights have long been at the heart of politics in rural China, and have shaped the allocation of property rights in the early decades of Reform and Opening.[53] The same is true of rural China today. In a clever study of illegal golf courses in China, Xin Sun shows how local governments allow their favored business partners to bend and break the law.[54] Firms connected to members of the Politburo on average receive discounts of 55–59 percent on land prices.[55]

[53] Whiting (2006).
[54] Sun (2015).
[55] Chen and Kung (2018).

Christopher Heurlin has shown how protests over land expropriations have forced officials to be responsive and make policy concessions.[56]

Village Officials and Land Expropriation

Village officials play important roles in land expropriations. First, survey evidence shows that in a majority of cases in which land is taken for commercial purposes (as opposed to infrastructural development) village cadres or investors initiate the confiscation, even though legally it must be approved by higher levels of government.[57] As Jean Oi notes, village political institutions are essentially "socialist landlords."[58] In the 1980s and 1990s, local officials used their power over land rights to ensure that collectively owned enterprises had preferential access to village land.[59] Through the mid-2000s, large-scale land reallocations – in which village officials redistributed the land holdings of large numbers of villagers – were the "preferred avenue" for land expropriations because they could be accomplished by making each villager's land holding slightly smaller with no direct compensation.[60] However, the Rural Land Contracting Law of 2003 placed tighter controls on when village officials could undertake such large-scale land reallocations, curbing though not eliminating land takings by village officials for the purpose of land development.[61]

Second, village leaders serve as representatives of the landholding village collectives during negotiations with higher levels of government over land use planning. They frequently work directly with firms and higher-level officials to attract investment to their village.[62] If they succeed, they bargain with higher levels of government or firms over the amount of compensation the village will receive in return for its land. One study found that in 39 percent of cases, village political institutions retained some portion of the compensation, in some instances more than 50 percent.[63]

Village officials and village political institutions often benefit directly from land expropriations. One survey found that 37 percent of a village's

---

[56] Heurlin (2016).
[57] In 55 percent of cases the taking is initiated by village governments Deininger and Jin (2009, p. 31).
[58] Oi (1991, p. 193).
[59] Oi (1991, p. 133n72).
[60] Deininger and Jin (2009, p. 23).
[61] Deininger and Jin (2009); Hsing (2010).
[62] Cai (2003).
[63] Deininger and Jin (2009).

own-source revenue comes from land takings.[64] Land sales are also important opportunities for corruption for local authorities.[65] In one three-year period in China between 1999 and 2002, the Ministry of Land and Resources investigated over half a million illegal land transactions; anecdotal evidence suggests that village officials can make many times their annual salary in kickbacks from land deals.[66]

Overall, land sales transfer hundreds of billions of dollars of wealth each year from village collectives to the state, although a precise estimate of the size of the transfer is not possible based on current statistics. Combining survey evidence on average compensation amounts and the total area of land expropriated in 2012 suggests that in that year, farmers in affected households were compensated approximately 30 billion *yuan* (4 billion US dollars), but that these sales generated 4.2 trillion *yuan* (682 billion US dollars) in profit, including the sale of land that was not expropriated from farmers.[67] Other surveys indicate that households receive 2 percent of the revenue from land sales.[68] Xin Sun shows that these land requisitions erode trust in local governments.[69]

The Negative Consequences of Land Expropriation
How do households fare after their land has been seized? Some China scholars, drawing on well-known cases of land expropriation in highly urbanized areas like Shenzhen, argue that households "want to be expropriated."[70] Yet Lynette Ong argues that compensation is often "paltry" and that after land expropriation "the incomes of displaced villagers declined or remained largely unchanged [while] their living expenses rose."[71]

These conflicting accounts leave us with an unclear picture of the consequences of property expropriation. In this section, I provide systematic evidence from across China that land expropriation has generally provided low levels of compensation that did not increase household

---

[64] Deininger and Jin (2009).
[65] Chen and Kung (2015).
[66] See Cai (2003); Zhu (2005). Sun (2015) shows how large-scale violations of land laws can go unpunished.
[67] Deininger and Jin (2009) estimate an average compensation of 7,700 per *mu* in 2012, during which 3,694,245 hectares were expropriated. Data on land use sales was gathered from Ministry of Land and Resources (2014).
[68] China Renmin University, Michigan State University, and Landesa (2011).
[69] Sun (2014).
[70] See Paik and Lee (2012).
[71] Ong (2014, p. 169).

wealth and that had durable negative impacts on household income. Qualitative evidence suggests that households' subjective well-being also suffers.

To estimate the effect of land expropriation on household material wellbeing, I draw on evidence from the 2012 China Household Finance Survey (CHFS, 中国家庭金融调查), a survey with a national sampling frame conducted by researchers at the Research Institute of Economics and Management at the Southwestern University of Finance and Economics.[72] The survey used remote sensing techniques and GIS to randomly sample over 8,000 households in eighty counties across twenty-five provinces.

The CHFS sample provides information on land expropriations and compensation amounts. About 4 percent of the sample reported having had their land expropriated, which suggests that around 20 million households or 60 million people have had land confiscated. Once households that have had their homes expropriated for demolition and redevelopment purposes are taken into account, it suggests that around 100 million people have had property confiscated by the local government.

In contrast to the picture painted by some qualitative research in peri-urban China, land expropriation is typically poorly compensated. Approximately 80 percent of households receive some sort of compensation.[73] However, the modal compensation amount is zero. Among those who do receive cash compensation, it is typically low relative to farming income. Figure 3.4 shows the distribution of cash compensation for households. The majority of households receive low levels of compensation. Some outliers receive lavish compensation, driving the mean to a relatively high level: about 8,300 *yuan* per *mu* of land.[74] If the average farmer generates about 1,000 *yuan* per *mu* of land every year, this level of compensation, while far below the market value, can increase household well-being in the short run.

Non-land compensation is common but does little to boost household material well-being. For instance, households whose land is expropriated may receive a township or urban residency permit (*hukou*), which in

---

[72] The sampling frame excludes Tibet, Xinjiang, and Inner Mongolia as well as Special Administrative Regions.

[73] The figures on compensation from the CHFS sample closely match the values in the separate World Bank survey conducted by Deininger and Jin (2009) and in the China Family Panel Studies, introduced in Chapter 4.

[74] This figure is higher than Deininger and Jin (2009), likely reflecting the gradual increase in compensation since their 2005 survey.

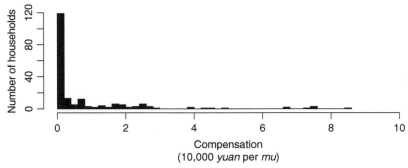

FIGURE 3.4 Distribution of land taking compensation amounts

theory gives them access to a wider range of social welfare benefits. Yet in practice local governments actually provide them with less costly welfare benefits, such as pension insurance.[75] As I show below, household material wealth does not improve following land takings, and income plummets.

Uncompensated or undercompensated land takings occur surprisingly frequently. Altogether, 45 percent of households received less than the value of a year's worth of their land's agricultural output in compensation, including the 18 percent that received no compensation whatsoever. These uncompensated land takings are significantly more likely to occur the further one travels from cities and county seats. Traveling forty minutes outside a county city doubles the probability of a land taking being uncompensated.

However, compensation has gradually improved. Article 47 of the 2004 revision to the Land Administration Law[76] stipulates that compensation should be six to ten times the average annual output of the land, but because of the ambiguous language this was often treated as a suggested ceiling for compensation, not an absolute minimum. The 2007 Property Law further strengthened land rights.[77] Since 2007, median compensation has jumped to around 3,900 *yuan* per *mu* of land.

How does expropriation effect household material well-being? To estimate the effect of expropriation on household outcomes, I preprocess

---

[75] Cai (2016).
[76] See www.gov.cn/banshi/2005-05/26/content_989.htm. For an English translation, see www.npc.gov.cn/englishnpc/Law/2007-12/12/content_1383939.htm. However, the English translation is not direct.
[77] For an English translation, see www.npc.gov.cn/englishnpc/Law/2009-02/20/content_1471118.htm.

the data using entropy balancing, which is a nonparametric technique for estimating causal effects using observational data.[78] The algorithm creates weights for each observation in the dataset (in this case, for each household) so that the re-weighted dataset is close to identical on observed covariates. The underlying logic is similar to that of an experiment, which seeks to create balanced treatment and control groups and a fair comparison. However, because I rely here on observational data, there is a strong possibility that the estimates might be confounded by unobserved household characteristics.

I re-weight the data on key pretreatment (pre-expropriation) characteristics of the household head.[79] These include whether the household head is a non-Han ethnic minority, whether they belong to the largest surname group in their village, number of years of schooling, whether they were a Communist Youth League member, distance to the nearest city, and age.

Figure 3.5 presents estimates for the effect of expropriation on key household outcomes. The first estimate is for the effect of land expropriation on household income. The estimates suggest that having land expropriated causes household incomes to drop by approximately two-tenths of a standard deviation. Separating agricultural income from commercial income shows that expropriated households see small gains

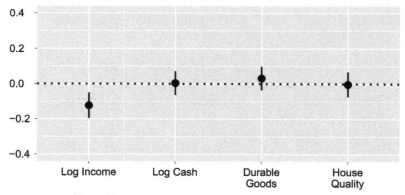

FIGURE 3.5 Effect of land expropriation on key measures of household material well-being. Estimated using entropy balancing with province fixed effects.

[78] Hainmueller and Xu (2011).
[79] Since controlling for post-treatment outcomes can bias the estimates, it is important not to condition on these variables.

in income from non-agricultural sources such as small businesses, but these gains are outweighed by lost agricultural income.

However, most expropriated households receive some form of compensation even if it is a small amount, so it is possible that lower income flows are offset by increases in other forms of wealth. To investigate this possibility, I examine the effect of expropriation on key measures of household cash, durable goods, and housing quality. The estimates show that expropriation does not lead to significant increases in households' cash holdings. Nor does it lead to increases in the log number of durable goods that households own such as TVs, satellite hookups, refrigerators, or furniture. Finally, it does not lead to increases in the quality of housing, measured here as households' log square footage (other measures, such as household head's assessments of the quality of household interiors, also show a non-significant effect of almost exactly zero).

In short, expropriations have historically left households worse off in terms of their material welfare. They lose an important income stream without, on balance, increases in nonfarm income to offset these loses. They also do not see significant increases in household assets, which, given the low median compensation for land takings, is not surprising.

The negative effect of land expropriations on households will be surprising to some China scholars, especially those whose work has focused on land development in peri-urban China. In contrast to the idea that farmers "want to be expropriated," the evidence presented here shows that the more typical story is one of lost farming income and no measurable increase in household wealth.

Over-time increases in compensation leave open the possibility that this dynamic has changed in recent years. Examining this will require more data and is an important avenue for future research on rural China.

3.3.2 Family Planning Policy

A second key mandate for village officials is to enforce family planning policies, which have had a profound impact on Chinese society over the past four decades. The policies are rooted in the 1970s "Later, Longer, Fewer" campaign, which encouraged families to delay having children and to have fewer of them.[80] Beginning in 1979, the state introduced mandatory birth quotas in a series of policies – created not by sociologists

---

[80] Whyte et al. (2015).

and demographers but by a team of missile scientists – designed to reduce China's growing population, which many felt posed a threat to its long-term economic growth and stability.[81] Although the resulting policies are generally referred to as a single "One Child Policy" (一胎制 or 独生子女政策), there has never been one single policy or a blanket limitation to one child. Instead, the policies have varied somewhat by province, and while they generally restricted urban families to one child, many regions made exceptions for ethnic minorities and often permitted a second child in rural areas, particularly if the first child is female.[82] Typical penalties for families that did not comply with the law included monetary fines, job loss, and even property seizure, while highly coercive measures such as forced abortions were real but relatively rare.[83] The policies were reformed in 2015 to allow for additional children, but state family planning policies have not been abolished altogether and still place limits on the number of births.

There is widespread agreement that the One Child Policy led to slower population growth, but there is significant uncertainty about its precise impact. Fertility was already declining before the policy was introduced, partly due to the Later, Longer, Fewer campaign, and the economic boom of the reform era also played an important role in decreasing China's fertility rate.[84] The widely cited statistic that the policy prevented 400 million births is surely an exaggeration. The effect of the policy was likely much smaller but still substantial.[85] Quantitative evidence suggests that at a minimum it prevented several tens of millions of births.[86]

Enforcement of family planning policies can have a profound impact on the career paths of village-level officials, for whom meeting birth quotas have long been a hard target. Failing to meet them can result in officials' losing their job or other bureaucratic penalties, such as a loss of income.[87]

At the administrative unit just below the village, the leaders of quasi-autonomous village wards have played a key role in implementing state family planning policy. These wards are a legacy of the collective

[81] Hesketh et al. (2005); Greenhalgh (2008).
[82] Hesketh and Zhu (1997).
[83] Hesketh and Zhu (1997); Greenhalgh and Winckler (2005).
[84] Cai (2010); Whyte et al. (2015).
[85] Feeney and Feng (e.g., 1993); Hesketh et al. (e.g., 2005); Chen et al. (e.g., 2009); Cai (e.g., 2010); Whyte et al. (e.g., 2015).
[86] McElroy and Yang (2000); Chen et al. (2009).
[87] O'Brien and Li (1999); Hesketh et al. (2005); Birney (2014).

agriculture system, which divided villages up into "production teams" (生产队) that collectively owned and cultivated land. The dismantling of the collective agriculture system led to reforms of the administrative structure of villages. The old production teams were, in most villages, renamed villager small groups (村民小组). To simplify matters, I refer to these sub-village jurisdictions as "wards."

Despite their nominal autonomy, village leaders implement state family planning policies by popularizing their details, helping the state collect information on compliance, and levying fines on villagers for over-quota births.

3.3.3 Stability Maintenance

Finally, the party seeks to curb collective protest and expression. There is a huge literature on collective protest in China and the incentives for local officials to suppress it.[88] For the central government, the incentives for repressing protest are clear enough, since it can threaten their hold on power (although Beijing may tolerate a limited amount of protest since it helps the government identify the most discontented populations and the most corrupt local officials).[89]

Higher levels of government create strong incentives for local party cadres to curb protest. When villagers engage in collective protest, lodge collective complaints, or submit petitions to higher levels of government, it can ruin an official's promotion prospects.[90] Birney writes that "one county official in charge of overseeing village elections explained ... his evaluation would take a severe hit if there were even a single protest."[91]

The party holds village-level officials accountable for protests or other forms of political instability. For example, township officials sometimes sack village party secretaries after incidents of collective protest or petitioning.[92] Village-level leaders may also have their salaries docked or receive no salaries at all if they do not meet the targets set out for them by township officials, which often include stability maintenance targets.[93]

---

[88] See, for example, O'Brien and Li (1995); Perry (2002); O'Brien and Li (2006); Lee (2007); Cai (2008); Li and O'Brien (2008); Deng and O'Brien (2013); O'Brien and Deng (2015a).

[89] Lorentzen (2013). See also Edin (2003, p. 44).

[90] Edin (2003, pp. 43–44).

[91] Birney (2014, p. 59).

[92] O'Brien and Li (1999, p. 178).

[93] Whiting (2004).

Land takings are perhaps the single largest cause of protest in rural China.[94] Disputes over land takings often escalate into court cases, especially if the land is taken by an outside developer or the local government.[95]

3.4 THE COMMUNIST PARTY'S GOVERNANCE CHALLENGE

The state tasks village officials in China with implementing important policies of control. Village cadres help implement land requisitions, which lead to drops in household income and effectively redistribute wealth from village collectives to the state in a highly regressive form of taxation. Cadres help implement birth quota policies, which place them in the position of trying to control women's bodies and highly consequential decisions about family planning. They must also serve as the grassroots arms of the state, helping de-escalate and defuse protest before it grows into a major political problem.

Given the importance of these grassroots officials for state control and state capacity, it is essential to understand their relationship to local society. What social and political ties shape village politics in China?

In this section, I present micro-level evidence on how social and political ties influence trust and political mobilization in rural China. The experiment, the first of its kind, uses a conjoint design that randomly varies the attributes of potential candidates standing for village elections. The results show that villagers tend to distrust CCP members, but have a high degree of trust in people from their lineage or neighborhood. Voters also heavily weight these social ties when casting ballots in village elections. These results suggest that the CCP faces a governance challenge at the grassroots level, where local CCP cadres are distrusted but must find a way to implement coercive policies.

3.4.1 Hypotheses about Political Trust and Mobilization

What sorts of political leaders do the citizens of rural China trust? In village elections in rural China, how do voters decide which candidate to support? We have little quantitative evidence about how voters make decisions about who to support or what type of political leader they trust the most.

---

[94] Hsing (2010).
[95] Whiting (2011).

In China, elections involve short campaigns with little policy debate. Surveys of two provinces in the early 2000s found that in most villages the candidates make a speech to villagers or the villager representative assembly shortly before the election, while other forms of overt campaigning, like house-to-house visits by candidates, occurred in only about a quarter of surveyed villages.[96] Some scholars of village elections argue that "little or no campaigning" occurs in Chinese village elections because electioneering is both "culturally inappropriate" and unnecessary since villagers all know each other.[97] When electioneering does happen, most candidates offer up simple platitudes about the need for village harmony and economic development that echo Communist Party slogans. In one village election I witnessed, campaign posters had slogans like "'Live in peace and work happily; collective stability and growth,' that's our motto!" and "Our slogan: Build a new prosperous and harmonious village."

Given the lack of policy debate, voters may be guided by the candidates' membership (or lack thereof) in the ruling party. Evidence from other authoritarian countries points in several directions. Where parties are weak, as in Jordan,[98] or effectively proscribed from competing altogether, as in Vietnam,[99] some previous studies relying on regression analysis have found that party labels have no discernible influence on voters. Another possibility is that voters favor candidates who belong to the CCP. Previous scholarship has shown that the CCP mobilizes its members quite effectively in village elections, and that Party members are more likely to run for village office.[100] Yet an important recent study by Melanie Manion finds that in elections for township Peoples' Congresses, voters nominate Party and other government leaders at a significantly *lower* rate than a separate Party nomination committee.[101] Given the unsettled state of the evidence, I test a hypothesis on the effect of party membership on voters' evaluations of candidates.

Voters may also be guided by candidates' class or occupational background. In elections for Local Peoples' Congresses, Manion shows that voters nominate self-employed entrepreneurs at higher rates than the Communist Party committee.[102] In addition, it may be the case that

---

[96] O'Brien and Han (2009).
[97] Pastor and Tan (2000, p. 496).
[98] Lust-Okar (2006).
[99] Malesky and Schuler (2011).
[100] Landry et al. (2010).
[101] Manion (2014).
[102] Manion (2014).

voters prefer well-educated candidates over less-educated candidates from the same class background, such as teachers. The preference for well-educated candidates would be consistent with evidence from Victor Shih, Christopher Adolph, and Mingxing Liu, who find that education provides an advantage in advancement for CCP members at the elite level.[103] Their experiment examines the effect of three occupations: entrepreneur, teacher, and farmer.

Community ties also play an important role in village politics. As discussed in rural China lineage and temple groups are important social organizations. Voters may also be influenced by their membership in neighborhood networks such as "villager small groups," which are based on place of residence. In the Mao era, these groups were called production teams, and they collectively owned and cultivated the village's land. While villagers now have use rights to private plots, the land itself remains collectively owned. Since villager small groups continue to control the allocation of land in many villages, they are still a feature of village economic and political life.

The candidate's gender may also be important. Throughout the world, there are fewer female than male politicians. In 2007, just 17 percent of members of parliament worldwide were female.[104] One potential reason for the low number of female political leaders in China is voter discrimination. Indeed, at higher levels of leadership in China, being female is a distinct disadvantage.[105] Given the evident discrimination against female politicians worldwide, as well as China in particular, it is possible that voters in village elections make their decisions based partly on the gender of the candidate.

Finally, voters may weigh the age of the candidate. Edmund Malesky and Paul Schuler find that in elections in authoritarian Vietnam, voters prefer older candidates.[106] Similarly, Shih, Adolph, and Liu find that age has a large positive effect on advancement in the Central Committee, but the effect is very imprecisely estimated.[107] However, Manion finds no difference in the age of candidates nominated by voters and the Party.[108]

In short, the existing literature suggests that trust and political mobilization may be influenced by some mix of party, class, clan,

---

[103] Shih et al. (2012).
[104] Wolbrecht and Campbell (2007).
[105] Shih et al. (2012).
[106] Malesky and Schuler (2011)
[107] Shih et al. (2012)
[108] Manion (2014).

neighborhood, gender, religion, and age. In the next section, I describe an experiment that tests the causal effect of each of these attributes on voters' evaluation of political leaders.

3.4.2 Results from an Experiment on Political Trust in Rural China

To test what candidate attributes influence vote choice, I asked villagers in a random sample of villages in a municipality in southern China to choose between two hypothetical candidates to serve as their representative. I used a multidimensional design in which I randomized each candidate attribute simultaneously; such conjoint designs have only recently been used in studies of politics.[109] The aim of the design was to present villagers with the sort of information that they might have about a real-world candidate. As I have discussed in village elections in China, information is generally limited to basic candidate attributes with no information about policy positions.

To test each of the hypotheses mentioned I presented voters with information about seven candidate attributes in a simulated ballot. The attributes were gender (male or female); age (thirty-five, fifty-seven, or seventy-eight years old); occupation (farmer, teacher, or entrepreneur); religious habits ("never goes to temple to worship" or "frequently goes to temple to worship"); clan ("same clan as you" or "different clan than you"); villager small group ("your small group" or "different small group"); and party membership ("CCP member" or "not CCP member"). Party membership was limited to CCP membership to reflect the fact that members of China's officially sanctioned minority parties essentially never run openly as minority party members in village elections. Respondents were presented with a mock ballot listing the attributes of each candidate. Once respondents viewed the ballot, they were first asked to select which of the two candidates they would prefer. Subsequently, they were asked to rate on a 1 to 5 Likert scale the degree to which they thought the candidate cared about the voters' material interests (利益) and the degree to which they trusted (信任) the candidate.[110]

---

[109] Hainmueller et al. (2014).

[110] In the Likert scale, 1 was "not at all" (完全不信任/在乎) and 5 was "a lot" (完全信任/在乎). A potential concern with asking multiple questions is some degree of contamination, especially that respondents will have an incentive to make their responses consistent with each other. The results should alleviate this concern. Like several recent experiments that have also asked respondents to assess hypothetical candidates *after* "voting" for them, I find that how respondents assess candidate trustworthiness and other qualities is not a simple function of their voting decision.

Each of the attributes was fully randomized with no restrictions, and the order of attributes was randomized for each respondent. Jens Hainmueller, Daniel Hopkins, and Teppei Yamamoto show that difference-in-means tests will provide unbiased estimates of average marginal effects for each attribute component.[111] Following their approach, differences in means for a given attribute are calculated by regressing the dichotomous choice variable on a set of dummy variables for each attribute component, excluding one comparison condition. As with most conjoint experiments in political science, respondents voted on multiple pairs of candidates, in this case three pairs per respondent; standard errors are clustered by survey respondent to account for within-respondent correlations.

The experiment was conducted in 2013 in a random sample of twenty-two villages outside Guangzhou. (See Appendix B for more details.) It is important to note that the sampling strategy did not produce a random draw of households, but the sample nevertheless closely approximates the characteristics of these villages. The sample was 50 percent male, with a lower middle-school education, and a mean age of fifty-four. While kinship groups are a relevant feature of local social life, they are not especially strong; 70 percent of villagers reported that they did not have an active ancestral hall or that they did not visit it. The attrition rate was low; less than 2 percent of respondents who started the task failed to rate all four pairs of profiles.

Figure 3.6 presents point estimates and confidence intervals for candidate vote choice. The reference categories are presented as a dot without a confidence interval, and other categories are shown with 95 percent confidence intervals.

The results show that Party membership has no influence on voter preferences. The point estimate is almost precisely zero, and the 95 percent confidence bounds suggest an electoral benefit of at most 4 percentage points, or a cost of up to 4 percentage points. (If additional parties were added to the list of tested attributes, it is possible that the CCP would be more popular than its potential rivals. However, as long as respondents' preferences are independent of irrelevant alternatives, the finding that voters do not prefer CCP candidates over those with no party membership should hold.) This finding clarifies the role of the Communist Party in elections in China: CCP ties are of negligible

---

[111] Hainmueller et al. (2014).

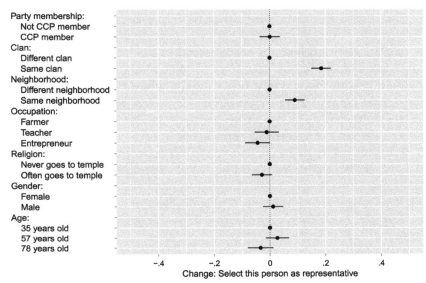

FIGURE 3.6 Point estimates of marginal effect of candidate attributes on vote choice with 95 percent confidence intervals.

importance in elections. Party membership neither hamstrings candidates nor provides them with an advantage.

By comparison, the candidates' lineage membership exerts a strong pull on voters. Results from the ballot experiment show that voters are 19 percentage points more likely to vote for a member of their own lineage group. The results hold if I restrict the analysis to the first of the three ballots that voters cast or correct for multiple comparisons.

These findings are consistent with a large body of work that under-scores the importance of lineage groups or clans in village elections, but provide more direct evidence than previous studies. Interestingly, the effect size is large among voters who regularly attend lineage hall activities (22 percent, SE=3.2) and among voters who report never going (17 percent, SE=2.1). This suggests that using lineage hall activity as a proxy for clan salience, as some studies do, may significantly undercount politically active clans.

Voters also strongly favored members who belonged to the same vil-lager small group. They were 9 percentage points more likely to support a candidate who hailed from their collective. This large effect size is unexpected, given how little has been made of neighborhood ties in studies of Chinese village elections.

The results also show that voters in village elections penalize candidates who are entrepreneurs. Voters are approximately 4 percentage points less likely to vote for an entrepreneur-candidate compared to a candidate who is a farmer. This could to some degree reflect the stigmatization of private enterprise earlier in the Communist era; however, given the central place of private business in the current economy, this seems unlikely. Instead, it is more likely to reflect the different economic and policy interests of farmers and business owners.

Religious habits play a less important role in voters' decision-making. If anything, there appears to be a slightly negative effect of being a regular temple attendee on voters' behavior, though the confidence interval overlaps with zero. This is surprising in light of previous work that has suggested that cadres who belong to temple organizations are more accountable to villagers.[112]

There is also evidence of male voters discriminating against female candidates. In the overall population, being female is slightly penalized by voters, though not at a statistically significant level. Once we break down respondents by sex, however, a divide emerges. Female respondents do not strongly discriminate on gender; however, male respondents are 6 percentage points *less* likely to vote for a female candidate, a statistically significant effect (SE=2).

Finally, age has no discernible effect on voters' preferences. Voters exhibit a slight preference for middle-aged candidates over young and post-retirement age candidates. This is generally consistent with findings that older candidates are preferred for promotions at higher levels of government in China, and that voters in Vietnamese elections prefer older candidates. However, it suggests that candidates over the retirement age may face a penalty.

The middling performance of CCP candidates seems to result, at least in part, from low levels of trust in CCP cadres. As a follow-up to the main vote choice question, I asked voters to rate on a scale of 1 to 7 how much they trust the candidate. Figure 3.7 presents estimates for this variable.

Voters clearly penalize candidates who belong to the Communist Party. They rate them about 8 percentage points less trustworthy than other candidates. One interpretation of this result is that villagers think Party members act to advance their own interests, which are separate from those of regular villagers.

---

[112] Tsai (2007a).

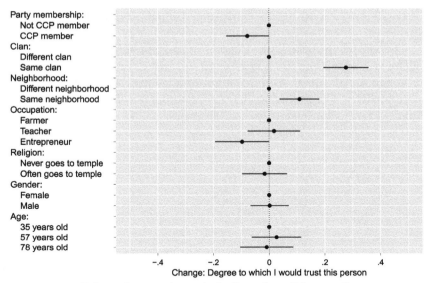

FIGURE 3.7 Point estimates of marginal effect of candidate attributes on trust. 95 percent confidence intervals shown.

On the question of whether candidates care about their material interests, voters specifically penalize the Party when it is associated with the local business class. Voters rate CCP members who are also entrepreneurs 10 percentage points lower (SE=7) than non-Party entrepreneurs, which is a statistically significant difference. However, they do not penalize farmers (estimate=-8, SE=6) or teachers (estimate=-4, SE=6) for belonging to the Party.

The Party nominally represents the interests of workers and peasants. Yet unlike China in the Mao era, the Party cannot count on being able to mobilize villagers based on the prestige of the Party alone.

3.5 CONCLUSION

In this chapter, I outlined the CCP's governance challenge in rural China. The CCP's core demands on village officials are that they help requisition land, enforce birth quotas, and curb protest. These policies help advance the party's key goals of economic growth and political stability. However, the party's grassroots agents are at a disadvantage when it comes to implementing these mandates: quite simply, people distrust them. The combination of low trust in the party and high demands on its local agents constitutes China's grassroots governance challenge.

The theory presented in Chapter 2 suggested a solution to this dilemma: officials can use non-state groups, which enjoy high degrees of trust and social capital, as tools of informal control that help strengthen state capacity. The following chapters examine the effectiveness of state building through non-state groups in detail.

4

Cultivating Civil Society

Cultivating civil society – encouraging the establishment of non-state groups like churches, temples, civic associations, lineage groups, labor unions, or clubs – can strengthen state capacity. In this chapter, I show how local officials in China encourage the establishment of lineage associations, temple organizations, and social clubs as a way to increase their informal authority and make local society more legible to the state. This, in turn, helps them suppress protest and requisition land. Drawing on examples from India to Appalachia, I argue that governments outside China have often engaged in similar strategies of top-down *informal control.*

The flip side of informal control is that if communities lack strong social organizations, activists can find creative ways to mount spontaneous, leaderless resistance. Consider, for example, the wave of student protests in Nicaragua in 2018 that demanded the ouster of President Daniel Ortega. Facing harsh repression, the students launched what one analyst described as a "spontaneous movement that was not the result of any organization," in which "the lack of a clear leader ... made the movement harder to quash."[1] In rural China, such seemingly spontaneous and leaderless protests are common. For instance, a small group of anonymous activists can organize a flash protest by hanging up posters that announce a date and location for people to gather. In addition to discussing informal control, this chapter highlights how the *lack* of state-dominated civil society organizations can sometimes help activists organize.

---

[1] See Robles (2018). I thank James Scott for pointing me to this example.

TABLE 4.1 *Longjin and Meilong case studies*

	Longjin	Meilong
Competitive elections	No	No
Distance to city center	10 km	8 km
Religious festival	Yes	Yes
Key explanatory variable:		
Lineage association	No	Yes
Key outcomes:		
Compliance with land expropriation	Low	High
Compliance with stability maintenance	Low	High
Compliance with birth quotas	High	Low

4.1 LINEAGE GROUPS AND INFORMAL CONTROL

Lineage groups are arguably the most important social group in rural China. They are extended kinship networks, and members of the lineage claim descent from a common known ancestor. These groups often share resources such as ancestral halls with spirit tablets, as well as formal lineage associations that organize group activities.[2] See Chapter 3 for an extended discussion.[3] How do lineage institutions facilitate informal control in rural China?

4.1.1 Structured Case Study Evidence

The cases of Longjin and Meilong villages illuminate the role that lineage groups play in strengthening political control. Like most of the case study evidence in the following three chapters, the two villages are "most-similar cases,"[4] with comparable economic, social, and political conditions. They differ, however, in one crucial respect: in Longjin Village, officials have not permitted or encouraged the revival of lineage associations in the reform era, whereas in Meilong they have allowed and nurtured them (see Figure 4.1).

Both Meilong and Longjin are highly urbanized villages near Guangzhou. They are unrepresentative of China as a whole, since their proximity to a major city means that residents enjoy a standard of living that is much higher than the typical farmer in rural China. Guangdong

---

[2] See Section 3.1.1 for more detail.
[3] See also Mattingly (2016).
[4] Przeworski and Teune (1970).

FIGURE 4.1 An active lineage hall in a nearby village during the Lantern Festival.

FIGURE 4.2 Many of the ancestral halls and temples in Longjin have become trash dumps and recycling centers.

Province also has much more active and organized lineage groups than much of the rest of China. The survey evidence presented below provides a more representative picture of the country.

However, focusing on case studies in relatively urbanized Guangdong has an important analytical payoff. A natural concern is that places with and without lineage groups are likely to be fundamentally different. In particular, villages without lineage institutions are likely to be poorer or may come from regions that have a weaker history of lineage activity. In these places local officials could not hope to cultivate lineage institutions even if they wanted to because they lack the economic and cultural raw material to do so. My cases address this problem: both villages have a centuries-long history of lineage activity, yet only in one village (Meilong) have officials permitted and cultivated a revival of the lineage associations in the post-Mao era.

Placing this matched pair of villages side by side has two potential benefits. First, to some degree, a paired comparison can provide some inferential leverage on what causes the different outcomes in the two villages.[5] However, there are some clear shortcomings associated with

---

[5] Przeworski and Teune (1970); Tarrow (2010).

relying on paired comparisons for causal inference, including insufficient degrees of freedom and the nonrepresentative nature of the sample.[6]

A second reason to use paired comparisons, as I do throughout this book, is that this approach better illustrates the logic of the argument by presenting one case where the main explanatory variable is present and one where it is absent (in other words, counterfactual cases). Unpacking causation happens in parallel *within* each case, through process tracing.[7] The following subsections describe the structured case studies, which help illuminate how lineage institutions can be effective tools of informal control.

Later in the chapter, I draw on a national dataset to show that the patterns I describe here hold across China.

Longjin Village: The Power of Seemingly Leaderless Protest

Longjin Village is located near where the Pearl River flows into the ocean in southern China. Its history stretches back to the Ming Dynasty (1368–1644 CE). Before the Communist takeover, lineage institutions governed the village's political, social, and economic life. Lineage elders mediated disputes between their members, gave their blessing to marriages and funerals, and helped oversee the lineage's corporate lands. When members of the lineage fell on hard times, they could count on charity from their kin to put food on the table until the next growing season.

The Communist Revolution changed everything for the lineages in Longjin. Local Chinese Communist Party (CCP) cadres pushed aside the lineage elders who had held sway in the imperial era. (The greater social equality this signified was a welcome change for many.) The CCP-led land reforms of the 1950s broke up the lineage's corporate landholdings and redistributed the land among village members. During the early years of the Cultural Revolution, the Red Guards rampaged through the village smashing ancestral tablets, painting Maoist slogans on the walls of the lineage halls, and setting lineage genealogies on fire. People stopped going to the lineage halls to worship, and the buildings gradually fell into disrepair.

In many nearby hamlets, lineages have enjoyed a striking revival starting in the 1980s. Lineages have used the wealth they earned in the reform era to rebuild lavish ancestral halls (see Figure 4.1). These lineages have

---

[6] Tarrow (2010, pp. 247–248).
[7] Brady and Collier (2010).

flourishing communities and hold massive celebrations during holidays like the Lantern Festival.

Yet the lineage revival that has swept across much of the region has passed over Longjin, where several of the ancestral halls and temples have become trash dumps and recycling centers (Figure 4.2). It is hard to conceive of a more inglorious end for buildings that once served as the kin group's spiritual heart. In Longjin, the village's longstanding Party secretary seemingly had little interest in rebuilding the village's main ancestral hall, and there the matter stopped. As one village elder said, "We don't count as a lineage any more."[8]

Longjin came to a crossroads in 2010, when the village's CCP secretary announced a plan to sell off all of the village's collectively owned land to a real estate developer. Land values in the area had skyrocketed, and political leaders saw an opportunity to "transform" (改造) the urban village by evicting villagers from their land and building a mall and apartment complex. The compensation they offered residents would have replaced a few years of lost income from the land and provided them with a modest apartment, but did not come close to matching the value of the land over the next decade or more. Initially some villagers held little hope of halting the plan. As one put it, "We're basically just ants who don't have any power."[9]

To implement the land confiscation and development plan, the village Party secretary had to rely on coercion rather than subtler techniques of persuasion. He announced the plan as a *fait accompli*. He extolled its value to the village and in the local newspaper, and misleadingly declared that the plan was approved by some 80 percent of the village. (This approval came from the villager assembly, rather than the villagers themselves. Some assembly members would later claim their signatures had been forged.) When residents tried to drum up some favorable news coverage from a sympathetic journalist, the Party secretary deployed the village's security forces to the village gates to prevent the media from entering. This type of blunt-force enforcement had worked in some arenas of village life, such as meeting the local family planning targets.[10]

However, the Party secretary lacked the moral authority to bring people on board. Since the village's lineage institutions had been

---

[8] Author interview, Fall 2013, Guangdong Province. 我们不算一个家族.

[9] Author interview, Summer 2013, Guangdong Province. 我们这些蚁民是没有权利的.

[10] Records showed an average of 0.75 children per female.

weakened, there was little respect for the fact that he was an elder. Nor had he built up a reservoir of trust and goodwill by doing good works for the group, such as helping organize village-wide feasts during traditional holidays.

The residents of Longjin turned their   lack of social organization into a surprising asset. An anonymous resident (or perhaps a small group of them) used their anonymity to their advantage. One day, around lunchtime, they plastered red posters in all of the public squares around the village: "Good tidings for those opposed to the demolition plan: 90 percent of Longjin villagers and shareholders oppose the plan."[11]

The village committee did not remove the posters for weeks. Cadres had evidently resigned themselves to the fact that enough people had seen them that taking them down would be futile.

In interviews, the residents of Longjin professed not to know who was behind the protest. It is possible the identity of the person was widely known, and that villagers did not want to endanger them by telling me. But given the village's population of close to 10,000 residents, it seems more likely that many honestly did not know who it was.

The seemingly leaderless protest movement soon escalated. Two weeks later, a second set of red posters called on local inhabitants to take to the streets: "To all residents of Longjin: On Tuesday ... morning at 8:30, gather at the basketball court. From there, we will go to the relevant government offices to make our feelings known. Please participate."[12] A throng of people assembled in the park. Someone circulated a petition (no one claimed credit for being its author, and with such a large crowd it was hard for most to tell who had started it). Each protester signed it and then dipped their fingers in red ink and left a print next to their signature, as if in blood. Then, they marched to the city government to deliver the petition to local leaders.

This seemingly leaderless protest put an end to the land requisition plan. Instead of jailing the protest ringleaders, the government sent everyone back to the village on air-conditioned buses. Not long after, the city government announced two surprising concessions: first, they would cancel the plan to confiscate land; second, there would be new elections for the village government.

---

[11] 反拆特大喜讯：龙津村股民，村民反对拆迁签约率已达90.

[12] 龙津村全体村民：定于X年X月X号（星期二）上午8:30时到球场集中，到有关部门反映民意，请谁时参加.

This is the power of leaderless collective action in China: it is not that no one initiates it, it is that it *appears* that no one does. Someone, or a group, wrote the posters in Longjin and paid to have them printed. Someone bought the glue and went around and put them up. Surely, some in the village know who this person is. Yet to the village cadres, to outsiders, and even to most of the people who participated in the protest movement, this person was anonymous.

How might the events in Longjin have unfolded differently? What if the village leadership had been more successful at cultivating institutions of informal control? In the next section, I examine the case of Meilong, which provides a kind of alternate history of Longjin Village.

Meilong Village: Using Kinship Ties for Repression

Meilong sits on the outskirts of the old city of Guangzhou. Like Longjin, it has been inhabited for centuries, and has since been swallowed by the growing megacity. While residents still collectively own small plots of land, no one farms anymore; instead, they use their land to build houses that they rent to migrants, which is more lucrative (and comfortable) than farming.

Meilong has a rich history of lineage activity. The village's dominant lineage has kept meticulous clan genealogies, which somehow survived the tumult of the Opium Wars, the War of Resistance against Japan, and the Cultural Revolution. The lineage histories document extended kinship networks that have farmed and fished on the same land for several centuries. Yet unlike in Longjin, traditional social institutions have enjoyed a renaissance in the reform era – in no small part because of the village's long-serving Party secretary, a man surnamed Pan. Pan invested considerable time and effort in reviving various elements of village civil society. He encouraged the formation of basketball, ping pong, and badminton clubs, a traditional lion dancing team, and competitive singing and wushu clubs. He also helped revive the village's dragon boat racing team, which brings the village together to cheer on their kith and kin against neighboring villages.

The centerpiece of Pan's effort to breathe life into local civil society was undoubtedly his effort to revive the Pan lineage association, which helped reinforce his authority in the village in ways that were sometimes subtle. For example, Pan helped oversee the renovation of the lineage's main ancestral hall, which was originally built in the 1880s and had turned into a rotting heap. Under Pan's guidance, the lineage association heads gathered funds from hundreds of people for the refurbishment.

Like many renovated ancestral halls, the donors' names were etched on the walls inside the renovated temple. Pan, residents told me, wanted recognition but was somewhat reluctant to have his name etched at the head of the list, since officially the CCP still frowns on its members partaking in "superstitious" activities like ancestor worship. Instead, Pan's immediate family members each made a lavish donation. Now, their names sit in a place of honor, reflecting some measure of glory onto Pan himself and serving as a clear symbol of his moral authority within the lineage group.

Other ways in which lineage institutions reinforced Secretary Pan's authority were a bit less subtle. Every year the Pan lineage association organizes a village-wide feast for the Lantern Festival, which features long banquet tables and skits and speeches to remind members of their kin's long history in the village. For years, Pan occupied a visible place of honor at the banquet. He also distributed patronage along kinship lines, providing members of his clan with jobs and other benefits.

While Secretary Pan exercised iron control over the village's political and social lives, he fell short in one area important to the government: the enforcement of birth quotas. Birth rates in Meilong are among the highest in the municipality.[13] While there are likely many causes of this, the prominent place of lineage associations in village life may be a contributing factor, given that they extol the values of kinship and descent.

The greatest test of Pan's authority in the village came when the government decided to expropriate the village's remaining land in order to redevelop it. The government offered a similar compensation plan to that proposed in Longjin. Once this land was gone, the city would have finally swallowed up the village completely. One villager, pointing to the skyscrapers ringing the village, told me: "The circle has been getting tighter every year."[14]

Unlike in Longjin, however, a majority of the residents of Meilong signed on to the plan within a few months. Given the stakes, why did the village fail to quickly organize like Longjin did?

An important factor in Secretary Pan's ability to control the village were kinship ties. The centerpiece of the pressure campaign was an effort to get government employees – and employees of companies

---

[13] There are 0.9 children per female, making Meilong's birth rate the second highest in the district.

[14] Author interview, Spring 2013, Guangdong Province. 圈子越来越小.

with connections to the local government – to pressure their kin to sign. Threatened with losing their jobs and livelihoods unless they produced signed relocation contracts, many had little choice but to comply.[15] Work unit heads tasked workers with getting sons, daughters, uncles, and cousins to sign the relocation agreement, placing those who did not on unpaid leave.

The pressure to get relatives to sign was enormous. A rumor swept the village that a government employee who could not successfully press his family to sign over their land committed suicide. The holdouts, seeing the pressure their relatives were under, often caved. Lineage-based social norms to protect and assist one's kin helped ensure that the tactic worked. One person summed up Pan's strategy as "using lineage ties to pressure us to sign."[16]

The effectiveness of this pressure campaign became evident when a few enterprising residents attempted to organize a protest movement patterned on what had happened in Longjin and other nearby villages. Pictures of the protest in Meilong showed at most three dozen people gathered around a red banner saying "Oppose the demolition, defend our homes!"[17] The protest outside the municipal government involved just twenty or so people, eventually dwindling to one brave woman alongside a banner.

Pan's strategy of informal control, along with economic inducements and the fear of more violent coercion, helped him successfully expropriate most of the village's remaining land – but this success came at a cost. A minority of villagers continued to hold out, delaying the construction plan and frustrating many residents who had already signed away their land and moved out of their homes.[18]

Pan's strong-arm tactics and the battle over the holdouts seemed to irreparably damage Meirong's social institutions. "Unfortunately," one villager lamented, "we have splintered."[19] I return to the theme of the long-term costs of using informal control later in the book. Sometimes using this tactic is not sustainable, especially when it comes to high-stakes

---

[15] See also O'Brien and Deng (2015a) on work units and "harmonious demolition."

[16] Author interview, Fall 2013, Guangdong Province. 带来压力.

[17] 反对拆迁，保卫家园. Image of protest collected by author.

[18] To make life miserable for the holdouts, Pan ratcheted up the pressure by installing loudspeakers around the village that, starting at daybreak and again in the afternoon, blared music and propaganda through tinny speakers. "This is something I haven't had to endure since the Cultural Revolution," one woman in her 80s said.

[19] Author interview, Spring 2013, Guangdong Province. 我们分成几个阵营.

land development, which can tear apart a community's social fabric. As one resident asked: "Will this be the end of the road for our 800-year-old lineage?"[20]

Since the case studies presented here are not representative of the country as a whole, in the next section I explore survey evidence from across China to unpack broader patterns of repression, compliance, and political instability.

4.1.2   Survey Evidence on Lineages

If my theory of informal control is correct, we should observe that across China the presence of lineage organizations is associated with more land confiscation and less protest, but more noncompliance with family planning policy. To determine whether this is the case, I examine survey evidence and find that the results are all strongly consistent with the theory.

Data and Key Variables

I created a dataset of 415 villages from across China, drawing on the 2010 wave of the China Family Panel Studies (CFPS).[21] The survey was conducted by researchers at Peking University. It has a nearly national sampling frame that includes most provinces in mainland China[22] It used a multistage sampling scheme that randomly sampled counties, communities (i.e., villages), and households. The CFPS surveyed an average of twenty-four households within each community and surveyed multiple people per household (an average of 2.8 individuals). In each village, the sampling team also administered a community survey that was completed by village cadres.[23]

Since the unit of analysis throughout this book is the village, I created a village-level dataset by aggregating household data and linking it to the survey of cadres. The analysis in this section focuses on the following explanatory and outcome variables:

Active lineage association: My main explanatory variable is the presence or absence of lineage organizations, measured as the presence

---

[20] Author interview, Fall 2013, Guangdong Province.
[21] See Xie and Hu (2014); Xie and Zhou (2014).
[22] The sample excludes Hainan, Inner Mongolia, Ningxia, Qinghai, Tibet, and Xinjiang, as well as the Special Administrative regions.
[23] Some 30 percent of respondents were village heads, 31 percent were village party secretaries, and 20 percent were village accountants.

or absence of ancestral halls (家族祠堂), which is recorded in the community survey. Ancestral halls are defined in the CFPS as a "site where lineages gather and worship their ancestors with spirit tablets."[24] The benefit of using this as the main measure of lineage activity is that it is easily observed by survey enumerators; it is also consistent with the measure used by Tsai and others.[25] A drawback of this measure is that some active lineages do not have spirit tablets or an ancestral hall.

Land seizures: The measure for land confiscations comes from the household survey, in which respondents were asked whether "their household has experienced their land being expropriated."[26] I create this indicator for whether a village has experienced a land expropria-tion based on whether any household answers yes to this question. The results remain robust when using other measures, like the percentage of households that answer yes to this question.

Net public goods spending: To assess the effect of lineage institutions and land confiscation on public goods provision and public investment, I use net spending on public goods in yuan, which I normalize by pop-ulation and log transform. The measure draws on the village budget information reported by the village cadres to the survey team. This measure combines money given directly to villagers, money spent on public goods, and funds invested in public infrastructure, and subtracts households' contributions to the village budget through levies.[27]

Over birth quota: Compliance with family planning policy is mea-sured as the percentage of households over the birth quota. The cadre survey has information on the birth quota allowance, as well as whether or not exceptions were made for households whose first child is a girl. I combine this information with the household survey that accounts for all members of the household.

Political instability: To analyze political instability, I examine both (a) whether people have grievances against the local government and (b) whether those grievances escalate to contentious activity. To measure grievances against the government, I create a variable that corresponds to the percentage of respondents in a village who feel they have been "treated unjustly by a government cadre."[28] To capture grievances that translate into conflict, I create a measure based on the percentage of

[24] 家族祠堂是指家族公共聚会的场所，也是家族供奉祖先牌位的地方.
[25] Tsai (2007a).
[26] Question E9: 您家是否经历过土地被征用?
[27] Specifically, this adds variables K302, K303, K304, and K305 while subtracting K201.
[28] Question N205: 受到政府干部的不公正对待.

households that report having engaged in contention with a government cadre.[29]

Villages with Lineages Experience More Expropriation, Less Protest

What is the effect of the presence of lineage organizations on the key outcomes I study in this book? Do they lead to more land expropriation and less protest, as hypothesized? To understand the effect of lineages on political control, I compare villages with and without lineage organizations; however, a natural concern is that these two types of villages may be inherently different from each other. One might suppose that villages with lineage organizations may be wealthier, less socially fragmented, and located in more rural areas. Or it may be, as Tsai suggests, that the presence of lineage groups is somewhat random and contingent on the presence of entrepreneurial villagers.

In fact, villages with and without lineage organizations are quite similar to each other on most observable measures, which lends credibility to the idea that the revival of lineage institutions is somewhat contingent on (or driven by) difficult-to-observe factors. Figure 4.3 plots differences between the villages with and without lineage groups on key measures: the distance to major cities, mineral wealth, social fragmentation, terrain, electoral institutions, whether it is in a disaster-prone area, whether it is in a tourist region, and ethnic minority presence. (I focus on these measures because they are all plausibly pretreatment and I do not want to condition on variables that the explanatory variable may also cause, such as contemporary measures of wealth, since these will contaminate the estimates.[30] The results are robust to including posttreatment measures like contemporary wealth.)

To correct for the remaining imbalances between villages, I reweight villages without lineage organizations so they more closely match the characteristics of those with lineages using a technique called entropy balancing.[31] Entropy balancing creates a weight for each observation in the comparison or "control" group, in this case villages without lineage groups. The basic intuition is that observations in the control group (in this case, villages with no lineages) that are very different from observations in the treatment group are given very little weight. In

---

[29] Question N206: 与政府干部发生过冲突。
[30] Montgomery et al. (2016).
[31] This technique was developed by Jens Hainmueller (2012).

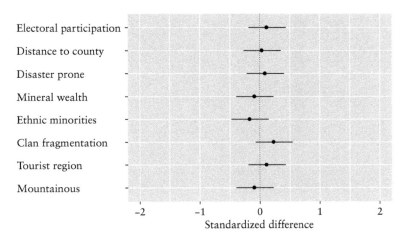

(a) Before entropy balancing

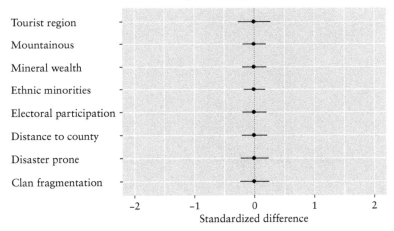

(b) After entropy balancing

FIGURE 4.3 Difference between villages with and without lineage
organizations, before and after entropy balancing

the reweighted dataset, the two groups are essentially identical on most
measures.[32]

[32] See Figure A4.3 in Appendix A for covariate balance before and after reweighting. The
covariates I use in the weighting algorithm are distance to major cities, mineral wealth,
social fragmentation, terrain, electoral institutions, whether it is in a disaster-prone area,
whether it is in a tourist region, and ethnic minority presence.

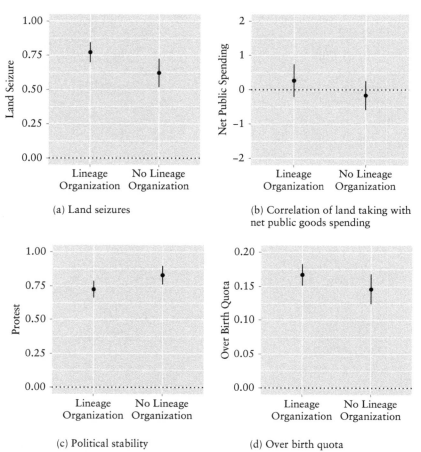

FIGURE 4.4 Mean values for lineage and non-lineage villages on key outcome measures with 95 percent confidence intervals. Non-lineage villages are reweighted using entropy balancing. Differences in means are statistically significant at the $p < 0.05$ level except for (b), which is not significantly different.

In Figure 4.4, I plot means for villages without and without lineage organizations along with 95 percent confidence intervals. I used entropy balancing to reweight the estimated mean for villages without lineage organizations.

Villages with lineage organizations are significantly more likely to experience a land expropriation – 79 percent, compared to 64 percent of those without lineage organizations. The difference is statistically significant ($p = 0.006$), and other ways of measuring the outcome (such as the percentage of respondents who have been expropriated) provide substantively similar estimates.

One possibility that runs counter to the argument that lineage organizations are being used for political control is that land takings may be beneficial rather than coercive. For instance, the revenue from land takings could be invested in local roads, schools, wells, and other public goods. To examine whether this is the case, I plot the correlation between land takings and net public goods spending in Figure 4.4(b). It shows that in villages with lineage organizations, there is no increase in public goods spending (and the difference between villages with and without lineage organizations is not statistically significant). While it is possible that higher levels of government may be spending these funds on local public goods, the data show no measurable increase in other outcomes like paved roads or school attendance after land takings, suggesting this is unlikely to be the case.

Do lineage group leaders target members of their own lineage group? If lineage leaders do not target their own groups for expropriation, we should expect that low levels of lineage group fragmentation leads to low levels of expropriation. That is, in villages dominated by a single lineage group there would be very few land seizures. On the other hand, if lineage group leaders expropriate from their own group, we would see high levels of expropriation in villages with one lineage group. Figure A.7 in the appendix shows a U-shaped relationship between lineage group fragmentation and land seizures. Of particular interest is the fact that the results show high levels of expropriation with low levels of surname fragmentation. It shows that in villages with a single surname group, expropriations are likely to occur. This is difficult to reconcile with the potential objection that lineage group leaders exclusively target other groups for expropriation.

The survey data also shows that lineage organizations help local cadres curb protest. Figure 4.4(c) plots the percentage of people with a grievance against a government official who engage in contentious activity with a government official (I condition on grievances since the difference may otherwise reflect the fact that in one type of village there is less reason to protest, not that officials are more successful at suppressing those who have incentives to protest.) In villages without lineage organizations, 83 percent of people who report having a grievance with an official also report having taken action on it. In villages without such organizations, only 73 percent of people with a grievance report having acted on it. The difference is statistically significant ($p = 0.02$). A potential unresolved concern with this measure is that respondents may misreport it, since it is politically sensitive. However, a large number of respondents (23 percent) reported having grievances with officials, and the pattern observed here is consistent with the qualitative data.

Finally, consistent with the hypotheses and qualitative evidence, villages with lineage organizations have higher rates of noncompliance with family planning policies – an estimated 17 and 14 percent, respectively. Again, the difference is statistically significant ($p = 0.01$). While lineage organizations are useful tools of political control, they do have their limits, especially when they propagate norms that run counter to state policies. In Appendix A, I present regression results with and without controls.

4.1.3 Beyond China: Caste and Kin in Moghul India

Do kinship organizations in other places also serve as tools of political control? Evidence from early modern India suggests that even in a drastically different state and time, traditional kinship organizations played a similar role. In India under the Moghul Dynasty, kinship and caste groups allowed the state to exercise control over the rural hinterlands in much the same way that lineage organizations help the Chinese state extend its own reach. In India, these groups organized social relations and the distribution of power: at the top of the social hierarchies of these groups were lineage chiefs, sometimes referred to as rajas or zamindars, who commanded small military forces and had hereditary rights to a portion of the harvest.[33] The central state saw these social institutions as potentially useful mechanisms of control – and the chiefs as important potential allies or adversaries. Anthropologist Richard Fox writes that "partly through the ascriptive office of lineage raja, partly through their investiture with state power, the elites of such kin, or caste, groups often presented both the greatest threat of local revolt and the most potent guarantee of the preservation of central authority at the local level."[34]

Like many early modern states, the challenge of raising revenue from an unwilling rural populace often frustrated the Moghuls, and its

[33] Richards (1996, p. 80).
[34] Fox (1971, p. 16).

rulers found that governing through lineage institutions was a valuable tool of control: "castes were ... state defined institutions for revenue collection, and were often delegated police and civil power over a designated area."[35] To control the chiefs, the pre-Mughal (pre-1526) Indian state introduced a system in which the lineage chiefs held official offices and received a fixed percentage of the collected tax revenue; to overcome potential agency problems, the state also appointed a local fiscal officer, generally from one of the higher castes but not from the raja's lineage, who received a slightly smaller cut of the revenue and monitored the chief.[36] Although this system helped the state collect revenue, it was irregularly implemented, and noncompliance and revolt were serious problems. As historian John F. Richards notes, "the state did not penetrate far below the surface of the average [rural district] prior to the mid-sixteenth century."[37]

The Mughal Empire's attempts to build a more modern state under Akbar the Great (who reigned from 1556 to 1605) eventually came to rely more heavily on these lineage chiefs. Akbar's initial efforts used classic state-building strategies to make the countryside more "legible" to the central state and, therefore, more controllable: he standardized weights and measures, oversaw the collection of extensive local data on market prices for crops, and undertook detailed plot-level cadastral surveys.[38] After introducing this new standardized taxation system, Akbar initially administered taxes directly through the central state instead of through the lineage chiefs. After five years the state returned control to the local chiefs, which increased revenue flows.[39]

Maintaining this state required further strengthening the lineage institutions. Akbar flattered the lineage heads with assurances that their power (and that of their councils) had some degree of autonomy and agency, as long as they supplied him with revenue. He cajoled them by providing them with a large share of a growth pot of revenue. And he threatened them, if perhaps only implicitly, with the powerful army

---

[35] Fox (1971, p. 16).
[36] Richards (1996, pp. 81–82).
[37] Richards (1996, p. 82).
[38] See Scott (1998) on state efforts at making society legible and Richards (1996, p. 84) on state building under Akbar.
[39] Richards (1996, p. 84). See also Fox (1971, pp. 98–99) on Akbar's attempts to weaken the lineage elite.

he commanded.[40] Richards writes that "over time the new regulation system would gradually convert the zamindars to a service class of quasi-officials, dependent upon the state."[41]

The economies and societies of contemporary China and Mughal India are radically different, but they employ roughly parallel strategies of state control. In both cases, relatively strong states, at least in their historical contexts, have relied on the social authority provided by kinship institutions to control their respective populations.

4.2 RELIGIOUS ASSOCIATIONS AND INFORMAL CONTROL

Does the presence of religious groups strengthen political control in the same way as lineage organizations? Folk religious, Daoist, and Buddhist groups all play an important role in the social lives of many people in rural China. These institutions propagate norms that encourage deference to the state, as I discussed in Chapter 2. However, there is also reason to be skeptical that these institutions are effective tools of control. Folk religious organizations form only weak social bonds between members, in part because their rituals are private rather than communal. As the evidence from the survey experiment in Chapter 3 showed, they are not salient identities for political mobilization; nor does membership in these groups automatically confer trust on their members.

This section examines the role of religious groups as tools of informal control. Overall, the evidence suggests that these groups can be useful for officials who want to encourage compliance with the state, but somewhat less so than lineage groups.

Not all religious organizations are effective tools of authoritarian control. Christian and Islamic organizations, in particular, have organizational structures that make state co-optation and control difficult, and they sometimes propagate norms that compete with secular authority.[42] Under Xi Jinping, the CCP has tightened control over Christian groups by arresting pastors of underground churches and through a cross-removal campaign. The CCP had undertaken an even more far-reaching crackdown on Islam. In Xinjiang, over one million Uyghurs

---

[40] Richards (1996, pp. 86–90).
[41] Richards (1996, p. 87).
[42] Consistent with this, Luo and Andreas (2016) show how Islam has helped encourage resistance to land expropriations in northwest China.

TABLE 4.2 *Chalong and Kaijia case studies*

	Kaijia	Chalong
Annual agricultural income	About 3,000	About 3,000
Competitive elections	Yes	Yes
Distance to city	30 km	25 km
Lineage association	No	No
Key explanatory variable:		
Folk religious festival	No	Yes
Key outcomes:		
Compliance with land expropriation	Low	High
Compliance with stability maintenance	Low	High
Compliance with birth quotas	High	Low

have been detained and the state has shuttered mosques and discouraged public religious practice.

4.2.1 Structured Case Study Evidence

To examine the influence of religion on political control, I return to the most-similar logic of design introduced above, comparing a village that has strong religious institutions with one that does not. These two villages lie in northern Jiangsu on China's eastern seaboard. While southern Jiangsu is one of China's richest regions, the northern part of the province is poor to moderately prosperous. The villages of Chalong and Kaijia both have broadly similar economic, political, geographic, and social conditions, as Table 4.2 shows. However, one has broad participation in temple fairs while the other does not.

Chalong: Seemingly Leaderless Protest and the Media

The residents of Chalong Village are by no means wealthy, but there are many signs of economic progress. Villagers live in two-story houses built from concrete, and satellite dishes decorate many rooftops. The country's high-speed rail system passes through village's wheat fields, a symbol of the country's meteoric economic growth. Yet economic development has brought drawbacks. When I walked with farmers to their fields, a nearby steel mill emitted a stream of smoke with a sweet, chemical odor.

Agriculture in this part of Jiangsu revolves around the wheat harvest, which is undertaken by combine tractors that tour through the area and

FIGURE 4.5 A temple in rural China

rent their services to farmers. The village committee organizes a group of them to come through, and farmers pay 50 yuan per acre. Everyone watches as the combines cut row after row. Gesturing to the steel mill and the plume of pollution, a farmer smiled and told me: "I don't eat this wheat myself."[43]

To celebrate the harvest, farmers place bottles of Qingdao beer in a pail, the bottle necks wrapped in a silver foil. The beer warms in the sun while they wait for the combines to finish their work. When the whole field is harvested, the farmers drink together, and someone will generally bring a small box of fireworks. As the combines move from field to field, from village to village, so does the sound of fireworks.

Being a wheat farmer in Jiangsu is not a path to great wealth. In the spring of 2013, farmers told me they expected around 700 dollars a year in income.[44] For most, wheat farming serves as a supplement (albeit an important one) to the income remitted to them by their children,

---

[43] Author interview, Spring 2013, Jiangsu Province.

[44] They expected about 1 *yuan* (about 15 cents in US currency) per *jin* (about a pound) of wheat. With an average yield of 500 to 600 *jin* per *mu* of land, about 4 *mu* of land per household, and two harvests per year, that works out to 4,000 to 4,400 *yuan*, or a little

husbands, and wives who generally work in manufacturing or service jobs elsewhere in China. Farming income is also a form of employment insurance for those who have been laid off.

Lineage ties are of little importance in Chalong. It is a mixed-surname village, with dozens of different surnames and none of them clearly dominant. Voting does not occur along lineage lines, and villagers I spoke to were not aware of any families with lineage histories (族谱).

Religion, however, is important in this part of Eastern China. Most houses have shrines and icons celebrating the Bodhisattva Guanyin, the Goddess of Mercy. Temple fairs (庙会) are also common in this area. These fairs mix a dose of religious content celebrating Guanyin and Chinese folk religious figures with more secular celebrations. Much like in the pre-Communist era, temple fairs are an important occasion for commerce. Local shopkeepers set up tents to sell all kinds of farm implements like hoes, shovels, and pitchforks.

These fairs might conceivably bind together citizens and village cadres and provide an avenue for informal accountability or informal control. Lily Tsai shows how participation in temple fairs by villagers in Hebei helps "reinforce a sense of obligation to the village community," and causes village officials to "strive to meet the temple festival association's ethical standards and ideals of public service."[45] Tsai describes these fairs as somewhat secular in nature but still having an important religious component, which is similar to temple fairs in northern Jiangsu.

However, Chalong Village does not hold a temple fair. Some villagers (but not cadres) participate in a nearby township's fair, but participation is low. Does the overall lack of social cohesion that this implies present an advantage or a disadvantage for village cadres?

The local government named Chalong a Model Work Unit for Family Planning (计划生育先进单位), which indicates that the village leadership is unusually effective at enforcing family planning policy. This is consistent with the hypothesis that the absence of social institutions such as lineage organizations is helpful for enforcing birth quotas. Unlike in some villages, families who exceed the quota actually pay their fines thanks to a rigorous enforcement, which helps deter others from violating the policy. The lack of strong religious institutions may to some degree help

---

under 700 US dollars per year using the conversion rate in 2013. After paying for the combine harvester, seed, and so forth, their incomes were likely closer to 400 dollars.
[45] Tsai (2007a, pp. 142–144).

cadres, since the Buddhist belief in reincarnation may subtly discourage the faithful from following the policy.

The village leadership has been less successful at controlling protest or eliciting compliance with land requisitions. Starting in 2009, county officials began to work with village officials to build a steel mill and coal-fired power plant. The government planned to expropriate 1,000 *mu* of land, affecting about 250 households, or roughly a third of the village (which has a population of 2,300).

The way the local government expropriated land in Chalong was almost certainly illegal, but reflected a common practice among some local governments throughout the 2000s and first half of the 2010s. As discussed in Chapter 3, the central government restricts the amount of land that local governments can expropriate and convert from agricultural to construction use. The district government that oversaw Chalong had already used up its entire land quota.[46] To get around this, the township claimed that Chalong's agricultural land had "subsided" (塌陷地) and could no longer be used for farming. It then proceeded to confiscate land without informing higher levels of government, and retroactively applied for approval. As the director of the district's Land and Resources Bureau explained, the township could face penalties from the municipal or provincial governments if the development was not retroactively approved. However, it was unlikely to be rejected, since this would imply that the mayor and provincial governor could not control their subordinates.

The village cadre's lack of informal authority made them ineffective at persuading villagers to sign over their land. Cadres went from house to house to encourage people to sign compensation contracts. Villagers were dismayed to learn about the compensation plan. Usually, payments for land expropriations in China come as a lump sum; even if the compensation is only a fraction of the land's value, the large windfall is often several years' worth of income. However, district officials and village cadres said they were afraid villagers would "squander" (乱花钱) a lump payment, and instead offered household heads a "living stipend" (生活费) of 150 yuan per month (a little over 20 US dollars), which is well short of what most made from farming. The documents indicated that these payments would end after about decade, depending on the

---

[46] Chalong was close enough to the prefectural seat that the county (县) had been converted to a district (区), but units underneath the district were still referred to as townships (镇) rather than subdistricts (街道).

recipient's age. Villagers were livid. "We're adults," one said, explaining that the offer of such a small stipend instead of a lump sum payment was insulting. "We just want to eat – we're not stupid!"[47]

The village's lack of a dominant social organization made it easier for discontented villagers to organize resistance without local cadres finding out. A key tactic was a coordinated push to draw media attention to an evidently illegal land expropriation. An anonymous villager started posting about the land taking on popular internet forums like Tianya as well as more niche sites like Grassroots Rights Awareness (草根普法论坛), which are sometimes monitored by local journalists. The posts asserted that the land takings violated State Council circular number 5668, and included an anonymized way for journalists to get in touch with the protest organizer.[48] This tactic paid off when a journalist from a newspaper from Shaanxi Province came to investigate, and wrote a muckraking report that embarrassed the local government. The fact that local cadres were not deeply embedded in village society likely made it harder for them to uncover the identity of the people who organized the media attention.

In addition to shining a spotlight on local corruption by calling on media allies, aggrieved residents also launched more traditional protests. Residents banded together to petition higher levels of government about the project. Somewhat similar to events in Longjin, this process emerged organically rather than through an organization with strong leadership. The petition was organized by a network of residents who launched it in the privacy of their own homes. The Party branch secretary did not have an effective network of informants and allies to help him identify and head off the petitioners ahead of time.

Since persuasion and prevention failed, Chalong's leadership turned to more violent tools of repression. One tactic was economic coercion. They destroyed the value of the fields to farmers by hiring heavy machinery to drive across them, tearing up the soil and killing the half-grown wheat harvest. They also had workers dump stones on the fields to make it impossible for combines to harvest the wheat. When this strategy failed to induce more farmers to sign, local officials resorted to violence. One night, according to locals, dozens of local security agents and

47 Author interview, Spring 2013, Jiangsu Province. 我们不是猪！
48 The contact information was an anonymous user name using the social media and communications platform QQ. In the early 2010s, it was straightforward to create a QQ address without linking it to an individual identity.

"hooligans" (小混混) rampaged through the village, barging into the homes of the villagers who had not signed over their land and beating them. (Villagers supplied photos of injuries and damage to their homes to corroborate this, but the village officials I contacted declined to be interviewed.) Villagers said that four people were detained.

As the next case demonstrates, village cadres with more informal authority might have been able to lessen anger over the compensation plan, and might have had the social networks to identify villagers whose grievances were especially sharp, and defuse the situation. Villagers' non-compliance meant that they got a better deal than they might have: at least they were compensated.

Kaijia Village: Where Associations Strengthen Informal Control

The nearby village of Kaijia is similar in many ways to Chalong. It is a moderately prosperous village whose agricultural economy revolves largely around the wheat harvest. By the time I visited Kaijia, the combine harvesters had already come and gone, and everyone was preparing their wheat for sale. After the harvest, farmers sun the grains to dry out the last bits of moisture. They do so by spreading the grains in a thin layer on whatever flat, hard surface is available – which generally means roads and parking lots. Farmers in Kaijia carpet nearly every inch of asphalt in freshly cut grain. On the major county road, farmers spread wheat along the edges even as buses, motorbikes, and cars drive over the grains and speed inches from their heads.

Kaijia's local temple fair, held in March, is more popular than the one near Chalong, and has resulted in the establishment of a number of social clubs. For example, villagers have organized a 100-person "drum and gong team" (锣鼓队) and a "popular custom cultural troupe" (民俗文化表演团) that practice throughout the year, strengthening bonds among residents. The informal accountability model suggests that these associations should be effective at holding officials accountable, in part because the increased ties provide a template for grassroots collective action.

Yet in Kaijia, local elites appear to support these groups precisely because they legitimate the power of village cadres and help them thwart collective protest. Kaijia's Party secretary, surnamed Meng, has taken the lead in promoting the temple fair and the troupes that perform in it. In the Mao era he was the head of the village's Mao Zedong Thought Propaganda Team, and he organized a series of Maoist musical and theatrical shows that brought him to the attention of local officials. By the mid-1980s he became the village Party secretary. An entrepreneurial figure, he quickly pivoted from putting on shows about Mao to putting on shows about the very "feudal" influences – traditional Chinese culture and Buddhism – against which Mao had fought so vigorously. He organized village events for the spring and lantern festivals, and gave his blessing to the drum and gong team and the cultural troupe. He declared: "I've learned from experience that traditional culture helps bind [villagers] together and increase cohesion."[49]

In Kaijia, the temple fair and other cultural groups have greatly strengthened Meng's informal authority. Villagers take pride in the fair and the active singing and dancing troupes, which have performed outside the province and have attracted attention from local newspapers. These groups add to the local quality of life and provide outlets for fun and recreation outside work and television that remain somewhat rare in village life, even in moderately prosperous areas of China. It is not difficult to find villagers willing to credit Meng for the temple fair and other cultural events, even if he is not formally the leader of these groups. As one villager said: "There have been positive changes here because of this kind of good village official."[50]

Nevertheless, in 2010, the local government appropriated over 400 *mu* of land to build a distillery. The district government officially converted the land from agricultural to construction use. However, it was village officials who attracted investment to the village, negotiated with the distillery owners over compensation, and moved villagers off the land.

Meng's popularity and credibility among villagers helped forestall large-scale mobilization against the land development. He initially promised that villagers affected by the land takings would have preferential access to jobs in the distillery, and offered compensation similar to the levels in Chalong. (Since both villages are in the same district, in principle compensation is consistent between the two.) Throughout China, farmers whose land is being requisitioned sometimes reject relatively generous offers because they fear that local officials will not follow through with them. However, in Kaijia the Party secretary could call on a reserve of positive sentiment and trust built up over the years he has spent leading the village through its cultural renaissance. Initially, many villagers expressed support for the plan.

---

49 Quotation from local newspaper article. (Not cited to preserve anonymity.) 加强了村民的凝聚力.
50 Author interview, Spring 2013, Jiangsu Province. 这样好的村官.

Meng's moral authority helped him ensure compliance with the land taking and forestall collective action. However, villagers were not compensated after the land was confiscated. As for the promised factory jobs, some villagers did work in local factories but most workers in the industrial park were evidently migrants from Sichuan Province.

In a village like Kaijia, going up against a village cadre with a high degree of moral authority can be frustrating and demoralizing, requiring a mix of courage and stubbornness. I did not meet anyone in Kaijia waging a lonely battle against the village government, but an activist I interviewed in Sichuan told me about her life-changing experience fighting against an entrenched local cadre. When he tried to expropriate and demolish her home, her son was detained by the police and disappeared while in custody (the police claimed he moved elsewhere but she presumes, I think with good reason, that he died in the police station). She then waged a long and often solitary battle against the local government on behalf of her son. She broke down as she related a police officer's threats: "Do you want me to kill your daughter? Do you want me to kill your grandson? Do you want them to suffer the same fate as your son?"[51]

Kaijia's success in strengthening social control through organizations that promote traditional culture has become a model for the provincial government, which issued a circular encouraging others to follow the "Kaijia experience" and strengthen the "cohesiveness" of local society through the promotion of traditional culture.

4.2.2   Survey Evidence on Religion

In this section, I use survey evidence to describe broader patterns across the country. The case studies suggest that religious groups – such as temple fair performance troupes – may be channels of political control and repression. Village cadres may help create and nurture these groups in order to bolster their moral authority and implement policies like land requisitions.

As in the previous section, the national survey evidence comes from the CFPS. The survey asks villagers to indicate whether or not they participate in religious organizations.[52] I code villages as having a religious organization if at least one respondent indicates that they participate in

---

[51] Author interview, Fall 2012, Sichuan Province.
[52] A7 您参加了以下哪些组织? 宗教/信仰团体.

an organization. The results are similar if I use other measures such as the percentage of villagers participating in religious organizations, and in some cases these results are more robust. To be conservative, I use the dichotomous measure here, which also allows me to use entropy balancing. In Appendix A, I also present regression results.

As was the case with lineage activity, the presence of religious organizations in villages appears to be somewhat contingent on whether entrepreneurial villagers revived them during the reform era. Appendix Figure A.6 presents balance tests, which show that villages with and without these organizations are similar on most measures.

To adjust for differences between villages, I use the same entropy balancing framework I introduced in the previous section, and the same set of plausibly pretreatment covariates to create the weights. After entropy balancing, the two groups of villages have identical characteristics on average (see Figure A.6).

The results suggest that religious institutions are likely to be effective tools of political control, but the statistical evidence is more tentative than the results for lineage groups. Figure 4.6 plots the mean values for the two types of villages across the same outcomes discussed in the section on lineage groups, along with 95 percent confidence intervals. The direction of the results is generally consistent with the hypotheses.

Consistent with the claim that religious institutions increase compliance with extraction, I find that villages with religious organizations experience more land expropriations (74 percent) than those without such institutions (65 percent). The unadjusted difference in means is statistically significant ($p = 0.03$), but after reweighting using entropy balancing the results fall short of the traditional threshold for inference ($p = 0.07$).

The data also show that land expropriations in villages with religious organizations are predatory, not beneficial. Figure 4.6(b) shows that land seizures in villages with religious organizations are correlated with a one-standard-deviation *drop* in public goods spending. While the relationship between land expropriations and public goods spending may not be causal, the evidence strongly suggests that these land takings do not benefit villagers. The results are statistically significant ($p < 0.001$).

The data also support the idea that religious institutions are not especially useful for eliciting compliance with birth quotas, and may in fact encourage noncompliance. Villages with religious organizations have

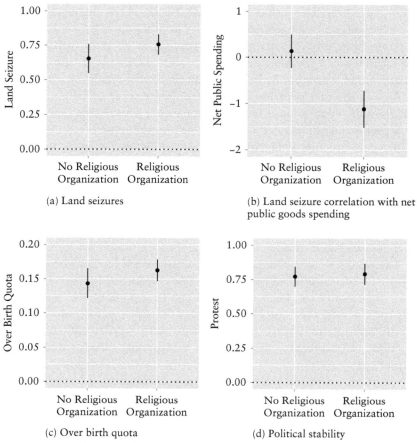

FIGURE 4.6 Villages with and without religious organizations on key outcome measures, reweighted using entropy balancing. Please see the text for more details.

slightly more over-quota births (16 vs 14 percent); this difference is not significant at the traditional level ($p = 0.08$).

However, the quantitative data do not provide strong evidence to support the hypothesis that religious organizations are effective at quelling contentious collective action. There is no substantively meaningful difference between villages with and without religious organizations. These results suggest that more work is needed to understand the role of religious groups as tools of political control in China.

4.2.3 Beyond China: Company Towns in the US

The use of religious institutions as a means of control is not limited to China. For example, at the turn of the last century, some 20,000 "company towns" sprang up across the southern United States.[53] These towns were generally run by coal companies that created entire communities from scratch to attract workers: they built (and owned) the town's homes, schools, churches, theaters, stores, and hospitals.

Company governance of these towns was deeply autocratic. An overriding concern was preventing unionization, which would mean higher wages and lost profits for the company. The nature of company towns made preventing unionization an especially vexing challenge: a closed community gave workers ample time to socialize, form bonds, and try to organize.

To combat unionization, many company bosses relied heavily on coercion.[54] In many cases, they hired private police forces to intimidate and beat union organizers and protect anti-unionists and replacement workers during strikes.[55]

Yet company bosses soon realized that softer forms of social control – including building churches – might be more effective in the long run. The companies built churches, handpicked ministers, and encouraged their workers to attend them regularly. In doing so, companies did not just have their workers spiritual welfare in mind. As the West Virginia Coal Operators' Association wrote: "It is a good business proposition for any coal company to take an interest in and to assist in the building up of religious and community activities."[56] A poem from Carl Sandburg captured the sometimes cynical relationship between company preachers and their employers:

> You live in a company house
> You go to a company school
> You work for this company,
> according to company rules.
>
> You all drink company water
> and all use company lights,
> The company preacher teaches us
> what the company thinks is right.

---

[53] Wagner and Obermiller (2011).
[54] For an overview, see Corbin (2015); Wagner and Obermiller (2011).
[55] Corbin (2015, pp. xvii–xviii). See Frye et al. (2014) and Mares and Zhu (2015) for discussions of the role of economic coercion in company towns in Russia and Germany.
[56] Corbin (2015, p.149).

Hand-picked company preachers often used their authority to vilify union organizers on religious grounds, calling them "ungodly and wicked."[57] They would also discourage strikes. One company boss, for example, built a Catholic church in the company town after witnessing how a priest in a nearby town helped break up a strike by "absolutely refusing to allow his flock to have anything to do with the union."[58] Some denounced the unions in vitriolic terms. For example, the famous traveling preacher Billy Sunday delivered a sermon in one West Virginia coal town that turned into a broadside against union organizers:

I cannot believe that God had anything to do with the creation of these human buzzards [i.e. union organizers]. I'd rather be in hell with Cleopatra, John Wilkes Booth and Charles Giteau than to live on earth with such human lice ... If I were the Lord for about fifteen minutes I'd smack the bunch so hard that there would be nothing left for the devil to levy on but a bunch of whiskers and a bad smell ... As a rule the strikes don't originate with the men, but with the walking delegate who comes around nosing for trouble. America, I call you back to God and if you don't come back God will deal with you as he did Carthage, and Rome, and Germany.[59]

The moral and religious authority wielded by preachers like Billy Sunday made many faithful miners feel obliged to listen to them. One union organizer disparaged these preachers as "nothing more than stool pigeons for the coal operators, and instead of preaching of the Gospel of the Son of God, they preach the doctrine of union hatred and prejudice."[60] While it is difficult to gauge the effectiveness of the widespread practice of using churches and preachers to repress unionism, the popularity of the tactic suggests that the company bosses considered it an effective tool of social control.

4.3 BEYOND KINSHIP AND RELIGION: WORKERS AND UNIONS

What types of organizations outside of kinship and religious institutions are effective for informal control? In this section, I continue with the theme of controlling workers and examine how states can also control the working class through unions and other seemingly autonomous grassroots labor organizations. This can occur at several levels, from the

[57] Corbin (2015, p.150).
[58] Corbin (2015, p. 150).
[59] Jameson (1922, p. 1).
[60] Cantor (1992, p. 22).

factory floor to the national stage. At the grassroots level, the state can exploit the moral authority of local labor leaders; at the national level, political control more often takes the form of state corporatism.

Andrew Walder's study of political authority and compliance in Chinese factories demonstrates how, at the grassroots level, the CCP relied on personal ties to exercise control over its workers. The party's authority over factory workers was driven in part by "a clientelist system in which public loyalty to the party and its ideology is mingled with personal loyalties between party branch officials and their clients."[61]

One of several ways that the party exerted control over workers was through informal leaders whose moral authority gave them significant sway. Walder notes that some veteran workers in factories served as informal "masters," who because of their skill, charisma, and longstanding ties cultivated large followings among other workers. Workers describe them as having "a strong sense of personal dignity" and "a sense of moral authority."[62] Walder quotes one of his informants as saying:

> The old masters controlled their workers ... Workers will do anything their master says, but not necessarily for the party leaders. So the party leaders are very polite and respectful to the masters, always asking for their option and so forth.[63]

Walder noted, "shop leaders, in these cases, have to work through or around masters, coopt, or manipulate them, in order to ensure that their orders will be followed."[64] Much like the lineage and religious leaders I described above, these factory leaders with significant informal authority can potentially be powerful allies, who can help the state ensure compliance.

One parallel to the type of control I have focused on in this book are attempts to control labor movements through systems of state corporatism. Ruth Berins Collier and David Collier write that after the initial political incorporation of labor movements in Latin America, "state control of the working class ceased to be principally the responsibility of the police or the army but rather was achieved at least in part through the legalization and institutionalization of a labor movement sanctioned and regulated by the state."[65] State incorporation of the labor movement in

---

[61] Walder (1988, p. 6).
[62] Walder (1988, p. 178).
[63] Walder (1988, p. 179).
[64] Walder (1988, p. 178).
[65] Collier and Collier (1991, p. 3).

countries like Brazil involved "repressing preexisting unions and replacing them with highly constrained, state-penetrated labor organizations that would avoid class conflict and instead 'harmonize' the interests of capital and labor."[66]

Co-opting labor movement leaders helped states and parties control the working class. For example, the Accion Democratica party in Venezuela initially used repression to deal with the labor movement. However, these laws were quickly repealed, and as Collier and Collier note, the party rapidly moved to "control derived from party ties and influence ... [P]rominent among these last was the co-optation of union leaders who also occupied party and electoral posts."[67]

In general, state corporatism at the national level sought to politically control the labor movement by institutionalizing and bureaucratizing it. The large size of working-class movements in Latin America meant that most labor leaders also lacked the kind of symbolic authority held, for instance, by national religious leaders and other communal elites.[68] These differences aside, the co-optation of labor leaders in Latin America had broadly similar consequences and aims as village cadres in China – political control and demobilization.

4.4 CONCLUSION

In this chapter, I have argued that autocrats in China cultivate non-state groups like lineage and temple organizations in an effort to control the societies they govern and encourage compliance with the state. Yet the tactic of cultivating non-state groups for the purposes of political control does not appear limited to China.

The findings outlined in this chapter suggest an important limit to the influential theory that in rural China, local civil society groups serve primarily as channels of bottom-up informal accountability. The theory of informal accountability suggests that civil society groups reward officials who perform well in office with additional moral authority, providing an incentive for them to supply public goods and services. This type of bottom-up accountability may be one function of these groups.

I argue that civil society groups tend to strengthen top-down political control. One indication that these institutions serve the state is the fact

[66] Collier and Collier (1991, p. 169).
[67] Collier and Collier (1991, p. 263).
[68] See also Slater (2009, 2010).

that village cadres themselves have in many places encouraged the revival of lineage and folk religious institutions; after all, these non-state groups reinforce the power of local elites and can be used as subtle channels of control and repression.

5

Co-optation

The previous chapter was devoted to understanding how officials some-times cultivate non-state organizations to increase their personal author-ity, allowing them to apply pressure directly on the people they govern. Yet these groups sometimes also empower potential political rivals: social elites, from clerics to clan elders to village leaders and union organizers, who may owe their allegiance to their group and not the regime. Civil society elites are important figures in authoritarian politics in part because they serve as brokers between the state and their commu-nity. As key local intermediaries, they sometimes pressure local officials to take action to benefit their group: to pave a road, for example, or to mend a schoolhouse roof or to fund a healthcare program. However, these brokers also often help the state press its demands on their groups: for instance, to comply with taxation or to give up their land.

In this chapter, I turn my attention to the dynamics of co-optation. A rich literature suggests that venues like national parliaments help author-itarian regimes share power and distribute rents among elites and the groups they represent.[1] Yet the way that co-optation works at the local level is different.

One might expect that the inclusion of civil society elites in local polit-ical institutions might serve as a form of representation that strengthens the voice of members of those groups. By contrast, I argue that when communal elites are included in formal political institutions in rural China, they help the state control their group. Co-opting local notables is

---

[1] See, among others Gandhi and Przeworski (2007); Blaydes (2010); Svolik (2012); Truex (2016).

effective at helping the state requisition land and enforce family planning policy while forestalling collective action. However, the strategy has its limits: when they take actions that clearly do not benefit their group, the moral authority of civil society elites often erodes.

In the chapter, I first examine the role of lineage group leaders as brokers for the local state in China. Next, I turn to the role of religious authorities. Case studies from Scotland and the United States suggest that the findings may have applicability beyond China.

5.1 LINEAGE ELITES, MORAL AUTHORITY, AND CONTROL

Lineage leaders serve as key brokers for local officials. This section begins with an overview of the role of lineage elites in rural society, showing that they have long been key political intermediaries in China. Next, I present evidence from a unique experiment showing the high degree of moral authority lineage elites have in high-stakes conflicts over redistribution. I then examine evidence from structured case studies and a national survey. These results show how co-opted lineage elites use their authority to requisition land, enforce birth quotas, and tamp down on protest – but in the long run their behavior can erode trust in local institutions.

5.1.1 The Role of Lineage Elites in Rural Society

Lineage group elites are key brokers in village politics in many villages in China. They have three important characteristics: (1) their advice and counsel is often required within the lineage, especially for life events (大事) like funerals or weddings; (2) they informally resolve disputes between group members; and (3) they are central nodes in village social networks, and important sources of information (and gossip) about the village. Different villages have different ways of referring to these leaders. These range from lineage chiefs (总理),[2] to lineage elders (长老) and lineage heads (族长).

Lineage elites have historically both aided and exploited less powerful members of their group. Lineage elites in imperial China aided their group by organizing mutual defense, by warding off especially predatory

---

[2] Yan (2012).

local officials, and by providing group charity. Yet the ways in which they distributed benefits in the group was often highly unequal. "The gentry used their power to provide minimal benefits for the humbler members of the lineage," notes Richard Madsen, "but most of the benefits to be obtained from their wealth and power were channeled through their closer relatives."[3] These highly unequal arrangements created obligations for weaker members of the lineage to comply with group elites. "In return for the assistance provided by their richer relatives, the poorer kinfolk were expected – indeed morally obliged – to give deference and loyal cooperation."[4]

The sway that lineage elites had over weaker members of their group made lineage heads crucial brokers between the Imperial state and local society. Michael Szonyi writes of how the Ming state "deputized semiformal and informal agents to collect taxes and perform other local [government] functions"[5] especially military conscription. The Ming promoted standardized lineage institutions and rituals that helped them lengthen the state's reach into rural society.[6]

The historical role of lineage elites in rural China as conduits of state control is not that different from the role of traditional elites in other contexts. In rural Vietnam, for example, the "prestige and power of notables on the council that administrated village affairs were considerable, for they handled relations with the state, collect taxes, allocated communal land, and conducted the rites of worship and the harvest festivals central to the folk religion."[7] As Kate Baldwin shows, chiefs in precolonial Africa played similar roles in helping the state collect taxes – although today chiefs are much less likely to do so.[8]

In imperial China, the relationship between the state and lineage elites was a fruitful but informal alliance, and the incentives of local gentry and the state did not always align. David Faure argues that while lineage institutions "bonded local society to the state," this should not be confused for direct "control" by the center.[9] Lineage elites had incentives to use their power to appropriate land and other property for themselves and, in turn, at times would help members of their group evade state taxation

[3] Madsen (1984, p. 59).
[4] Madsen (1984, p. 60).
[5] Szonyi (2017, p. 218).
[6] Faure (2007, pp. 93–108).
[7] Popkin (1979, p.92).
[8] Baldwin (2016, pp. 22–41).
[9] Faure (2007, p. 108).

or conscription.[10] This lack of alignment in incentives is a theme I will return to shortly.

In the late nineteenth and early twentieth centuries, the Chinese state attempted to incorporate lineage elites into the state through more formal channels in order to remedy the problems of inconsistent control. Under the Qing and Republican governments, lineage heads were sometimes absorbed into the state through their membership in village councils and infiltrating institutions similar to the *baojia* system.[11] These institutions allowed the state to assess land, monitor the population, and collect taxes, albeit imperfectly.

The Communists extended the state's reach into villages, and in the Mao era pushed lineage institutions underground (and in some villages destroyed them altogether). Before the Communist takeover in 1949, the CCP was pragmatic about using existing social organizations like lineages to help further party goals like setting up rural cooperatives.[12] However, the more radical changes of the 1950s and 1960s stripped local gentry and lineages of their property. Land was collectivized. The party vilified the pre-1949 local gentry as part of the old "feudal" social order. Communist ideology replaced the old lineage-based moral order.[13]

Yet, as the state retreated from village life in the wake of decollectivization, lineage organizations saw a significant revival starting in the 1980s, and in many places lineage elites re-emerged as important local brokers. (See the discussion in Chapter 3.) Lily Tsai shows that in 2000, 17 percent of villages have a lineage or clan head; such villages are more common than those with ancestral halls and spirit tablets.[14] As we have discussed, lineage heads today still serve important social and political functions in villages. Yiqing Xu and Yang Yao describe an example of the role of a lineage head in one village in Zhejiang:

My father used to be the *zuzhang* (lineage chief) of our clan. The village chief (chairman of the village committee) was also a member of the clan. Whenever the village committee had some great undertakings to accomplish, like collecting money for building a road, he came to my father and other seniors of the clan. If the seniors thought the chief's plan could work, they would convene a meeting

---

[10] Madsen (1984); Duara (1988); Huang (2008).
[11] Duara (1988, pp. 101–115), Huang (2008). See also Schurmann (1966, pp. 411–412) who argues that the Republican and Qing governments were not successful in linking these institutions of control to "existing local groupings or relationships." Duara and Huang's more recent work suggests that Schurmann likely overstated his case.
[12] Schurmann (1966, pp. 423–424).
[13] Madsen (1984, pp. 60–61).
[14] Tsai (2007a, pp. 155–157). See also Xu and Yao (2015).

of household heads, together with the village chief, to convince the villagers to support the project, either by giving money or donating working hours. Since in our village, the majority of households are from the Fu family, the meeting is almost like a villagers' assembly. People took it quite seriously. They trusted my father because they thought he's impartial and experienced. The seniors didn't enjoy formal titles, and they didn't take charge of daily matters, but they were (moral) authorities of the village.[15]

Xu and Yao's account suggests that lineage institutions have a dual role, not just as a provider of public goods but also as a control mechanism for the state (something they leave unexplored). This control mechanism, they argue, works through the moral authority of lineage chiefs.

Is the moral authority of lineage elites powerful enough make people change their minds about decisions with important material payoffs? In the following section, I turn to a quantitative test of this proposition.

5.1.2 An Experimental Test of Moral Authority

I argue that informal institutions encourage deference to group elites; as a consequence, other members of their group have strong incentives to comply with decisions that these elites endorse. To test this quantitatively, I conducted a survey experiment in a rapidly urbanizing municipality in southern China. This municipality had recently announced a plan to "redevelop" (改造) dozens of surrounding villages, some of them still agricultural and others highly urban "villages in the city" (城中村). The redevelopment plans called for seizing villagers' land and homes in most of these villages, and the plan had received extensive local media coverage.

Villages were randomly selected using a multistage procedure, stratifying on whether or not the village was on the land seizure list, and by district. Within each randomly selected village the enumeration team canvassed door-to-door and in public spaces. It is important to note that the canvassing did not produce a random draw of households, but the resulting sample nonetheless closely matches the characteristics of the population that remains in these villages.

An experimental manipulation measured whether villagers would be more likely to have confidence in information that came from lineage group leaders about property seizures. The prompt was meant to elicit

---

[15] Xu and Yao (2015, p. 375).

opinions about the very real possibility that the government would act to seize their property. I randomized whether a statement supporting a property seizure plan was endorsed by either a village official, a lineage group leader, or a villager (which served as a baseline condition). Enumerators read villagers the following statement:

This municipality has plans to "redevelop" dozens of villages by 2020. Suppose a [villager] [lineage leader] [village official] from your village said: "This redevelopment plan benefits us, we should all support it." Do you have faith (信心) in this [villager's] [lineage leader's] [village official's] statement? [Yes] [No] [Don't know][16]

Each respondent only saw one prompt, so it was impossible for them to compare the identities of endorsers.[17]

There were several reasons to suspect that the endorsement experiment would not change respondents' confidence in the statement. Respondents faced the real likelihood that their property would be seized, and may have already had solidified attitudes toward existing plans. Respondents lived in an environment where lineage group ties were not particularly strong. (Seventy percent of respondents reported they had no active ancestral hall or that they did not visit it.) Moreover, respondents were presented with a prompt that did not mention a specific kinship group leader whom they knew and respected.

Even with these hurdles, villagers were significantly more confident in messages supplied by hypothetical kinship group leaders. Figure 5.1 shows the percentage of respondents that expressed confidence in the endorsement made by each type of figure. Respondents were 16 percentage points more likely to be confident in the endorsement of a kinship group leader when compared against a baseline condition, that of an anonymous villager. This difference is statistically significant at the $p = 0.05$ level. Villagers are also more 9 percentage points more confident in statements made by lineage leaders than village officials. This difference is suggestive but is not statistically significant at the $p = 0.05$ level, though arguably the political sensitivity of the village official condition may have created a floor effect for this endorsement.

---

[16] In the prompt, the term used for village official was 村干部 and the term used for kinship leaders was 家族长老, or "lineage elder." Extensive pre-survey interviews suggested that in these villages the influential members of lineage groups were referred to this way. The precise number of villages to be redeveloped has been slightly altered here to protect the anonymity of respondents.

[17] The prompt is similar to a "confidence experiment" implemented by Chhibber and Sekhon (2014) in India.

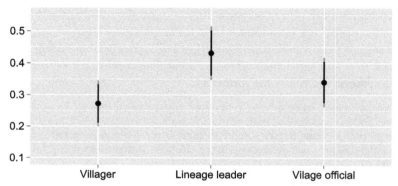

FIGURE 5.1 Survey experiment results. Percentage expressing confidence in statement supporting expropriation plan, by type of leader endorsement. Dark lines show 90 percent confidence intervals and light lines 95 percent confidence intervals.

The level of faith that individuals expressed in statements by lineage leaders is striking, especially given the limitations of the survey experiment. Village redevelopment has enormous stakes. Bad compensation can break a family financially by tearing away their most important source of income. Good compensation, on the other hand, can help them live in comfort for years. Not surprisingly, feelings about the development projects run hot. Yet over 40 percent of respondents have confidence in the statement that the redevelopment plan will benefit them, compared to just over a quarter of respondents in the baseline condition (the anonymous "villager"). In the context of local politics, this represents a substantively large shift in public opinion.

In real life, the effect of a lineage elder trumpeting the benefits of government policy may have even larger effects – after all, it is more likely to be a sustained campaign, not a one-off prompt, and likely to be conducted by someone that villagers know and respect, instead of the anonymous version presented here. Next I turn to structured case study evidence to examine how lineage elite endorsements of state policy strengthens political control when the material stakes are high.

5.1.3 Structured Case Study Evidence

My basic argument in this chapter is that when lineage group elites are included in village political institutions, they use their moral authority to help officials control society and enforce policies in ways that can

TABLE 5.1 *Wucun and Rivertown case studies*

	Wucun	Rivertown
Agricultural income in *yuan*, median	2,000	1,800
Competitive elections	No	No
Driving time to county seat	1.25 hours	1.5 hours
Lineage groups	Yes	Yes
Key explanatory variable:		
Lineage leader on village committee	No	Yes

sometimes be predatory. When they are outside these formal institutions, however, they are more likely to act as a check on the power of the local state, and help protect the interests of their group.

The villages of Rivertown and Wucun in Hunan illustrate this logic (see Table 5.1). In this case, both villages were the sites of major road building efforts. Yet while farmers in both villages lost land, they were compensated only when lineage elites remained outside the state. When lineage elites had been integrated into local political institutions, they helped officials requisition land without compensation.

The two villages I discuss in the following sections are remote and relatively poor, and in a province not famed for having especially strong lineage institutions. These two case studies also illustrate the broader applicability of the theory to poorer regions with weaker kinship institutions.

The Case of Rivertown
The remote mountain village of Rivertown lies along a gently flowing mountain stream, about an hour and a half's drive from the county seat. Sheer karst cliffs surround the village on all sides, and two decades ago it was impossible to reach Rivertown by car. Several locals and the village Party Secretary (who was my host) said that I was the first foreigner to ever visit the village, although there is no written record of the village's history before 1949 and no way to verify this.

Until very recently, the villagers cultivated rice, but now the villagers grow a tea varietal called *huangjin gui*,[18] largely because the government pays a subsidy to do so. Bamboo shoots are another local specialty. The shoots grow at the top of the valley, requiring a vigorous forty-minute hike from the village. Because the shoots sprout on a steep slope, villagers

---

[18] 黃金桂.

foraging for shoots must cling to mature bamboo trees in order to avoid sliding down the mountain. As if this were not enough, the mountain is covered in aggressive red ants, so foraging for bamboo shoots requires villagers to keep constantly moving from tree to tree to avoid getting covered in painful welts.

Nearly all villagers in Rivertown belong to the Tang lineage. The lineage lacks either an ancestral or a written history because literacy came late to this part of China. Nevertheless, there is a sense of group solidarity reinforced by a strong oral tradition, which holds that the lineage was founded during the Song Dynasty by two brothers from Jiangxi province.

The village Party Secretary is a member of the Tang lineage. He has served in the village government since 1983, and enjoys a great deal of informal authority in the lineage. He has earned this respect by being one of the few men of his generation who can read and write competently, and by being an industrious farmer. He also has a talent for putting people at ease; as soon as I met him, he started to crack self-deprecating jokes about his height.

The informal authority of the Party Secretary was integral in getting a paved road built to the village. To be clear, the road has brought significant benefits to villagers. The road opens up the village to local markets, schools, and hospitals. Yet the cadres compensated villagers nothing for the land they lost in order to accommodate the project. As both villagers and the Party Secretary told me, the project required significant "thought work"[19] on the part of the Party Secretary in order to persuade villagers who would lose land. According to the Party Secretary, he went around from house to house in order to cajole villagers to give up their land without compensation. His status within the group made such a request difficult to deny.

In rural China, these road building projects are often beneficial to the public – yet can still be a major source of rents for village officials. Higher levels of government generally initiate a road building project and supply village governments with compensation funds for the lost land. But sometimes only a portion of those funds, or sometimes none of them, actually make their way to villagers. Instead, much of the money finds its way into the hands of local cadres. This pattern occurred in a village I visited in the same county as Rivertown. In this village, the Party Secretary split

---

[19] 思想工作.

most of the road compensation fund of 100,000 *yuan* between himself and his younger brother, who served as the head of the village committee. Then he made sure his nephew's company won part of the contract to build the road itself. Villagers who lost the land were incensed over the lack of compensation. As one told me, "We rely on the land to make a living."[20]

As we shall see in the next case study, villagers are more likely to be properly compensated for this type of project when lineage institutions act as a check against the local state rather than an extension of it.

The Case of Wucun

Like Rivertown, Wucun is fairly remote. Getting to Wucun requires an hour and a half bus ride from the same county seat that serves Rivertown. The minibus route follows a paved road through a lush valley and then abruptly swings right onto a pock-marked dirt track that veers at an impossible angle up a mountain. The village is perched at the top.

Wucun is just as poor as Rivertown. About half the homes in the village are made of carefully masoned slate stone on the bottom half and, on the top, mud bricks. I also counted five concrete homes, built by richer families. Since disrupting bird nests is terrible luck, many houses have swallows living inside.

Nearly all agriculture focuses on wet rice cultivation. Many but not all families seem to own water buffaloes, and many own pigs, dogs, and chickens. The sight of smoked pork (a local delicacy) curing on the inside of houses was common.

As with Rivertown, elections are not free. The township government decides both the Party Secretary and village committee lineup. The ballot box is brought house-to-house and people must write in the preferred candidate while the cadres supervising the election stand over their shoulders.

The Long lineage group dominates Wucun. Although the lineage is divided up into three informal factions, each with its own informal leader, group obligations and rituals strengthen ties among all members of the lineage, even in the absence of formal lineage resources like an ancestral hall. For example, when a member of the lineage dies, every family must contribute a peck of rice to help feed people for the funeral. There is also an obligatory financial contribution for funerals.

---

[20] Author interview, Spring 2013, Hunan Province. 依靠土地为生.

Lineage group elders play important social roles in the village. When there are weddings, funerals, and other big social events, everyone comes to consult the group's informal leader. He instructs them on the proper rites and on practical matters, like how much food they need to lay out for guests; he also helps solicit contributions from other members of the lineage group. These leaders also mediate conflicts within and, to a degree, between families. Two of the most common disputes include marital strife and conflicts over land boundaries. As one villager noted, "We trust them to resolve things fairly."[21]

Lineage leaders also act as brokers or intermediaries in village politics. As the village Party Secretary put it: "Lineages play an influential role in the village. Within each lineage and sometimes within each sub-lineage faction there is usually an influential person. When I need to get things done I need to go and talk to them and get them on my side first, because they can talk to the rest of their clan and move them along."[22]

These autonomous lineage leaders also supervise the village government – and help ensure that, in contrast to Rivertown, Wucun's major road building project compensated villagers who lost land. The road leading into the village was financed partly by villagers, who gathered funds to compensate the farmers whose land would be seized in order to build the road.

In order to get villagers buy-in to the project, the Party Secretary needed the lineage leaders on board. He called a meeting that included the village committee, the leaders of the villager small groups, and the influential members of the lineage groups. He focused on persuading the elders of the Long lineage to back the plan. They agreed to back the Party Secretary, but the meeting also set a precedent that these informal leaders would be consulted about the project.

The supervision of the lineage leaders helped ensure that no corruption took place and that villagers were fairly compensated. The village committee collected several hundred yuan from each villager for the road building project. Lineage leaders spread word about the compensation amounts and contributions, and this information would have made it difficult if not impossible for leaders to skim from the top. In return, the leaders helped officials collect funds from villagers. Their presence alongside village officials, as informal auditors of a sort, helped convince villagers to part with their money.

[21] Author interview, Spring 2013, Hunan Province.
[22] Author interview, Spring 2013, Hunan Province.

What would have happened if village officials had stolen the compensation funds? While we cannot observe the alternate history of Wucun itself, the nearby village of Jiucai provides a glimpse at the counterfactual. In Jiucai, each lineage group has a formal leader called a *zuzhang*, a position that is reached through consensus within the clan. Just like in Wucun, the village cadres have little informal social authority in comparison to these lineage heads.

Yet unlike in Wucun, the village committee head and the Party secretary took cash from a road building project – and they paid a price. When it emerged that villagers would not be compensated for their lost land, the village erupted in turmoil. Village notables organized a mass petition. The lineage leaders gave their blessing to the petitioning effort, which was crucial in erasing any doubts that petition signers had about the safety and wisdom of taking on the local cadres. Nearly every household in the village signed the petition.

As a result of this remarkable level of collective action, driven partly by these lineage leaders, the citizens of Jiucai won. After delivering the petition to higher-ups in the county government, the local government removed the village Party Secretary and village committee head from their posts and delivered compensation to the villagers. Had the Party Secretary in Wucun also tried to embezzle funds, it is possible that the lineage elders might have organized their group in a similar fashion. This threat provides an incentive for officials to refrain from corruption.

5.1.4 Survey Evidence on Kin Group Brokers

While the case studies show the theory at work in particular cases, it leaves open the question of whether the theory applies to the rest of China. To answer this question, I constructed a unique dataset to make inferences about national patterns. Many of the measures draw on data from the Chinese General Social Survey (CGSS), which collects data on lineage elites and their political participation. The survey wave that I draw on was conducted in 2005 by researchers from the Hong Kong University of Science and Technology and the Peoples' University of China. (More recent waves of the CGSS and the CFPS survey data used in the previous chapter do not ask about lineage group leader incorporation.) The survey's rural sample was created by stratifying among regions, then sampling seventy-five county-level units; within each county, the survey randomly sampled four townships, and within each township, two villages. The survey sampled a total of 408 villages.

I draw on the CGSS for data about village-level lineage institutions. To be consistent with previous analyses, I proxy for lineage group salience by measuring the presence or absence of ancestral halls. (The CGSS also asks villagers directly whether "there is a lineage group network in the village" and the results are consistent using this broader and more informal measure of lineage group salience.) In addition, the survey asks whether "the leaders or most influential members of the lineage network [are] also village cadres." I create dummy variables for the presence of lineage groups and lineage leader composition.

I combined data from the CGSS with outside sources to create a unique dataset with a rich set of village characteristics. These covariates include a measure of economic activity using nighttime luminosity data from 1992, which is a plausible pretreatment measure of wealth. (The results do not change if I use a more contemporary, and posttreatment, measure of wealth.) I also created measures of the village's distance from the township and county seats, agricultural suitability, and terrain roughness. I drew on the CGSS for measures of surname and ethnic fragmentation, township control over elections, and the number of households. In Appendix A, I present a detailed breakdown of how each variable was constructed. Table A.1 provides some basic descriptive statistics and Table A.2 explains in more detail how each variable was created.

When Do Lineage Elites Join the State?

What types of lineage elite join village governments? When do they do so? The question is crucial for understanding the dynamics of political control in rural China. If different types of lineage elites chose to join village governments – or if they do so in very different types of villages – it will require a research design to overcome this selection problem and find a comparable set of villages.

There are two main selection effects at work: first, lineage elites tend to enter politics in rapidly developing villages; second, especially powerful lineage elites tend to enter politics, especially those who already play roles as local brokers. These two trends are consistent with the theory that the state wants to incorporate local power brokers into the state in order to develop land in villages where it is most profitable. However, it also poses real challenges for untangling cause and effect.

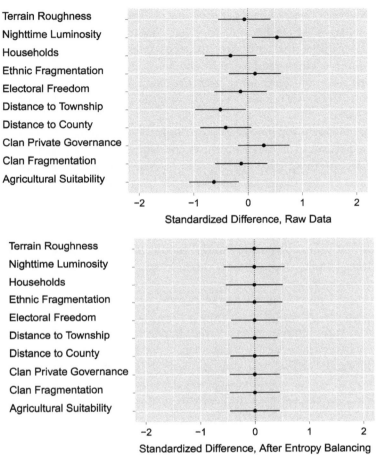

FIGURE 5.2 Difference between villages where lineages are village cadres and villages where elites are *not* village cadres, before and after entropy balancing. $N = 69$.

Figure 5.2 plots standardized difference in means results for different variables, comparing villages where lineage elites have joined the local government with those where they have not.

These villages are comparable on some important dimensions. There are no significant differences between the two groups of villages in terms of terrain roughness, the quality of elections, clan fragmentation (measured using surnames as a proxy), and ethnic fragmentation.[23]

---

[23] The clan fragmentation index captures the likelihood that two randomly selected villagers will belong to different surname groups. The surname fragmentation index is:

However, these villages differ on a couple of key dimensions. First, villages where lineage elites have joined the local state tend to be in locations that are ripe for economic development. In particular, lineage elites tend to join the local government when the village is close to the county and township seats. They also tend to be in villages with high levels of wealth, proxied for by nighttime luminosity.

The tendency for lineage elites to join the local state in villages with a high potential for development is consistent with my hypothesis. For officials, co-opting local notables can be costly: they may need to spend time and energy flattering them in order to convince them to join local government. In the case of development projects, they may also need to line their pockets with money. In remote or agricultural villages, where the prospects for growth are barren, co-opting traditional elites may be a waste of time, effort, and money. In villages ripe for development, on the other hand, co-opting elites can help speed development and may be worth the cost.

For the elites themselves, the prospect of rapid local development also changes the calculus of joining the village government. In wealthy areas, village committees have larger budgets, meaning local cadres have more resources to distribute among their group. This can make the job more rewarding and prestigious.[24] It also potentially makes the position of village head or party secretary more lucrative for the office-holder. They can use their authority to ensure that favored allies get land and in return receive kickbacks; or they can pocket a portion of the compensation for larger projects driven by county, city, or prefectural authorities.

Lineage elites are also more likely to join the local state when they already serve as local power brokers. In villages with insider elites, lineage institutions serve different functions than in villages with outsider elites.[25]

In villages with insider elites, lineage institutions tend to provide more private governance than in villages without – making lineage elites

---

1 − (percent of village in largest surname group)^2 − (percent of village in second largest surname group)^2 − (percent of village in third largest surname group)^2.

[24] However, as Oi and Rozelle (2000) note, it can also motivate villagers to focus their attention outside the village.

[25] Since the survey was conducted after these elites joined office, it is possible that the differing answers reflect recent changes. However, in most cases, my fieldwork suggested that these particular function, of lineage institutions tends to change relatively slowly, making it unlikely this was the case.

key political intermediaries. Groups with insider elites tend to do more to privately organize the provision of public goods and services. For example, in some villages that I visited lineage elites helped organize the collection of funds that the group gave to the poor or elderly members of the clan who had no children.[26]

One important possibility is that the leaders who join office are different from those who do not. Some scholars have found substantial heterogeneity in the degree to which leaders are pro-social or antisocial.[27] While it is possible that more antisocial or selfish leaders sort into office, there is little quantitative evidence to that effect. Instead, as mentioned, the leaders who join office are *more* likely to privately supply public goods.

The informal authority of lineage elites makes them especially useful allies of the local state. As the survey evidence shows, the stronger lineage institutions are, the more local actors have an incentive to incorporate lineage leaders into the state. However, from a research design perspective it does make it more challenging to ensure that the comparisons between villages capture the effect of incorporating lineage leaders into the state, not the differing strengths of lineages. In the qualitative case studies, this is accomplished by pairing villages with similar sorts of lineage institutions; in the quantitative analysis, which because it is observational can only capture correlations, I take a similar approach of matching villages with comparable lineage institutions.

To create a more credible comparison group, I again use entropy balancing, introduced in the previous chapter (see Section 4.1.2).[28] The underlying intuition for entropy balancing is that, like a randomized experiment, the researcher's aim in an observational study should be to create a control group that is comparable to the treatment groups. In a randomized study this is accomplished by design. With entropy balancing, the researcher instead creates weights for each observation in the control group (here, outsider elite villages) to make the group more comparable to the treatment group (here, insider elite villages). As the lower half of Figure 5.2 shows, entropy balancing leads to nearly perfect balance on observed covariates.

---

[26] See also Tsai (2002).
[27] Kosfeld and Rustagi (2015).
[28] Hainmueller (2012).

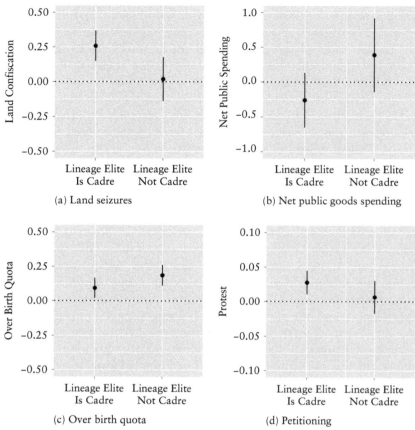

FIGURE 5.3 Key outcome measures with 95 percent confidence intervals.
Villages where lineage elites are not cadres ($N = 38$) are re-weighted using
entropy balancing. Villages where lineage elites are cadres ($N = 31$) are not
re-weighted.

Main Results

What is the consequence of including lineage elites in village governments? Figure 5.3 examines key outcomes, including land requisitions,
public goods spending, birth quota compliance, and protest. Villages
where lineage elites are not cadres ($N = 38$) are re-weighted using
entropy balancing while villages where lineage elites are cadres ($N = 31$)
are not weighted.

The results show that, first, having insider elites is helpful for requisitioning land. I use an indicator variable for whether CGSS respondents indicated land had been expropriated in a village under the current village committee.[29]

In villages where lineage elites have joined the village government, land expropriations are much more likely to occur ($p = 0.004$). The implied effect is substantively very large: in villages with outsider lineage elites, close to zero land requisitions occur, but land requisitions occur in about a quarter of villages with insider elites. Appendix Figures A.3 and A.4 show a reduction in cultivated land and an increase in revenue from land in villages where lineage elites have joined political institutions. Since the measure of land expropriation used here is imperfect, these alternative measures are important.

Moreover, villages where lineage elites are included in village governments have lower levels of net public goods spending. (The difference is statistically significant at $p = 0.02$.) This is largely because these villages collect significantly more in taxes and levies through the *Yishi Yiyi* (一事一议) program of participatory governance. Do land takings by lineage elites lead to higher public goods spending? In most villages, land expropriations are not strongly correlated with either decreases or increases in net public spending (defined as the amount that villages spend on all public services and infrastructure minus the amount they collect directly from villagers in cash contributions). On the other hand, in villages with insider elites land takings are associated with sharply lower net public spending.[30] Mostly, this drop occurs because insider elites who take

[29] More specifically, the indicator takes a value of 1 if CGSS respondents indicate land was reallocated for the purposes of a state land expropriation (国家土地征用) or the development of an enterprise (发展企业用地), which is another form of land appropriation. This captures an important subset of all land expropriations but not all of them, since not all expropriations are followed by land reallocation. For this reason, I also examine results for other variables.

[30] See Appendix Figure A.5. The figure draws on village-level data from the CGSS, and shows that in villages with insider elites, land expropriations in fact correlate with *lower* overall public spending. To analyze the relationship between land expropriations and other outcomes, I use a simple interaction framework. I use the following specification:

$$y_i = \alpha + \beta x_i * \mu z_i + \gamma_i + \theta_j + \epsilon_i \qquad (5.1)$$

For each village i in the dataset, y_i is the outcome variable. The variable z_i is an indicator for whether or not the village has experienced a land requisition and the variable x_i is an indicator for whether or not the leader of the lineage group is also a village cadre. In Appendix A, I present full results that include conditioning variables γ_i and province fixed effects, θ_j for each province j.

village land are also directly taxing villages at higher rates than other villages.

In addition to helping implement land requisitions, Figure 5.3(c) shows how lineage group elites also help implement family planning quotas, a second key priority of local governments. When lineage elites join local governments, there are significantly fewer over-quota births ($p = 0.02$). In villages with insider elites, the estimated number of families of over-quota births drops by 10 percentage points.

Finally, there is more tentative evidence that when lineage elites are cadres there is more protest, albeit small in scale. Figure 5.3(d) shows that in the typical village where lineage elites are cadres, virtually no one reports petitioning. In villages where lineage elites are cadres, that rises to about 3 percent of respondents. The difference is not statistically significant at the traditional 95 percent confidence level ($p = 0.08$). The results are largely driven by villages that have experienced land requisitions. This is suggestive of the way in which elite co-optation can erode trust in the long run.

In Appendix A I provide additional results, including a section exploring the role of social structure (such as the number of lineage groups in a village).

In short, the results suggest that lineage elites are effective intermediaries for the state, who help implement policies including land requisitions and birth quotas. However, when they extract too much, as arguably happens during land requisitions, it can lead to a backlash.

5.1.5 Beyond China: The Enclosure Movement in Scotland

Highland clans in Scotland have many of the same characteristics as lineage groups in China. They were based on bonds of real (and sometimes fictive) kinship. Clan members were entitled to own land by virtue of their membership in the kin group, through the right of *duthchas*, but clan membership also obligated them to provide rents to their clan chiefs. Historically, these rents came in the form of food, including grain and livestock, rather than cash.[31] In return, the these chiefs provided their clan with safety and protection. In this way, chiefs also served the central state: "[W]here the authority of central government was weak or spread

---

[31] For example, in one region tenants handed over 30 percent of their barley and 15 percent of their oats to clan chiefs. See Dodgshon (1998, p. 63).

thinly, order was provided by the authority which chiefs exercised over their clans."[32]

Beginning in the 1600s, the British government sought to bring rural Scotland under greater Crown control and increase the revenue they could extract from it. In order to do so, they slowly co-opted and assimilated the clan chiefs. The Statutes of Iona, passed in 1609, outlawed important clan traditions and encouraged highland clan chiefs to send their sons to lowland Protestant schools; they also created incentives for chiefs to collect regular cash rents and participate in markets.[33] While the statutes were not always faithfully enforced, this process began to align the interests of clan chiefs and the Crown, and started to transform the relationship between chiefs and their clans as well.

The critical juncture for Scotland came when the Crown began to encourage chiefs to consolidate their landholdings. Consolidating landholdings meant, of course, that the people living on it had to be removed; as historian T. M. Devine notes, "eviction and forced removal became an integral part of the destruction of the traditional settlements throughout the Highlands and this was the most direct violation of *duthchas*, the obligation on clan elites to provide protection and security of possession for the people within their lands."[34] The removal of peasants for large-scale sheep farming was, for many, cataclysmic. Devine writes that "the most notorious removals took place on the Sutherland estate and between 1807 and 1821 the factors of the Countess of Sutherland and her husband Lord Stafford removed between 6,000 and 10,000 people from the inner parishes to new crofting settlements on the coast in the most extraordinary example of social engineering in early nineteenth century Britain."[35]

The Scottish chiefs' co-optation by the state – and their subsequent betrayal of their kin – made it enormously difficult for their clans to effectively resist land appropriation. Historians have tended to attribute this to a mismatch between cultural expectations and actual behavior. Devine writes that "the relentless violation of the values of clanship caused enormous collective disorientation throughout the Gaelic world and hence a basic difficulty in resisting landlord action in any effective fashion."[36] Another historian writes that clan rank-and-file "adhered tenaciously to

[32] Dodgshon (1998, p. 32). See also Cathcart (2006, pp. 60–75).
[33] Dodgshon (1998, pp. 102–118).
[34] Devine (1994, pp. 34–35).
[35] Devine (1994, pp. 34–35).
[36] Devine (1994, p. 41).

the traditionalist concept of *duthchas* long after clanship had been abrogated by the conduct of chiefs."[37] He goes on to write that they "seem prisoners of their own culture, thoroughly perplexed, demoralised and disorientated by the process of anglicisation effected by the assimilation of the clan elite into the British establishment."[38]

The role of clan leaders in nineteenth century Scotland suggests that this pattern of elite co-optation has a long history that extends well outside China. Much like in China, clan chiefs helped facilitate the transfer of wealth away from their group. But is this theory limited to traditional kinship groups like clans, lineages, or tribes? In the next section, I turn to consider the role of religious groups in China.

5.2 RELIGIOUS LEADERS, CO-OPTATION, AND CONTROL

Folk religious groups in contemporary China generally do not have the types of traditional leaders that some lineage groups have. Instead, these groups often have councils or committees that tend to be made up of the village's social elite. The way to think about religious authority, then, is that it generally helps reinforce the authority of preexisting intermediaries, like the leaders of lineage groups. As I will show, a mix of religious and kin-group based authority allows brokers to exert especially powerful control over their groups – but also makes them especially vexing adversaries for local officials when they are not included in local government.

5.2.1 Structured Case Study Evidence on Religious Brokers

Two structured case studies illuminate the way that co-opting the leaders of religious organizations can strengthen political control, especially when these organizations overlay other social groups like lineages. The case studies I present here are from two villages in the same prefecture in Eastern Guangdong (see Table 5.2).

These cases were selected based on survey data. Using the CGSS dataset, I determined that Headwater and Peng Village would be interesting high-leverage cases to examine. Both are identical across many key characteristics. Importantly, both are relatively close to the prefectural

---

[37] Macinnes (1988, p. 72).
[38] Macinnes (1988, p. 72).

TABLE 5.2 *Headwater and Peng Village case studies*

	Headwater	Peng
Annual income in *yuan*, median	12,000	10,000
Years schooling, mean	5.7	5.9
Competitive elections	No	No
Distance to city	20 km	26 km
Annual religious festival	Yes	Yes
Lineage groups	Yes	Yes
Key explanatory variable:		
Religious/lineage authority on village committee	No	Yes
Key outcomes:		
Percent expropriated	0%	40%
Comply with birth quotas	45%	90%
Petitions (before land taking)	No	No
Petitions (after land taking)	No	Yes

seat and in regions that are developing rapidly, so it is reasonable to suppose that land might be expropriated in both villages and that villagers would have the resources to petition and have children over the local birth quota, even if they have to pay a fine. Yet the two villages have experienced quite divergent outcomes.

The Case of Peng Village

Peng Village has a single dominant lineage group, with resources including an ancestral hall and a genealogical record or *zupu*.[39] The village chief has for years been an unofficial leader of the kinship group. Even before he took his position, he had emerged as someone to whom others would go for information about village politics, to resolve disputes, and to consult with on matters like weddings. When asked who the most influential member of the kinship group currently is, villagers generally mentioned the village chief; when asked who the leader was in the years before he joined the village committee, most still named him.

Folk religious institutions reinforce the power of lineage elites and village cadres. Like many other villages in the region, Peng Village holds a yearly deity procession; in this village, the procession honors the Lords of the Three Mountains, a legendary trio of mountain deities

---

39 族谱.

famed for their role in suppressing a rebellion against a Song Dynasty emperor.[40]

The centerpiece of the festival is a deity procession. Statues of the Lords of the Three Mountains patrol the village in a prearranged order. On the first day they travel in sequence to the eastern part of the village, and then the south, followed by the northern and western reaches. On the second day the Lords of the Three Mountains parade south, north, west, and east. The deities stop at the main lineage ancestral hall and villagers line the main parade route, lighting candles, incense, and fireworks as the deities pass.[41] The parade includes lavish helpings of food for celebrants, who drink expensive tea and liquor and chew on betel nuts (a mild narcotic).

A village elder's council (老人理事会) organizes the religious procession and fair. The council gathers contributions from each villager to pay for it: there is a mandatory 3 *yuan* contribution for each adult, and an additional 2 *yuan* must be paid by men who wish to honor the passing gods by lighting a candle and placing it on their palanquin. (In the patriarchal culture of Chaozhou, this is a task generally performed by men.) Men who have recently married must pay an additional 80 *yuan*, for which they receive the honor of helping carry the gods for part of their journey, which brings good fortune to their new household.

Village cadres have substantial influence over the religious council and give it its marching orders (quite literally, since they determine the route of the deity procession). The village head and Party Secretary do not serve on the council. However, a small group of lineage elites sit on the council and hold its key offices, and these socially influential households also happen to be allies of the village's political leadership. The village head has cultivated these ties through old-fashioned patronage. When influential families want to build new houses, the head has used his power over land reallocations to give cultivated land to these families for use as residential land.

Religious institutions reinforce lineage elites' power and in doing so strengthen the power of village cadres. Organizing the festival requires substantial social authority in order to convince villagers to donate money, time, and resources; at the same time it strengthens the council members' moral authority and reputation among villagers. For example, the careful sequence in which the deities parade through the village,

---

40 三山国王. See Chen (2001) for an overview.
41 See Eng and Lin (2002, p. 1259) describe similar practices in other villages in Chaozhou.

which is announced on posters throughout the village beforehand, makes it plain to everyone in the village that all households, rich or poor, have equal access to the deities. All villagers regardless of means also enjoy the same food and liquor. In this manner, the parade reinforces the council members' reputations for being equitable and fair social arbiters.

In many villages in Guangdong, local officials have quietly encouraged the revival of deity processions and folk religious institutions, since they sometimes see them as useful for governing the village and exerting political control. Irene Eng and Yi-min Lin in their study of religion in Guangdong note that "since the late 1980s, many village cadres have not only taken a tolerant attitude toward the deity procession but have actually provided tacit support for it, so as to add legitimacy to the authority they hold based in the state system."[42] Eng and Lin note that religious institutions increase the popularity of social elites, who can be powerful allies of village officials who need their help with family planning policies and revenue collection.

The content of Peng Village's religious institutions – that is, the symbols, narratives, and rituals used by these groups – also to some degree reinforce cadres' symbolic political authority. For example, the Lords of the Three Mountains are known for their role in quelling a rebellion against the Song state, for which the emperor awarded them an honorary title. The rituals and symbols of the deity procession legitimate secular state authority, rather than defying it, by deifying figures whose most notable achievement was to support the central state against an insurrection.

In 2009, the village chief and Party Secretary used their power over the land reallocations to distribute, probably illegally, about thirty plots of farmland to an entrepreneur from a nearby city. The leaders used what one villager called "dirty tricks"[43] to prevent immediate mobilization against the plan, taking advantage of their moral authority (and others' lack of information about the development plan). First, they persuaded other lineage leaders – the heads of the village's "big families"[44] – that the expropriation scheme would benefit everyone. Once they had the backing of these key allies, they moved on to persuading the "little families"[45] to support the plan. Officials then collected several thousand dollars from

---

42 Eng and Lin (2002, p. 1276).
43 Author interview, Spring 2013, Guangdong Province. 变相手法.
44 Author interview, Spring 2013, Guangdong Province. 大户.
45 Author interview, Spring 2013, Guangdong Province. 小户.

nearly every household as a down payment on a new apartment, an amount which for many farmers represented most of their savings.

However, the housing never materialized, leaving villagers with bull-dozed farmland and empty bank accounts.[46] The leaders fled to the nearby township. Villagers suspected township officials protected them because they, too, had benefitted from the scheme. As one villager lamented, the committee chief and Party Secretary treated their kin group members like "lackeys"[47] and then betrayed them. As one villager put it: "They set a trap to cheat us."[48]

When local cadres dominate religious institutions, they can use their moral authority to pressure villagers to support land and other expropri-ation schemes. Villagers face steep costs organizing against the local state. They also face high levels of uncertainty about the value of any expro-priation deal on the table. Overcoming the collective action problem is difficult under these conditions of uncertainty, especially when socially influential villagers have expressed support for the plan.

The Case of Headwater Village

In the hamlet of Headwater, by comparison, a few miles down the road, the influential members of the religious group have not joined the govern-ment. The key village committee members and Party officers have little moral authority or prestige (威望) within the lineage group.

The village of Headwater holds a yearly festival to honor the Queen Mother of the West, a Daoist goddess who become extremely popular in China during the Tang Dynasty.[49] The Queen Mother holds an important place in the Daoist pantheon: she cultivates the peaches of immortality, which bloom once every three thousand years, and which she feeds to other deities in ritual feasts to ensure their longevity. According to legend, she has also fed the peaches to certain mortal devotees, including the seventh emperor of the Han Dynasty.[50]

In Headwater, the deity procession honoring the Queen Mother is the village's largest social gathering. Celebrants parade a representation of

---

[46] Deininger and Jin (2009) find that in about a third of land takings, the project is not completed.

[47] Author interview, Spring 2013, Guangdong Province. 助手.

[48] Author interview, Spring 2013, Guangdong Province. 设局骗我们.

[49] 西王母. See Cahill (1993) for a scholarly overview of the history of the Queen Mother of the West.

[50] Evidently, the peaches did not confer immorality on the Emperor Wu, who died just short of his seventieth birthday. See Cahill (1993, pp. 54–55).

the Queen Mother of the West between three local villages. Each of the three neighboring villages takes a turn holding the parade, so that each village organizes the festival once every three years. Villagers told me that the villages compete to match or top the quality of the parade and festival held by their neighbors the previous year. In southern China, this type of deity procession is an important ritual. Helen Siu describes a similar parade honoring the god of the south seas in the Pearl River Delta: that procession of the god's idol generally lasted four days, traversing several settlements, with some villages putting on as many as six operas at the same time to serve as entertainment.[51]

In Headwater, the parade once required villagers to shoulder a heavy statue of the Queen Mother and walk it for miles down dusty dirt tracks, a backbreaking task. Now, to tour the Queen Mother, villagers place her statue on the back of a pickup truck and drive her slowly down newly paved roads, proceeded by a line of trucks that delivers vollies of fireworks.

Villagers say that organizing the religious festival unifies Headwater's three major lineage groups and reinforces the power of the group of elders that head them. Putting on the festival is an impressive logistical feat. Festival leaders must wheedle donations from the village's three lineage groups to pay for food, costumes, fireworks, decorations, a stage, and a sound system. They must recruit a cast of hundreds, clothe them in traditional dress, and provide them with the appropriate objects to carry, which range from silk banners to replica jade swords. The effort requires months of planning by the festival council, which is composed of Headwater's lineage elite.[52]

Not coincidentally, the festival reinforces the authority of the village's social elites. During the procession, lineage elders march in a place of honor just behind the deity. The celebration that concludes the day-long festival also includes speeches by key elders, who put their personal stamp on the festival's success. Writing about temple festivals in a group of villages in the same prefecture, Irene Eng and Yi-min Lin note:

For those who wanted to play a leading role in lineage organizations, the [temple festival] council provided a useful avenue, as according to local tradition the

---

[51] Siu (1989, pp. 79–82).
[52] The pattern of temple councils being staffed by lineage elites seems to be a general one. In a study of a nearby set of villages, Irene Eng and Yi-min Lin note that "all the leading members of the elders' councils in the villages we studied were also leading members of their clans." See Eng and Lin (2002, p. 1276).

worship of deities assumes greater significance than the worship of ancestors. A prominent status in council affairs could help enhance or reinforce one's status in clan affairs ... Since the deity procession is a vital test of their leadership, they cannot afford to make it a less than spectacular event if they want to maintain their influence in the village.[53]

It is much the same in Headwater, where many credit the festival with uniting the village's three lineages. As one leader put it, "Even though we are a mixed-surname village, we all help each other."[54]

The core of lineage group elites plays an almost daily role in bargaining with the government and even providing private governance. They gather funds to provide a modest stipend for retirees and the poor, and put on a religious festival that requires a high degree of collective organization. When asked who they would go to if they had a dispute with the local government, villagers frequently mentioned one of the lineage leaders. Despite a favorable location near a highway to the prefecture's administrative seat, there have been no land requisitions by village officials in Headwater. There is also widespread noncompliance with the local birth quota.

The threat of violent collective action organized by independent kinship group leaders is not an abstract threat for village cadres in Headwater. Indeed, a half hour's drive down the road from Headwater is a village whose tight-knit lineage groups forced the Party Secretary and village committee to flee during violent protests over land expropriations; another hour or so down the road is the village of Wukan, whose lineage leaders organized a similar protest that ousted leaders. As a village committee member in a nearby village put it, "You can't get anywhere around here without negotiating with the lineage leaders first."[55]

5.2.2   Survey Evidence on Religious Brokers

The case studies showed the process by which religious institutions can strengthen the informal authority of village elites, and indirectly strengthen the state's control over local society. I now turn to survey evidence to examine whether this pattern holds across mainland China. The evidence is drawn from the CGSS dataset.

---

[53] Eng and Lin (2002, p. 1276).
[54] Author interview, Spring 2013, Guangdong Province. 我们都互相帮助.
[55] Author interview, Summer 2013, Guangdong Province.

To examine whether religious festivals strengthen the authority of lineage elites, I examine whether the outcomes of lineage leader incorporation differ in villages with and without folk religious activity. To estimate these correlations, I interact an indicator for village participation in temple fairs with an indicator for whether or not lineage leaders have become village cadres.[56] I present graphical results here, relying on specifications without controls, but full regression results with controls are consistent with the results here.

The fusion of lineage and religious authority can make local elites powerful allies, or adversaries, of the local state. Figure 5.4(a) presents correlations with land confiscations. It plots the estimated marginal effect of lineage leader incorporation by whether or not the village has festival activity.[57] In villages that hold festivals, including lineage elites in village political institutions correlates with a more than 25 percentage point increase in the likelihood of a land requisition. On the other hand, in villages with no festival activity, the effect of lineage leader inclusion on land expropriation is close to zero.

To some degree, then, the power of lineage leaders hinges on the presence of complementary religious institutions that legitimate their authority. When local elites organize religious festivals and other cultural activities it increases their prestige. Their high levels of social capital can make them powerful authoritarian brokers.

Do villages that have festivals also tend to spend more on public goods and services? Figure 5.4 (b) presents estimates for the marginal effect of lineage leader incorporation on net public spending (see previous chapter for definition). When a village holds a festival, the inclusion of lineage leaders in village governments is associated with a decrease in net public spending. The results are not statistically significant, but the relationship is more consistent with these elites playing an extractive role than a benevolent or developmental one.

---

[56] I use the following specification:

$$y_i = \alpha + \beta x_i * \mu z_i + \gamma_i + \theta_j + \epsilon_i \qquad (5.2)$$

For each village i in the dataset, y_i is the outcome variable. The variable z_i is an indicator for whether or not villagers participate in a temple fair or festival and the variable x_i is an indicator for whether or not the leader of the lineage group is also a village cadre. In the appendix I present full results that include conditioning variables γ_i and province fixed effects, θ_j for each province j.

[57] Effect is not meant to imply that the regressions themselves represent a causal estimate.

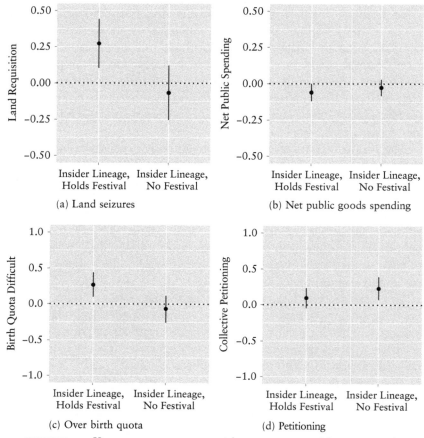

FIGURE 5.4 Key outcome measures with 95 percent confidence intervals
(N = 388).

However, it seems likely to be the case that religious associations help improve the *private* supply of public goods like roads and schools, as Tsai shows.[58] In fact, villages that hold festivals do have higher levels of education, consistent with Tsai's findings. This leaves the overall welfare implications of these groups somewhat ambiguous.

The results for birth quotas and protest suggest an important control function for religious organizations. Figure 5.4(c) on the other hand, shows that lineage elites in villages with festivals have a slightly easier time enforcing birth quotas, but the relationship is a weak one. There is

[58] Tsai (2002).

also some weak evidence that the additional informal authority created by religion may help insider elites quell collective action. Figure 5.4(d) presents results on collective petitioning. In villages with religious festivals, lineage elite inclusion is correlated with low levels of collective petitioning. The authority of these elites may to some degree contain collective action by dissatisfied members of their group. However, the results are not statistically significant.

Perhaps religious organizations lead to improved nonmaterial outcomes, such as generalized trust? Festival associations can link people to each other and strengthen social capital.

On balance, the evidence suggests that the presence of religious organizations is correlated with *less* social trust, not more. Appendix Tables A.16 and A.17 show correlations between whether a village has a festival and two measures of generalized trust. It may be the case that local elites introduce festivals in places with low levels of trust or that some third factor causes both. Still, the results suggest that it is unlikely that the festivals cause large increases in trust.

Of course, religious organizations also bring *private* psychic rewards, such as a sense of moral purpose, personal salvation, or spiritual fulfillment. After all, this is their core reason for being. This makes it even more difficult to interpret the overall welfare implications of the presence of these groups. These organizations can strengthen elite control *and* make members better off in important ways.

5.2.3 Beyond China: Urban Renewal in New Haven

Urban politics in the United States differs from rural politics in China in many respects – not least the vastly different national political regimes they operate under – yet informal arrangements are crucial in both contexts for governance. This fact has long been recognized by scholars of American politics. "Even though the institutions of local government [in the United States] bear most of the formal responsibility for governing, they lack the resources and the scope of authority to govern without active support and cooperation of significant private interests," wrote Clarence Stone in his classic work on urban governance. "An urban regime may thus be defined as the informal arrangements by which public bodies and private interests function together in order to be able to make and carry out governing decisions."[59]

---

[59] Stone (1989, p. 6).

In this section, I turn from the developing world to the United States in order to examine urban redevelopment in New Haven, a case made famous by Robert Dahl's classic book *Who Governs?* In New Haven in the 1950s and 1960s, a strong mayor, Richard C. Lee, used participatory, quasi-democratic bodies to bring local elites over to his side to help elicit the community's acquiescence with redevelopment policies that forcibly displaced a fifth of the city's population.

Mayor Lee wanted to redevelop New Haven at least in part to make his city look and feel "modern," using language which is echoed by the efforts of many Chinese officials seeking to "transform" or "remodel" rural China. In a letter to Yale art historian Vincent Scully after he left office, Lee wrote:

New Haven was a mess when I became Mayor on January 1, 1954 a rotten, stinking, decaying mess. When I think of the gin mills, the pool parlors and flop houses which dotted our main avenues. ... The old days, which I remember very well, were the stinking, rotten slums of Oak Street; the decaying, dilapidated, abandoned structures which disgraced our central city.[60]

To remake New Haven, Lee sought to tear down these "slums" and replace them with gleaming new infrastructure: public spaces, highways, and civic buildings. Scully and many others would ultimately regard this far-reaching redevelopment program as a social and aesthetic disaster.[61]

Whatever its ultimate consequences for the city, the implementation of Lee's plan was a remarkable exercise in state power. New Haven's redevelopment required the relocation of some 30,000 individuals, willing or not, from homes that some families had lived in for generations.[62] Altogether, New Haven relocated 20 percent of its residents from their homes over the course of about a decade, starting in 1956, in a redevelopment scheme that disproportionately effected African-American families, and to a lesser degree New Haven's other ethnic out-groups, especially the Catholic and Jewish communities.[63]

How did Lee elicit compliance with a redevelopment program that disrupted the lives of a fifth of the community? A key element of the mayor's urban regime was a set of councils and committees that played

[60] Rae (2008, p. 335).
[61] Rae (2008, pp. 312–432).
[62] Rae (2008, p. 340).
[63] Rae (2008, pp. 340–342).

an advisory role, especially the Citizens Action Commission (CAC) and its sub-committees. These councils had no meaningful formal power, and served mainly to help coordinate New Haven's social and business elite and rally their support for the project. Dahl writes that "[the commission's] members had been shrewdly selected to represent many of the major centers of influence or status in the community."[64] Lee ultimately appointed over 400 of New Haven's elites to the CAC and various other urban renewal committees. The members were "drawn mainly from the educated, activist, middle-class segments of the community" including labor leaders and influential members of key ethnic and religious blocs.[65] These local elites were placed on these committees not to provide meaningful feedback to the mayor in the decision-making process but, Dahl writes, because these civic leaders "were counted on to form a group of loyal supporters who would help enlist a community following."[66] This was a strategy that Lee found effective in other areas of city governance. For example, he was careful to appoint to the school board members drawn from the Catholic, Protestant, Jewish, and African-American communities, partly in order to help him gain support in each of those groups for his proposals.[67]

These participatory institutions helped win the buy-in of key local elites for New Haven's redevelopment, but after the projects had been completed the mayor faced substantial backlash when the costs for the affected communities became apparent. Racial discrimination had prevented some African-American families from finding new homes.[68] Partly in response, the mayor set up a separate government-funded organization called Community Progress, Inc. to help provide services to the poor. In a similar fashion to the redevelopment councils, "the organization had, from the outset, hired as its own staff many of the people living among the poor who might have become critics of its programs."[69] However, this was not enough to prevent others in the community from organizing against the mayor.[70]

The dynamics of New Haven's urban renewal has rough parallels to redevelopment projects elsewhere, including in many Chinese villages,

---

[64] Dahl (2005, p. 131).
[65] Dahl (2005, p. 131).
[66] Dahl (2005, p. 134).
[67] Dahl (2005, p. 150).
[68] Rae (2008, p. 338).
[69] Rae (2008, p. 349).
[70] Rae (2008, pp. 348–355).

in which initial acquiescence is followed by popular anger. Even a bad deal can sound good when trusted local elites and the state sing the same tune about the benefits of the project for the community.[71] However, the consequences of these deals for the distribution of wealth and power eventually become evident. While there are important differences between the two contexts, the importance of co-optation of local elites runs through both cases.

5.3   CONCLUSION

In this chapter, I have argued that civil society elites are important local brokers who can help the local state control society. When these elites are co-opted in local political institutions, they help the state implement policies like protest control, land requisitions, and birth quotas. When these elites do not belong to formal political institutions, they are more likely to organize their group in resistance to the state.

There are intriguing parallels between lineage and religious elites in China and traditional leaders in other contexts, such as chiefs. Kate Baldwin finds that national leaders cede control over land to traditional chiefs in order to increase electoral support among non-coethnics.[72] Interestingly, Baldwin also finds that voters tend to cast their ballots for political candidates endorsed by chiefs because they infer, correctly, that politicians with connections to chiefs will provide higher levels of public goods.[73] This is broadly consistent with the idea that traditional kinship institutions can help buttress public goods provision, which occurs in a context of repeated interaction and relatively low stakes.[74] But it leaves open the question of what role these elites might play in large-scale land requisitions. Lauren Honig shows that it is *autonomous* chiefs with power that is independent of the state that protect their constituents from land confiscation, which is broadly in line with the finding that autonomous lineage elites in China help protect the land rights of their group.[75] Consistent with the findings in this book, work by Daron Acemoglu, Tristan Reed, and James Robinson shows that chiefs in Sierra

[71] As Julia Chuang notes, when resistance does arise the state generally attempts to "bureaucratize" conflict in order to mute it. See Chuang (2014).
[72] Baldwin (2014).
[73] Baldwin (2013).
[74] See also Wilfahrt (2018a,b) on cooperation between traditional elites and how an overlap between formal and informal institutions can strengthen public goods provision.
[75] Honig (2015). See also Honig (2017).

Leone exploit their control over local civil society to control local politics and development.[76]

What about places where civil society groups like lineages or religious organizations are weak, absent, or difficult to govern? In the next chapter, I examine a third strategy available to autocratic states: infiltration.

[76] Acemoglu et al. (2014).

6

Infiltration

> We're going to set up a system of revolutionary collective vigilance so that
> everybody will know everybody else on his block, what they do ... what
> they believe in, what people they meet, what activities they participate in.
>
> Fidel Castro[1]

Civil society groups can help autocratic states strengthen their control over local society. The previous two chapters examined two ways
in which seemingly independent social organizations end up reinforcing the strength of autocratic states. First, cultivating these groups can
help front-line bureaucrats collect information and use social pressure to
encourage people to comply with the state. Second, co-opting the leaders
of local civil society can indirectly strengthen state control.

In this chapter, I turn my attention to a third strategy: the use of infiltrating organizations. The strategy of *infiltration* – creating networks of
grassroots informants, each of them in charge of a local "cell" – can
substitute for the strategy of using non-state groups to govern.

Many autocratic states build networks of informants and operatives
who have responsibility over small local cells. The most famous case may
be the network of informants created by the Stasi in East Germany. Yet
many other regimes have created similar systems. In Cuba, for example, Fidel Castro set up grassroots Committees for the Defense of the
Revolution which were explicitly created to help the state collect information on citizen behavior and curb noncompliance. Other regimes from

---

[1] Castro here is discussing the establishment of the Committees for the Defense of the
Revolution. See Fagen (1969, p. 69) cited in Read (2012, p. 250).

Indonesia under Suharto to Rwanda under Habyarimana have created similar systems.

This chapter shows how the Chinese state has constructed a modern system of infiltration organized around grassroots cells and their leaders. This decentralized, nominally autonomous system of cells and cell leaders (who are effectively informants) enables local officials to closely monitor local society. Case study and quantitative evidence show how small-group leaders help local officials implement policies including land confiscation and family planning quotas.

In theory, it could be the case that relying on a large number of informants with small cells might have drawbacks for autocratic regimes. The small size of these cells might encourage cell leaders to develop closer bonds to the people they are supposed to be monitoring and encouraging to comply with the state. Moreover, a large number of informants would be relatively difficult for states to monitor and control, and would be more expensive.

In contrast to this expectation, the central finding of this chapter is that hiring more informants and putting them in charge of smaller cells increases compliance with state policies. Villages with relatively small cells (and larger numbers of cell leaders) find it easier to confiscate land and to enforce state family planning policies while controlling protest. However, investing in infiltration has tradeoffs, including lower satisfaction with government.

This chapter begins with a discussion of the use of infiltration as a governance strategy by the CCP, and its roots in China's long history of state-building. Next, it turns to qualitative and quantitative evidence showing how infiltration is an effective strategy of control. Finally, it examines the interaction between the strategy of infiltration and the presence of other non-state groups like lineage and religious organizations, showing that infiltration is largely a substitute for cultivating civil society and co-opting local elites.

6.1 INFILTRATION AND THE REACH OF THE STATE

For centuries, China's emperors harnessed neighborhood social networks for the purposes of authoritarian control and infiltration. Formally, the imperial state did not generally extend much below the county level. Under the Song (960–1279), Ming (1368–1644), and Qing (1644–1912) Dynasties, China's emperors controlled rural society through decentralized administrative systems called the *baojia* (保甲) and *lijia* (里甲). Under this system of mutual responsibility, groups of a hundred or so households were divided into subgroups of around ten households.[2] The system required that the leaders of each *baojia* or *lijia* cell monitor their neighbors, report on their movements, inform on dissidents and traitors, encourage compliance with the law, and collect taxes.[3] These systems mimicked of infiltration the "cellularized"[4] or "honeycomb"[5] structure of rural society.

Ensuring compliance with extractive policies was a core function of the *baojia* and *lijia*.[6] The Qing, for instance, held the heads of these neighborhood groups personally liable for collecting revenue. When taxes came due, the heads of the groups reminded tax payers of their obligations. The amount owed was "deposited by the taxpayer personally in wooden chests installed in front of the yamen gate"[7] and counted by administrators, but if the count fell short, it fell to the heads of the *lijia* to pay. Hsiao notes that "as a consequence ... the entire clan of the person serving his one-year turn [as head of the *lijia*] had to postpone all weddings, and some of the inhabitants were thus compelled to foresake their home villages,"[8] and flee. Plainly, this placed pressure on tax collectors and their kin to meet their obligations.

The imperial state recognized that smaller cells could, somewhat paradoxically, strengthen central control by allowing the state to take advantage of the strong social networks that bind neighbor to neighbor. Franz Shurmann writes that "when the traditional state was primarily intent on strengthening its [taxation] functions ... it aimed at developing organization within the natural village."[9] (In China, a natural village is a geographically contiguous grouping of houses, something that an outsider might recognize as a single organic settlement; an administrative village can contain several natural villages.) Schurmann notes that by developing ties within the natural village, the state can take advantage of

[2] The exact numbers in each unit shifted over time but this was the approximate configuration during much of the Qing Dynasty. The imperial state in some periods employed both a *baojia* and a *lijia* system, which roughly paralleled each other but had distinct functions. In general, under the Qing, the *lijia* system was used to collect taxes and the *baojia* maintained law and order.

[3] Hsiao (1960, p. 7).

[4] Siu (1989).

[5] Shue (1988).

[6] Schurmann (1966, p. 409).

[7] Hsiao (1960, p. 95)

[8] Hsiao (1960, p. 100)

[9] Schurmann (1966, p. 410).

TABLE 6.1 *Rural administrative structure in China in the Imperial, Maoist, and Reform eras. These are approximations – the size of these units shifted over time even within these eras*[10]

Late Imperial Era	Mao Era	Reform Era
Bao	Brigade	Village
1000 households	220 households	531 Households
10 *jia*	7 production teams	10 Small Groups
Jia	Production Team	Small Group
100 households	33 households	52 households

neighborhood ties in a way that is less likely with a larger grouping of several natural villages. This is an important point to which I will return – increasing state penetration into villages by increasing the number of cells can help the state exert control.

The Communists greatly disrupted the old rural order and penetrated much further in to rural China than the imperial state. However, the administrative structure they created to replace it had clear parallels to the old *baojia* and *lijia* systems. The process of collectivization replaced the administrative village with the production brigade (生产大队), and divided each brigade into production teams (生产小队) based around village neighborhoods. These production teams became the focus of peasant life. Teams collectively cultivated their land and had collective responsibility for providing the state with grain levies.[11] As Vivienne Shue notes, these reforms "had the effect of accentuating the salience of the small locality – that is, the salience of the hamlet and the village – for the organization of peasant economic and social life."[12] The Communist system of collective agriculture was even more decentralized than rural administration under the late Qing. Table 6.1 shows the average size of the rural administrative units used by the Qing and the Communists.[13] This

---

[10] Data on imperial era from Schurmann (1966) and Hsiao (1960), data on Mao Era from Oi (1991, p. 5), data on reform era from author's dataset.

[11] See Oi (1991).

[12] Shue (1988, p. 132).

[13] Although the table elides this difference, in the imperial era, the *bao* was distinct from an administrative village, often referred to as a *xiang*. So an administrative village could conceivably include several *bao* and a *bao* might in some cases include several administrative villages. In practice, the *baojia* was somewhat irregularly organized since local officials preferred the units to coincide somewhat with natural administrative boundaries.

reliance on smaller cells helped the state control rural society and extract more effectively than the more centralized Qing system.

Collective agriculture turned the leaders of production teams into intermediaries and in the struggle over the harvest they often used what tools were available to them to help their neighbors. Oi writes that "evasion, illegality, and a 'facade of compliance' became necessary strategies of survival for team leaders who needed to function as both agents of the state and representatives of their localities."[14] Shue concurs that "low-level officials became wily and dogged defenders of their localities, constantly resisting ... within the scope that was legitimately and not-so-legitimately available to them."[15] This placed team leaders and other village cadres in an uncomfortable position. While "fellow villagers expected them to behave like traditional leaders, and in fact pressured them to do so, the party did not intend to share power ... and the political middlemen were soon to become men in the middle."[16]

The reform era and the process of de-collectivization did away with the system of production teams and replaced them with villager small groups.[17] Instead of cultivating the land collectively, individual households now have long-term use rights to plots of land – but villager small groups continue to formally own the land in most areas. These groups are quasi-autonomous organizations and not part of the formal state hierarchy.

A rich literature examines urban neighborhood organizations, which have some parallels to villager small groups. Ben Read describes neighborhood committees as the urban "nerve tips" of the state that "play a quietly powerful role in the political, social and economic life of many urban neighborhoods," in some cases taking on roles such as service provision and the implementation of policies such as family planning quotas.[18] In many ways, these neighborhood committees take on the same function as villager small groups, which have similar duties. However, these neighborhood groups have been complemented by homeowner associations that sometimes have a more adversarial relationship

---

[14] Oi (1991, pp. 11–12).
[15] Shue (1988, p. 139).
[16] Siu (1989, p. 136).
[17] In some villages, these are referred to using other terms, such as a village "districts" *pian* (片) or "teams" (生产大队). A small minority of villages lack villager small groups or the equivalent. In the Chinese General Social Survey, 95 percent of villages reported having a villager small group system.
[18] Read (2000, p. 807) See also Read (2012).

with the local state, and which have no clear equivalent in rural China.[19] Parallel to this, the state has rolled out an urban "grid management" (网格化管理) system, which divides neighborhoods into smaller cells; the staff of these grid management systems are responsible for monitoring small segments of neighborhoods in a manner reminiscent of the *baojia* system.[20]

While these urban neighborhood organizations have received considerable attention, state penetration of rural society, and in particular villager small groups, has received relatively less notice by Western scholars in recent years. Oi notes that in the early Reform era, "the power of these cadres did not just end, ... because of their positions and the prevalent clientelist politics in the Maoist period, those who had been cadres may have lost their offices but not necessarily their power."[21] However, to the extent that these groups are discussed by scholars at all, it has been to dismiss them. Jonathan Unger, for example, notes that "the villager small-group heads have very few functions and almost no power."[22]

While they are certainly not as powerful as they were in the Mao years, villager small groups and their leaders remain important because they are the state's rural nerve tips. They also often have authority over a village's most crucial resource: land. As Unger notes, "farmers take seriously their villager small group's continued ownership of the land."[23] Most villager small groups undertake land reallocations to readjust land holdings, with one survey finding that 95 percent of small groups have reallocated their land.[24] The leaders of villager small groups are generally but not always elected democratically by their peers, and they often govern by consensus.[25]

Despite being quasi-autonomous, officials nevertheless have significant control over the leaders of these neighborhood-based small groups. Officials I interviewed said that while these leaders were often elected, the village Party Branch or village committees could block the election of certain villagers or even potentially dismiss them from office. Village governments sometimes compensate small-group heads, which provides an

---

[19] Read (2003, 2007); Cai and Sheng (2013).
[20] See Chen and Kang (2016, p. 606) and Hu et al. (2018).
[21] Oi (1991, pp. 185–186).
[22] Unger (2012, p. 23).
[23] Unger (2012, p. 23).
[24] Kong and Unger (2013, p. 4)
[25] Unger shows that small groups in Anhui generally require a supermajority vote of all members in order to reallocate land. Kong and Unger (2013, p. 11).

additional tool of control, although the compensation is quite modest. The median village in the Chinese General Social Survey reports paying its small group and team leaders a salary of 200 yuan per year (about $30 US dollars).[26]

The heads of villager small groups serve as the lowest-level link between the Chinese state and society. When village cadres need to implement potentially unpopular or complex policies, they rely on small group leaders to help them disseminate information about these policies and persuade villagers to comply with them.[27] Village Party Secretaries I interviewed in Hunan noted that when they needed to reallocate land for road building projects they called a meeting of the heads of the villager small groups, and asked the heads of these small groups to conduct "thought work" (思想工作) with their teams to persuade them to voluntarily comply with the requisitions. In one village, the Party Secretary noted that he went door-to-door with small group heads to help persuade people to give up some land for the project. As he noted, the team leaders "are important allies." In many places, this is a matter of official policy. County governments throughout Jiangxi and Zhejiang, for instance, have issued documents noting that the primary duties of small-group leaders include "ensuring the smooth operation of important projects, such as land requisitions, housing demolition and relocation, [and] family planning."[28]

There is some evidence that local officials have come to recognize the effectiveness of having relatively small villager small groups as a tool of control. The number of small groups per village increased by 35 percent between 1997 and 2008 – that is, it increased from 5.9 small groups per administrative village in 1997 to 8 small groups per administrative village in 2008.[29] This is consistent with the idea that officials have recognized

---

[26] This may overestimate the amount that team leaders are paid and the frequency with which they receive salaries, since it asks about the salaries of "group and team cadres" (队组干部) which could be construed to include other village teams and groups.

[27] In addition to land policies, officials view villager small group leaders as potential allies in eliciting compliance with the One Child Policy, and encourage small groups to appoint households as leaders for promoting birth control policies. See Mattingly (2020). See also "Village Self-Government Family Planning Regulations" (计划生育村民自治规范). www.china.com.cn/policy/txt/2008-10/12/content_16598517.htm, last accessed February 14, 2019.

[28] "Strengthening Team Building among Villager Small Group Leaders" (关于加强村民小组组长队伍建设的意见). Author's Collection.

[29] This has also occurred in the context of growing village administrative consolidation, and to some degree this trend is also the result of a decrease in the number of administrative villages. Note also that this figure does not match the data in Table 6.1 which

TABLE 6.2 *Wujia and Taiping case studies*

	Wujia	Taiping
Population	1300	1400
Income	2000 yuan	2000 yuan
Township interferes in elections	No	No
Vote buying	Common	Common
Infiltration (sub-village cells)	Low	High

the utility of these close social ties as a tool of control and repression, and have adjusted rural China's administrative structure accordingly.

The remainder of this chapter investigates the role of grassroots cells and their leaders. When do these cells serve as effective channels of political control and infiltration?

6.2 STRUCTURED CASE STUDY EVIDENCE

The comparison of two nearby villages in Henan illustrates the importance of grassroots cells as tools of political control. The two villages are about an hour's drive from the provincial capital. As Table 6.2 shows, the two villages are very similar on most dimensions, including their population, level of development, and political institutions. For example, both villages hold elections without much interference from township authorities, although vote buying is common in both.

The key difference between the two villages lies in the way the state has invested in grassroots cells. In Wujia, the state has invested relatively little in growing these networks of grassroots operatives. There are relatively few of them, which means that each cell leader must monitor a larger population, and village cadres have only weak ties to these leaders. By contrast, in Taiping, leaders have created smaller cells, which eases the monitoring problems cell leaders face, and have also developed relatively close relationships with the leaders of these cells by drawing them into local patronage networks.

is from survey data, and excludes villages that have not introduced the small-group system. Data from the China Social Statistical Yearbook of 2009, www.stats.gov.cn/ztjc/ztsj/hstjnj/sh2009/201209/t20120904_72952.html, last accessed February 4, 2019.

6.2.1 Wujia Village: Low Infiltration, Weak Control

Wujia Village sits near a major county road in Henan Province on the dusty North China Plain. In most years, the village plants two crops per year: one of corn and one of wheat. Rice and pork, however, are the staples of the local diet, and the village has five small-scale pig farms. While farmers continue to tend the fields and raise livestock, most nearby villages also have small enterprises that employ a few dozen villagers and migrants. One village close to Wujia houses a factory that makes clothing and a plant that processes agricultural by-products; another has started to build an auto parts factory. In Wujia itself, there is a food processing plant, a business that rents construction equipment, and a half dozen greenhouses that grow flowers.

Henan is famous for being a leader in information disclosure, and the local government has been relatively effective at channeling political conflict into formal channels such as elections, courts, and the media instead of relying on less formal channels like petitions and protest.[30] A prominent local rights activist told me that petitions are "useless," and that "what you need is to go to the courts first and the media second."[31] He explained that the legal action forces bureaucratic wheels to start turning, which forces governments to look at residents' cases. Subsequent media coverage can intensify the government's focus on the issue and help claimants reach a resolution.[32] Residents also reported that they were free to vote for whomever they like and anyone can run for office on the village committee.

However, these formal institutions of accountability have not eliminated patronage, vote buying, and corruption. While voters in village elections can cast their ballot for whomever they like, they generally do so for the candidate who offers the most money for their vote. Vote buying plainly benefits candidates, who have calculated that the value of office exceeds the tens of thousands of dollars that some spend buying voter's support. It can even in some ways benefit villagers, who receive an upfront payment in return for their ballot rather than an abstract promise of future benefits which may or may not materialize. Yet this type of vote buying also reduces the incentives for officials to provide villagers with

---

[30] See Lorentzen (2013) for a discussion of how authorities allow protests to gather information on grievances.
[31] Author interview, Spring 2013, Henan Province.
[32] This activist's view of how to resolve disputes is consistent with Distelhorst (2013) and the idea of "publicity-driven accountability."

public goods and services once in office and encourages officials to treat office holding as an opportunity to seek rents rather than impartially serve the public.

A local rights activist explained that he thought that village cadres could be distinguished based on their dominant patron-client networks. First, he said, are officials who rely on patronage networks outside the village, especially higher levels of government and business interests. These cadres focus on trading political and economic favors among local elites. A second type are cadres who rely on patronage networks within the village, especially among lineage and neighborhood networks. These cadres focus on distributing rents among their networks of clients who, in return, support them at the ballot box and make sure they stay in office. A third type of village official has no real patronage network. As he noted, "This type is unusual."[33]

From the perspective of voters, a common danger is that officials signal they are focused on their village patronage network during elections – especially by buying votes in order to win office – but then once they become cadres they have incentives to turn toward patronage networks among local elites. In 2005, for example, a village entrepreneur named Wu Qiangguo ran for the village committee. Tapping his substantial (by the standards of rural China) personal wealth, he bought votes with cash and promises that he would work on the village committee toward promoting villagers' interests. Wu handily won the post of village head. Yet once in office he used his authority to requisition a large amount of cultivated village land, 41 *mu*, for a factory and market project. It was almost certainly illegal for the village committee to rent out cultivated land for this construction project, and a former village head told me that the village committee members kept all the rental money for themselves while compensating villagers nothing. Villagers also suspected that Wu had an ownership stake in the market project so that he benefited on both ends of the deal. The process greatly angered villagers, and even members of Wu's own clan.[34]

Perhaps because of the long-standing strength of clan ties, village cadres have *not* invested in dense networks of grassroots informants in

---

33 Author interview, Spring 2013, Henan Province.

34 Wu Qiangguo was an elite member of his clan, and consistent with what I have argued in previous chapters, his prestige and authority within his clan is one reason he was able to win office and undertake the initial land expropriation. But clan politics were not the only important dynamic at work within Wujia.

Wujia. Cadres have broken up the village into just seven small groups, which have on average 185 people per group. Village cadres have weak relationships with the leaders of these cells, who operate relatively independently.

The lack of effective control over villagers through the small-group system ended up turning into an advantage for villagers. Once the one-sided terms of the land deal emerged, a group of influential villagers, including small-group leaders, went door-to-door to help rally their neighbors in collective protest. The buy-in of socially influential leaders helped assuage peoples' concerns that they were taking a risky step by opposing a wealthy local entrepreneur who evidently enjoyed political protection from the township government. In taking collective action in an authoritarian regime, there is often safety in numbers: being one of a small number of villagers who signed such a petition could make one a target for political retribution; being one of an overwhelming majority of villagers signing a petition would be much safer. The participation of neighborhood leaders helped assure villagers that the protest would be broad-based. In the end, around 80 percent of villagers signed a petition demanding the head's ouster, including former members of the village government. The village committee head was forced to leave office.

Effective collective resistance organized by these neighborhood leaders has discouraged further illegal land takings in Wujia and helped protect farmers' property rights. When officials requisition land illegally and it goes unpunished, they have few incentives to stop, especially when the potential rents from selling land are so high. By mobilizing in such large numbers against Wu Qiangguo, the village demonstrated that future leaders would face some form of accountability if they appropriated village land. The comparative success of the mobilization in Wujia has strengthened the bargaining position of villagers, protecting their land rights and helping ensure that in the future villagers will not have their land taken without adequate compensation.

What would have happened if Wujia's neighborhood elites had been more closely tied to local officials? The case of nearby Taiping Village examines how investing in infiltration can pay off in the long run for local leaders.

6.2.2 Taiping Village: High Infiltration, Strong Control

Taiping Village is a short drive from Wujia Village, in the same prefecture but just across county lines. Farmers generally cultivate a combination of wheat and corn, and many villages are home to small factories and other enterprises, from plastics companies to agricultural processing facilities. Farmers in Taiping are not poor but not prosperous either, just as they are in Wujia.

Yet unlike in Wujia, the leaders of Taiping have invested a great deal in building infiltrating institutions. The long-time village head has two tools at his disposal to ensure the loyalty of the leaders of villager small groups. First, the leaders of these cells are in practice not democratically elected and instead are selected by the village head in consultation with the village Party Secretary. This ensures that he can select subordinates with the right mixture of loyalty (to himself) and competence (especially influence among their small group). Second, once they take office, the village head draws them into local patronage networks. Most consequential of all, he allows the leaders of villager small groups to use excess land within the group for their own purposes, such as building homes and small enterprises. Using land this way is probably illegal, which strengthens their loyalty to the village head. Neighborhood leaders know that if he leaves office the village head will not be able to protect them and their claim to the land will be in doubt, and their investment in it will be lost. As one villager put it, the small-groups leaders "owe their allegiance to the village head."[35]

Cell leaders are effective informants and operatives in part because of the small size of the groups they oversee. In Taiping, each village cell is smaller than in Wujia. Instead of being divided into seven cells, Taiping has been divided into ten, and each cell has about 140 people instead of nearly 200. This makes it a little easier for cell leaders to monitor their neighbors and develop closer relationships with them.

The head of the village committee, Wang Jianmin, used his authority to requisition village land for a factory project. He did so at the same time that the county government was requisitioning land to build a road through the village. The use of eminent domain to build roads is often fairly well-compensated in China (though as previous chapters showed, the compensation does not always reach its intended recipients). In this case, however, the village head evidently attempted to use the project as cover to requisition extra land near the road without compensation in order to build a factory on it. Villagers, not surprisingly, noticed that they were not being compensated for a substantial portion of the land they were losing.

---

35 Author interview, Spring 2013, Henan Province.

The land requisition in Taiping had some striking parallels to Wujia. In both cases, the village head attempted to requisition a few dozen *mu* of land to build a factory that, in villagers' eyes at least, had close connections to the village head. In both cases, villagers were given no compensation. And in both cases, many villagers expressed anger at the evidently illegal use of village farm land for an industrial project that brought few jobs to the village. Yet in Taiping, there was no broad-based collective action targeting Wang Jianmin, the village head. What explains this failure of collective action?

First, local officials used the coercive power of the state to their advantage. Two villagers I spoke with told me that they suspected that Wang Jianmin had a villager arrested for relatively trivial matters related to the land conflict, including raising some objections to the project in a public meeting called for the purpose of soliciting feedback. The village head then feigned ignorance of the reason the villager was arrested and offered to help him get rid of his trouble with the government if he would support the land development. As one villager put it, "the village head is particularly cunning."[36]

Just as important, the village head used small-group leaders as key allies. As discussed above, the village head used his control over appointments to select loyal subordinates and his control over village land to buy their continued allegiance. When he requisitioned land for the factory project, small group leaders played a very different role than in Wujia. Instead of going door-to-door to rally villagers in opposition, they went door-to-door doing "thought work" (村民小组) to convince villagers to accept the land requisition. In some cases, they promised they would help the villagers negotiate for better compensation and benefits (which never materialized). In the words of one villager, "The villager small group leaders bullied us."[37]

Taiping Village illustrates the high hurdles that villagers face when trying to organize against a powerful local state and the importance of having allies among the grassroots elite. First, local officials have all the coercive powers of the state at their disposal. They can jail villagers who resist them, even when they do so through evidently institutionalized channels like raising objections in public meetings. This makes it clear to villagers that anyone who stands out has made a powerful enemy. Second, they can use softer tools to convince people not to organize, like

[36] Author interview, Spring 2013, Henan Province.
[37] Author interview, Spring 2013, Henan Province.

having neighborhood leaders weigh in on the side of local officials. Since standing out can have harsh consequences, having local cell leaders on the side of the state can make organizing especially difficult.

Does the pattern observed in these two villages in Henan hold for the rest of China? The following section turns to survey evidence to assess the relationship between neighborhood groups and land requisitions, protest, and birth quota enforcement across China.

6.3 SURVEY EVIDENCE ON INFILTRATION

To examine national patterns, I use the dataset introduced in Chapter 5. As discussed previously, the data comes from a random sample of villages in China with a national sample frame (excluding Xinjiang and Tibet). This allows me to assess patterns beyond the villages in which I conducted qualitative field work.

The main explanatory variable is the number of small-group leaders per natural village. I standardized the measure so that the mean is zero and 1 is equal to one standard deviation from the mean. This measure of state penetration of neighborhood groups has advantages as well as drawbacks. It directly captures the idea that the more the state relies on neighborhood networks as a tool of authoritarian control, the more it invests in networks of cell leaders. This echoes Shurmann's argument that when the Chinese state "was primarily intent on strengthening its exploitation functions ... it aimed at developing organization within the natural village."[38] It is also consistent with the qualitative evidence, which showed how in the more decentralized village of Taiping officials used neighborhood leaders' social influence and access to information to their advantage. One drawback of the measure is that it does not directly take into account the number of people in each village. In the regressions, I control for village size and in the Appendix I present results using an alternative explanatory variable, the number of people per villager small group (Table A.18).

6.3.1 Infiltration Helps the State Requisition Land

The first set of analyses, presented in Table 6.3, examines the relationship between the number of cell leaders per natural village, which

---

[38] Schurmann (1966, p. 410)

TABLE 6.3 *Relationship of cell leaders to land requisitions*

	Ordinary least squares			
	Land requisitions			
	(1)	(2)	(3)	(4)
Number of cell leaders per village	0.051*** (0.020)	0.056*** (0.020)	0.051** (0.020)	0.049** (0.022)
Number of households (log)		0.007 (0.028)	0.002 (0.028)	0.011 (0.037)
Distance to county seat		−0.001 (0.001)	−0.00001 (0.001)	0.0002 (0.001)
Terrain roughness		−0.027 (0.021)	−0.025 (0.021)	0.005 (0.029)
Agricultural suitability index		0.039 (0.024)	0.035 (0.023)	0.049 (0.033)
Wealth (1992 nighttime lights proxy)		−0.0003 (0.003)	−0.0002 (0.003)	0.0001 (0.003)
Township control over elections			0.108 (0.091)	0.108 (0.104)
Distance to township			−0.011*** (0.004)	−0.011** (0.004)
Surname fragmentation index				0.283*** (0.097)
Ethnic fragmentation index				−0.063 (0.218)
Constant	0.161*** (0.020)	0.088 (0.175)	0.139 (0.176)	−0.006 (0.258)
Province fixed effects	No	No	No	Yes
Observations	348	346	346	333

Note: $^*p<0.1$; $^{**}p<0.05$; $^{***}p<0.01$

captures state infiltration into neighborhood networks, and land seizures. My theory would lead us to expect that more decentralized villages would experience more land seizures, since these smaller wards would allow the state to take better advantage of neighborhood social networks. The first column of the table presents results for the bivariate relationship. It shows that a one standard deviation increase in the number of informants correlates with a 5 percent increase in the likelihood of a land expropriation. The results are statistically significant at the $p < .01$ level.

Next, I gradually add control variables to the model. The second column adds controls for plausibly pre-treatment village economic characteristics. These the distance to the county seat, terrain roughness, agricultural suitability, and a measure of village wealth derived from nighttime lights. I also include province fixed effects to account for geographic heterogeneity. In the third column I add controls for political characteristics, such as the degree to which elections are controlled by the township instead of being free and fair and the distance to the township. Finally, I add in controls for village social characteristics including population and measures of social and ethnic fragmentation. In each of the specifications, the result for the main explanatory variable remains significant and substantively unchanged.

6.3.2 Infiltration Helps Enforce Family Planning Policies

Are neighborhood networks used to strengthen authoritarian control in other areas? In this section, I examine a second policy area of central importance to the Chinese state: family planning.

In rural China, neighborhood leaders play a key role in implementing state family planning policies by popularizing its details and – perhaps most importantly – by using neighborhood social networks to collect information and directly pressure people to comply with state policies. From the early years of the One Child Policy, the Chinese state has emphasized implementation at the ward level.[39] Ward leaders have helped the state "monitor and enforce birth limits"[40] and have become "an indispensable workforce for the state's birth-planning policy."[41] Ward heads often "mobilize the women in their group to submit to quarterly check-ups at the township birth-planning station.... [and]

---

[39] See Zhang (1999, p. 205), Alpermann (2001, p. 55), Greenhalgh and Winckler (2005, p. 195), and White (2006, p. 220).
[40] White (2006, p. 220).
[41] Alpermann (2001, p. 55).

persuade women who have given birth to a second child to undergo sterilization."[42] In some locations, ward heads must also attend regular meetings with village cadres and report on unauthorized pregnancies.[43] State regulations also encourage ward heads to appoint households as leaders for promoting birth control policies.[44]

Although the role of ward leaders in implementing family planning policy has been noted by others, we have little systematic evidence about their effectiveness. When are these ward leaders effective at eliciting compliance with this key state policy?

Table 6.4 shows OLS regressions on household compliance with birth quotas, drawing on CGSS household survey. I begin with a simple, transparent bivariate specification that shows that the number of cell leaders is negatively correlated with over-quota births, consistent with my hypothesis. The results suggest that a one standard deviation increase in the number of cell leaders in a village (that is, an increase of 4 cell leaders) leads to a decrease in over quota births of 2 percentage points (when the average is 10 percent).

Conditioning on plausibly pre-treatment variables does not substantively change the estimates. First, I condition on the size of birth quotas and local fines as well an ethnic fragmentation index (since there are exemptions for ethnic minorities). Then I add more conditioning variables for other economic, political, and social covariates. The results remain unchanged and statistically significant.

In the Appendix, I present additional results. These results include evidence on whether or not cadres report that enforcing birth quotas are difficult and the amount of time that cadres spend enforcing the policy.

---

[42] Alpermann (2001, p. 55).

[43] See Changtai County Family Planning Association. "Implementing the 'Four Guarantees' While Advancing Villager Autonomy and the Strong Establishment of the National Family Planning Policy Grassroots Autonomy Model County" (*Luoshi Sige Baozhang Tuijin Cunmin Zishi Zhashi Chuangjian Quanguo Jihua Shengyu Jiceng Qunzhong Zizhi Shifan Xian*). http://npsjsx.np.gov.cn/cms/html/npsjhsyxh/2015-10-14/585701091.html, last accessed August 15, 2016. County governments throughout Jiangxi and Zhejiang have also issued documents noting that the primary duties of small group leaders include "ensuring the smooth operation of important projects" including "family planning." "Strengthening Team Building among Villager Small Group Leaders" (*Guanyu Jiaqiang Cunmin Xiaozu Zuzhang Duiqu Jianshe de Yijian*). Author's collection.

[44] See also "Village Self-Government Family Planning Regulations" (*Jihua Shengyu Cunmin Zizhi Guifan*). www.china.com.cn/policy/txt/2008-10/12/content_16598517.htm, last accessed on June 27, 2016.

TABLE 6.4 *Relationship of cell leaders to birth quota compliance*

	Ordinary least squares			
	Percent over birth quota			
	(1)	(2)	(3)	(4)
Number of cell leaders per village	−0.018*** (0.006)	−0.018*** (0.006)	−0.018*** (0.006)	−0.014** (0.007)
Birth quota		−0.023 (0.027)	−0.023 (0.027)	−0.081 (0.093)
Over quota fines		0.004 (0.012)	−0.001 (0.013)	0.008 (0.040)
Ethnic minority index		0.015 (0.063)	0.012 (0.064)	0.007 (0.066)
Number of households (log)			0.013 (0.009)	0.017 (0.011)
Distance to county seat			0.0004 (0.0003)	0.0004 (0.0003)
Terrain roughness			0.010 (0.007)	−0.006 (0.009)
Agricultural suitability index			0.008 (0.007)	−0.007 (0.010)
Wealth (1992 nighttime lights proxy)			0.0001 (0.001)	0.001 (0.001)
Township control over elections				0.006 (0.031)
Distance to township				0.0002 (0.001)
Surname fragmentation index				−0.041 (0.030)
Constant	0.084*** (0.006)	0.110** (0.044)	0.016 (0.067)	0.111 (0.123)
Province fixed effects	No	No	No	Yes
Observations	348	348	346	333

Note: *p<0.1; **p<0.05; ***p<0.01

The results from the separate cadre survey confirm the results from the villager survey, lending additional credibility to the results. (See Tables A.19 and A.20.)

Of course, incentives for misreporting are an important problem on a politically sensitive topic such as China's family planning policy. However, several factors suggest that this is not a major problem for this data. First, the questions posed in the survey were not sensitive, and were instead the sorts of questions that respondents are generally willing to answer in interviews.[45] Second, some of the observed patterns run counter to the incentives for misreporting. In areas where officials exert high levels of effort enforcing family planning policies, citizens have an incentive to exaggerate their compliance in order to avoid punishment. Yet the pattern I demonstrate here is the opposite: where officials report high levels of effort, citizens report low levels of compliance.[46] Third, official's evaluation of whether the policy has been difficult to enforce accords with the reported number of children in each household in a separate survey, which is consistent with truthful reporting.

Another concern is that cadres in some villages may forgo enforcement to be more responsive to citizen demands, and may be seeking more individual exemptions from higher-level officials.[47] However, these exemptions are obtained on a case-by-case basis and require significant effort from village cadres. The low amount of time that cadres in villages with high numbers of over-quota births spend on family planning matters in these villages (Table A.20) is not consistent with the idea that they are spending time obtaining exemptions.

Overall, the results support the idea that villages with more frontline 'informants' are better able to enforce state family planning mandates. When the state can penetrate neighborhood social networks, these ties can help local officials monitor their constituents and make it easier to coax and coerce them to obey state policies.

---

[45] That is, while officials may be reluctant to report truthfully the number of out-of-quota births in the village, they are often quite willing to complain about what parts of their job are difficult, including enforcement of family planning policy. Citizens, as a practical matter, cannot hide out-of-quota children from village cadres.

[46] A remaining concern is that officials who do not enforce the policy are exaggerating their effort in areas with low levels of compliance. However, this suggests a pattern in which officials in both high- and low-compliance areas exert similar levels of effort, and also suggests relatively low levels of enforcement overall. Both of these patterns are not consistent with the existing qualitative accounts that officials in many villages exert considerable effort trying to enforce birth quotas.

[47] See work on forbearance of enforcement by Holland (2014, 2016).

TABLE 6.5 *Relationship of cell leaders to satisfaction with government*

	Ordinary Least Squares		
	Gov. justly enforces law (1)	Gov. impartially handle affairs (2)	Gov. cares about poor (3)
Number of cell leaders per village	−0.087*** (0.028)	−0.100*** (0.029)	−0.096*** (0.028)
Constant	2.900*** (0.028)	2.784*** (0.029)	2.823*** (0.028)
Observations	348	348	348

Note: *p<0.1; **p<0.05; ***p<0.01

6.3.3 Infiltration Decreases Satisfaction with the State

Relying on infiltration for control does come with a significant drawback: it decreases satisfaction with the state. The other strategies of informal control discussed in this book rely on the social authority of village cadres and influential local brokers. The trust and legitimacy that these figures enjoy can help them sell state policies.

Infiltration is by comparison a more coercive strategy. Rather than relying on actors' legitimacy to control groups, relying on grassroots operatives and informants does not necessarily add to the luster of the local state or the legitimacy of local policies. Instead, it relies on information gathering and persuasion by people with considerably less social authority and prestige. It is a strategy that may in the long run decrease satisfaction with the state.

In Table 6.5, I present bivariate correlations between the number of cell leaders per village and different measures of satisfaction with the government. Increases in the density of cell leaders is strongly correlated with small but statistically significant decreases in satisfaction with government performance across several measures.

The density of cell leaders is correlated with a reduction in people's ratings of whether the government "impartially enforces the law."[48] A high degree of infiltration also correlates with a decrease in the degree

---

48 公平执法. Respondents answered on a five-point scale. I take the village average of the 1 to 5 rating.

TABLE 6.6 *Relationship of cell leaders to percent of villagers petitioning*

	Ordinary least squares			
	Percent of villagers petitioning			
	(1)	(2)	(3)	(4)
Number of cell leaders per village	−0.001 (0.003)	−0.001 (0.003)	−0.001 (0.003)	−0.001 (0.003)
Economic controls		✓	✓	✓
Political controls			✓	✓
Social controls				✓
Observations	348	346	346	333

Note: *p<0.1; **p<0.05; ***p<0.01

to which people believe that "government branches impartially handle affairs."[49] Finally, a large number of cell leaders per village is associated with lower assessments of whether governments care about poor people and maintain societal fairness."[50]

The estimates suggest that the degree to which these ward leaders decrease satisfaction with local government in meaningful but small. A one-standard-deviation increase in the number of ward leaders per village is, on average, correlated with a drop of a tenth of a point on a five-point scale. In other words, the relatively intrusive nature of these informants may lead to a decrease in satisfaction with the state, but only a small one.

There is little quantitative evidence that informants are effective at quelling protest. In Table 6.6, I show OLS regressions using the same specifications as Table 6.3 and Table 6.4. The results show no correlation between the density of cell leaders and the percentage of villagers protesting. The estimate is very close to zero.

6.3.4 Results from a Natural Experiment

To identify the causal effect of infiltration on political control, I take advantage of plausibly exogenous variation in the process of agricultural de-collectivization in the late 1970s and early 1980s caused by weather shocks. During this era, the administrative structure of villages changed

49 政府部门秉公办事.
50 帮助穷人，维护社会公平.

substantially. From 1978 to 1983, in the lead-up to the final dismantling of the commune system, the government dramatically reduced the size of production teams across China. The size of the average production team dropped from 167 people to 136 people, a 19 percentage point decrease.[51] These production teams would later become the villager small groups that exist today.

Weather shocks during this era influenced the degree to which local leaders invested in infiltrating institutions. Many have noted that weather shocks have shaped the course of rural reforms in China during the 1970s and 1980s.[52] In the case of sub-village reforms, weather shocks shaped decisions at the grassroots level about how to best structure village administrative organization. In an era in which reforms were often led from the bottom up, local leaders had considerable discretion over how best to structure local political administration.[53]

The logic of the research design is straightforward. As Justin Yifu Lin argues in an influential article on this era in China, "the larger the size of membership in a team, the harder it is to monitor" and lower the per capita output of that team.[54] Droughts induced team leaders to move to smaller production teams in order to ease monitoring problems and increase output in a time of scarcity. The idea that scarcity induces local leaders to reduce the size of production teams is consistent with qualitative evidence from the era.[55] Ying Bai and James Kung have also demonstrated that areas that experienced severe drought during the early Reform era (1978 to 1984) decollectivized agriculture later, conditional on famine severity during the Great Leap Famine and public goods provision.[56]

---

[51] For data on this transformation, see National Bureau of Statistics of the People's Republic of China (1983), p. 147 and, for further discussion, see Parish (1985).

[52] For example, important work by Yang (1998, pp. 134–138) shows that areas of China that experienced disaster during the Great Leap Forward of 1958 to 1961 undertook decollectivization earlier than areas that did not. Yang suggests that experiencing the drought-induced disaster of the Great Leap pushed farmers toward conservativism (i.e., reform) rather than agrarian radicalism (i.e., collective agriculture).

[53] Kelliher (1992) and Zhou et al. (1996) show that the process of de-collectivization was led at least to some extent by peasants rather than elites.

[54] Lin (1988, p. S212).

[55] Vermeer (1982, p. 22).

[56] See Bai and Kung (2014). Interestingly, the article shows that while the first production teams to abandon collective agriculture – in Xiaogang, Anhui – did so in part because of severe drought, this was very much an exception to the more general relationship between drought and reform. The authors argue that "household farming is not conducive to providing ... indivisible public goods" like irrigation (Bai and Kung, 2014,

Consistent with this line of reasoning, villages that experienced drought during the period of village reform were more likely to create smaller sub-village groups.[57] The relationship between drought severity and the size of villager groups is negative.[58]

To estimate the causal effect of infiltration (specifically, the size of village groups) on policy implementation, I use an instrumental variables approach.[59]

Table 6.7 presents two-stage least squares results, instrumented by drought, for the effect of infiltration on key outcomes. These results of this natural experiment show that higher levels infiltration (induced by weather shocks) leads to more land requisitions, although the results are not quite significant at the traditional cutoff. There is more robust evidence for a relationship between infiltration and birth quota enforcement and dissatisfaction with the government.[60]

The instrumented results, in combination with the qualitative evidence, suggest a plausible causal interpretation of the results. However, this type of research design has important limitations. It could be the

p. 8), which are essential in times of scarcity. Rather than move toward household farming, production teams in drought-stricken areas banded together to delay the move toward household agriculture so that they could make use of collective resources and thereby reduce the impact of the drought. See also Kelliher (1992); Zhou et al. (1996).

[57] See Mattingly (2020) for relevant figures and tables.

[58] I measure drought severity using historical data on the Palmer Drought Severity Index. With this index, values of -4 and below indicate severe droughts while values of 4 and above indicate unusually rainy weather. To aid interpretation, I reverse the index so that 4 is severe drought and -4 is unusual rain, and then standardize the variable. I measure infiltration as the log number of village wards per natural village divided by the log number of households in the village.

[59] The first stage equation models the effect of drought Z on village decentralization x_i. In some specifications, I also control for village characteristics W_i and include regional fixed effects δ_j. I estimate the relationship between the instrument and decentralization using the following first stage model:

$$x_i = DZ_i + DW_i + \delta_j + \epsilon_e \tag{6.1}$$

The second stage is estimated using the following model:

$$Y_i = \alpha + \beta x_i + \gamma W_i + \delta_j + \epsilon_e \tag{6.2}$$

Where Y_i is the outcome of interest and β is the main coefficient that I interpret. The next section uses this framework to test my hypotheses. In the following section, I conduct robustness tests. In Mattingly (2020) I present second stage results and reduced-form results for One Child Policy enforcement outcomes.

[60] See Mattingly (2020) for additional results on birth quota enforcement. The results also pass a weak instrument F-Test.

TABLE 6.7 *Two-stage least squares estimates for the effect of infiltration on key outcomes, instrumented by weather shocks during de-collectivization*

	Dependent variable:			
	Land requisition (1)	Birth quota enforced (2)	Petitions (3)	Government justly enforces law (4)
Infiltration	0.130* (0.074)	0.285*** (0.093)	0.079 (0.061)	−0.479*** (0.122)
Observations	348	348	348	348
Weak instrument F-Test	33.2	33.2	33.2	33.2

Note: $*p<0.1$; $**p<0.05$; $***p<0.01$

case that weather shocks induced other changes to village society, and that this other factor had a direct effect on key outcomes. For example, it could be that weather shocks lead to lower long-run economic development, which in turn led to lower fertility, more dissatisfaction with the government, and different land use decisions. In a paper drawing on material in this chapter, I examine this threat to inference in more detail, and show that the most obvious alternate pathways, such as the relationship between weather shocks and economic development, are unlikely to drive the results.[61]

6.4 INFILTRATION AS A SUBSTITUTE FOR OTHER STRATEGIES

How does the strategy of infiltration interact with other strategies, like co-optation? In Chapter 2, I argued that infiltration was a substitute for cultivating civil society and co-opting its leaders. The argument was that there were high levels of infiltration in villages that lacked strong civil society institutions like lineages. Villages that had lineages but non-co-opted leaders had moderate levels of infiltration. The lowest level of infiltration occurred in villages with co-opted local notables.

[61] See Mattingly (2020). The problem described here is a violation of the exclusion restriction assumption.

TABLE 6.8 *Relationship of cell leaders to percent of villagers petitioning*

	Ordinary least squares					
	Land requisitions		Birth quota enforced		Petitions	
	(1)	(2)	(3)	(4)	(5)	(6)
Infiltration	0.145**	0.113*	0.207**	0.211**	−0.001	−0.0003
	(0.060)	(0.065)	(0.081)	(0.085)	(0.008)	(0.009)
Lineage leader	0.223**	0.196**	0.201	0.155	0.027**	0.014
is cadre	(0.090)	(0.094)	(0.123)	(0.123)	(0.012)	(0.013)
Infiltration X	−0.079	−0.095	−0.141	−0.150	−0.004	−0.011
Lineage	(0.228)	(0.229)	(0.311)	(0.299)	(0.031)	(0.031)
cadre						
Economic controls		✓		✓		✓
Political controls		✓		✓		✓
Social controls		✓		✓		✓
Observations	348	333	348	333	348	333

Note: $^*p<0.1$; $^{**}p<0.05$; $^{***}p<0.01$

To examine how these strategies interact, I return to the CGSS data. To captures villages with especially high levels of infiltration, I create an indicator variable "infiltration" that takes a value of 1 when a village has 1 standard deviation above the mean number of small group leaders.[62] Using an indicator variable simplifies interpretation of the interaction results.

Table 6.8 presents results including an interaction between the infiltration indicator and an indicator for whether a lineage group leader is a cadre (using the same indicator from the previous chapter). I return again to the main outcomes: a land requisition indicator, an indicator for whether cadres indicate the birth quota is difficult to enforce, and an indicator for the number of petitions.

---

[62] The results remain consistent at other cutoffs, but at two standard deviations above the mean there are no enough villages that both have lineage leader cadres and high levels of infiltration.

The results are consistent with the idea that infiltration substitutes for co-optation. The first row of Table 6.8 shows that in villages with high levels of infiltration and no lineage leader cadres, land takings are about 10 to 15 percent more likely, cadres are about 21 percent more likely to report that enforcing the birth quota is easy, and petitions are no more likely. When lineage leaders are cadres and there are low levels of infiltration (row two in the table), land takings are about 20 percent more likely, and birth quota enforcement easier (though the results are not statistically significant).

The small values, negative signs, and non-significance of the interaction terms (in the third row of the table) suggest that the combination of infiltration and co-optation does not pack a greater punch. This is consistent with the hypothesis that the strategies are substitutes. The qualitative evidence earlier in the chapter suggested that at times village cadres can take advantage of both their position in groups like lineages and the strategy of infiltration. However, the CGSS data suggest that this pattern is not widespread.

These interaction results should be interpreted with caution. They are correlations, not credible causal estimates. Moreover, the number of villages with high levels of infiltration *and* lineage cadres is exceedingly small: there are only three villages in the sample. This is partially because villages that have co-opted lineage cadres tend to invest very little in infiltration. Of course, this feature of the data is also consistent with the idea that local leaders treat infiltration and co-optation as substitutes.

6.5 CONCLUSION

In this chapter, I have argued that networks of local informants are a key element of political control in China. The evidence showed that when local cadres invested in dense networks of neighborhood informants, it made it easier to implement land requisitions and family planning policies, although it came with a cost: lower levels of satisfaction with the state.

Many other countries outside China rely on similar grassroots networks of informants and pro-regime operatives. In Indonesia under Suharto, neighborhood chiefs helped the authoritarian state to implement family planning policies in much the same manner as in China. In Cuba, neighborhood Committees for the Defense of the Revolution play much the same role as neighborhood leaders in China. And in Venezuela, Maduro has turned to *colectivos* that repress dissent and protest.

Is relying on infiltration and other strategies of informal control sustainable over the long run? In the concluding chapter, I plumb the limits of informal control and consider the sometimes uneasy relationship between autocratic states and the grassroots groups they rely on for political control.

7

Conclusion

The Duke Ai asked, "What can be done in order to secure the obedience of the people?"

Confucius, *The Analects*

Nothing appears more surprising to those who consider human affairs with a philosophical eye than the easiness with which the many are governed by the few, and the implicit submission with which men resign their own sentiments and passions to those of their rulers.

David Hume, "Of the First Principles of Government"

How do rulers control the ruled? How, in turn, can the governed control their governments? This book has described how the Chinese government strengthens its coercive capacity through means other than violent repression. Local officials cultivate civil society, co-opt local elites, and infiltrate social groups. These tools of informal control help local officials in China limit protest, generate revenue by confiscating property, and enforce mandates like the One Child Policy. When citizens can evade state control, however, they can organize resistance and hold their local leaders accountable.

In an era of heightened political repression under President Xi Jinping – and concerns that China is becoming a model of "digital authoritarianism"[1] – a focus on grassroots social organizations may seem quaint. Press coverage sometimes suggests that mass surveillance, artificial intelligence, facial recognition software, and social credit scores will allow the Chinese state to effortlessly monitor citizens' everyday lives. These are valid concerns, but the reality is that this techno-dystopia has

---

[1] Abramowitz and Chertoff (2018).

not yet come to pass.[2] When these digital tools reach maturity, the state will still face age-old problems about how to act on the vast amounts of data collected by its information-generating bureaucracies.

For the time being, China still mostly relies on human, not digital, tactics of authoritarian repression and control. Even in an era of heightened control under Xi Jinping, infiltration and co-optation remain key tools in the state's arsenal. For example, the "grid management" (网格化管理) system used in cities across the country relies on person-to-person tactics of infiltration like networks of informants and block captains.[3] The state's efforts to control religious groups still often relies on elite co-optation. For example, the Chinese Communist Party (CCP) recently struck a deal with the Vatican that gives state authorities the power to nominate bishops.[4] Even the harsh crackdown on Islam in Xinjiang – which has used highly coercive tactics like mass internment, mosque demolitions, and police checkpoints – uses infiltration as well as hard repression. For example, local governments have sent officials to stay in the homes of Muslim community members in order to track their behavior and beliefs.[5] These methods of informal control can be every bit as invasive and coercive as digital surveillance.

In this concluding chapter, I briefly recap the book's main findings and then examine their broader implications. An underlying theme of this book has been China's transformation from a rural, agrarian society to an urban, industrialized country. As Chinese society has transformed itself, the state has begun to evolve. In the long run, I argue, it is far from clear that these tactics of control, as widespread as they are, will be sustainable.

7.1 MAIN FINDINGS

My argument in this book has been straightforward. Chinese citizens distrust the ruling CCP, at least at the local level, and believe party cadres do not care about their material interests. By contrast, civil society groups such as lineage organizations are reservoirs of trust and fellow-feeling. Cadres can exploit these ties to help control society, defuse dissent, and implement policies. In short, state power in China comes from an unlikely source: society itself.

---

[2] See, for example, Horsley (2018) on misconceptions about the social credit system.
[3] See Chen and Kang (2016, p. 606) and Hu et al. (2018).
[4] Johnson (2019).
[5] See Economist Staff (2018) on the *fanghuiju* (访惠聚) program.

I examined three strategies of informal control. First, cultivating non-state groups such as lineage and religious organizations can enhance cadres' informal authority and help them collect information about local community members. This, in turn, allows them to implement coercive land requisitions and reduce protest.

In a second strategy, officials can co-opt communal elites, such as the leaders of lineage groups. After convincing them to join local political institutions, local officials integrate these community elites into patronage networks. These local brokers then have incentives to use their informal authority to help the state implement its policies, sometimes at the expense of their group.

Finally, officials can build networks of grassroots informants, often instead of investing in local non-state groups. These networks of informants help the state collect information about society and control it.

My findings suggest an important limit to theories that link civil society groups to increased political accountability and democratization. When social institutions encourage deference to group authorities, and when these group authorities have been co-opted by the state, they can serve not just as channels for bottom-up accountability but for top-down control as well. Officials nurture these institutions partly to reinforce their own authority.

These findings also contribute to our understanding of elite co-optation in authoritarian regimes. Previous work has shown how co-optation at the national level helps the regime reduce potentially destabilizing conflict between national elites who might otherwise pose a threat to its hold on power.[6] I have shown how the logic of political co-optation at the local level is rather different. Co-opting *local* elites in *local* institutions does not necessarily forestall a potential coup or national uprising; instead, it helps the regime govern and implement policy.

Finally, these findings also shed new light on the nature of state power in autocratic regimes. In contrast to Joel Migdal's theory that strong societies tend to lead to weak states,[7] I show how a strong society can in fact *complement* a strong state. And contrary to Michael Mann's idea that "despotic" states govern without the consent of civil society,[8] I show

---

[6] For important treatments, see Blaydes (2010, pp. 48–63), Malesky and Schuler (2010), and Svolik (2012, pp. 53–119).

[7] Migdal (1988).

[8] Mann (1984, 2012)

184 7 *Conclusion*

how authoritarian regimes can co-opt civil society leaders and use civil society to wield state power.

7.2 WHEN THINGS FALL APART

How durable is informal repression as a tool of control? One the one hand, it *is* durable in the sense that many states throughout history have used this set of tactics. The Imperial Chinese state, after all, used local communal groups and the *baojia* system in much the same way as local officials today exploit communal ties and use networks of local informants.

On the other hand, using this strategy can tear local communities apart and erode the legitimacy of political regimes. The case of a village in southern China illustrates some of the strengths, limitations, and tensions of using the strategy.

7.2.1 The Strange Case of Wukan

In December 2011, the sleepy farming village of Wukan on China's southern coast erupted in a protest movement that captured the attention of much of the country.[9] The people of Wukan were furious: for years, local officials had slowly been selling off village land while providing very little compensation. When village and township cadres devised a plan to sell off most of the remaining land to a developer, villagers began to stage protests. The initial protests garnered little attention from the outside world, but then one of the protest leaders, a man named Xue Jinbo, was detained by the police and died in custody under suspicious circumstances. The death triggered a massive outpouring of grief and anger. The residents of Wukan took to the streets, and the village cadres, fearing for their own lives, were forced to flee the town.

Wukan's village-sized revolution at first seemed to be a resounding success. Media-savvy villagers attracted the attention of the Hong Kong media and a wave of sympathetic, real-time international coverage followed. Instead of breaking up the protest with truncheons or guns, the government, as it often does in such cases, made concessions. It agreed to hold new elections for the village committee and work toward returning the land to villagers. The elections were held months later amid

---

[9] See Chapter 2, Section 2.3.1.

FIGURE 7.1 "Wukan Free"

FIGURE 7.2 Land in Wukan

great fanfare, and elevated the protest leaders to key posts in village government. People began to talk optimistically about a "Wukan model" (乌坎模式) of political action. Traveling around another province in China that year, I observed graffiti demanding (or perhaps celebrating) a "free" Wukan (see Figure 7.1).

Yet the case of Wukan took a few more twists. The village committee, now under the control of the protest leaders, never returned the land to villagers. Some in the village started to grumble that the protest leaders were either ineffective or corrupt. In 2016, the local government charged the former protest leader, Lin Zuluan – a distinguished military veteran in his 70s – with taking bribes. Lin made a public confession, but many suspected it was forced. Protests roiled the village yet again, but this time the police responded swiftly and with force.

The case of Wukan, strange as it is, in some ways symbolizes the paradoxes and contradictions inherent in the ways in which the local state controls society in China. Strong social solidarities can help the state keep a lid on grievances, until they seemingly do the opposite and facilitate widespread protest. Communal elites fight for their brethren when they are on the outside of political power, until they seemingly do the opposite once they are given political authority. And social ties slowly fray.

When Informal Control Succeeds

One of the paradoxes of Wukan is that the social institutions that helped its villagers organize the protest in 2012 were, for years, the same institutions that helped local cadres hold the village together. Wukan is a potentially fractious village: it has forty-seven separate lineage groups, each of which has a lineage head clamoring for the local government's attention and resources.

Folk religion has long knit together the village's forty-seven clans and helped ensure order and stability. The village hosts over a dozen large temples and a smattering of smaller shrines venerating a mix of Daoist, Buddhist, and folk religious deities. Yet these deities do not appear to divide villagers into competing groups. The villagers I talked to noted that they might pray to one deity one day and another the next, depending on the circumstances; each god serves a different purpose and can bring good fortune to a different aspect of life.[10] In a study of Wukan's religious life, Yuxin Hou quotes one prominent villager as saying:

There are loads of different deities involved in the religion indigenous to Wukan. In one temple you'll find offerings to a whole load of different gods. Every year on the birthdays of the gods, when they hold the divinity plays,[11] money just gets tossed around like confetti. Even when it comes to poorer people, they'll still spend 3,000 *yuan* [about $470 in 2012] making offerings to the gods, so who knows how much the rich people are spending.[12]

What ultimately brought the village together was a festival that celebrates its tutelary deity, the Immortal Father of Wukan, *Zhenxiu Xianweng* (真修仙翁). According to village lore, in his mortal incarnation, this figure was a prodigiously talented doctor who moved to Wukan from Fujian. During his lifetime, he served the poor and helped protect the village from disaster; after his death, he was reincarnated and has since served as the village's local deity. To honor him, residents hold a yearly festival on Immortal Father's birthday during the seventh lunar month. The statues of gods from the village's other dozen or so temples join the birthday celebration, as do those from neighboring villages. The festival centers around a set of lavishly produced religious plays that are put on for the enjoyment of the assembled immortals.[13]

Holding this lavish festival each year has created a template for cooperation that unites the village's fragmented lineage groups and gives civic leaders experience in collective organization. For years, it has also served the interests of the local state to some degree. A Deity Council (神明理事会) – composed of representatives from all the village's major clans – organizes the festival, which is a serious undertaking. Each year, they raise tens of thousands of dollars from

[10] Author interview, Summer 2013, Guangdong Province.
[11] These are performances held in the seventh lunar month, organized around a central festival honoring Wukan's tutelary deity, who is discussed shortly.
[12] Quoted in Hou (2013, p. 158).
[13] See Hou (2013, pp. 159–163) for additional background information.

villagers, much of it from people who have left the village (funding these religious plays is thought to bring good luck to businesses). The council also supplies the food and costumes, and coordinates with nearby villages.

Religious and clan-based organizations helped the local government better understand (and control) society. The lineage heads served as intermediaries between their groups and village cadres. They also helped local cadres press their demands on their group.[14] The Deity Council provided a regular and visible forum to ensure unity and order and reduce the potential for inter-clan feuds. One mark of the success of this system of hidden control was that village cadres were able to obtain tens of millions of dollars for themselves by expropriating land for more than a decade without providing adequate compensation.

When Informal Control Backfires

There is a limit to the degree to which hidden forms of control can work over the long run. Norms matter, but material incentives matter too – often more so. And social solidarity can also be used to organize *against* the state.

In Wukan, the same religious and social institutions that helped the state maintain order also helped villagers mobilize. The movement's leaders frequently delivered major speeches to the crowd from the large stage in the center of the village named after the Immortal Father of Wukan. Protest leaders also invoked a Daoist ritual to show villagers how urgent it was to act. Like many other Daoist spirits, the Immortal Father of Wukan has a "flag of command" (令旗), which symbolizes the authority delegated to him by the Emperor of Heaven.[15] The flag could be invoked to aid the village, but only under circumstances of dire need. According to villagers, it had not been used for over a hundred years, even during the warlord era, the Japanese invasion, civil war, or the Cultural Revolution.[16] During the initial failed uprising in September 2011, villagers did not use the command flag; not coincidentally in the eyes of some villagers, local officials efficiently quelled the protest.[17] Morale in the village declined and fissures began to appear among villagers, some of

---

[14] Author interview, Summer 2013, Guangdong Province.
[15] See DeBernardi (2006, pp. 134–136) for a discussion of flags and folk religious practice.
[16] This may well be more legend than fact, but in this case perception may be more important since it enhanced the flag's symbolic potency.
[17] See Hou (2013, pp. 169–171), which provides a more detailed description of these events.

whom thought another round of protest would be foolish; the prospects for future collective action seemed to be dimming.

To secure the support of wavering villagers, the protest organizers got permission from the Deity Council to invoke the flag on the morning of the second mobilization in November. They prayed to the deity's statue and asked him to protect the protesters. According to Yuxin Hou's account, the leaders cast a two-sided religious instrument called a *shengbei* on the ground three times and each time it landed with the lucky side facing up, an encouraging sign.[18] The flag took a place of honor at the head of the procession. As the director of Wukan's Deity Council described the event to Yuxin Hou:

In the end, Xianweng told us that we had to staunchly guard the village of Wukan, we shouldn't leave, otherwise people would die and we'd fail. Because everyone really believed in what Xianweng [the Immortal Father] said, after the village was sealed off and we started protecting it, everybody stuck to what [the Immortal Father] had guided us to do, that's why after that nothing else bad happened. If it hadn't have been for that, more people would have died. You could put it this way, [the Immortal Father] rescued Wukan. He really is truly incredible.[19].

In Wukan, political entrepreneurs appropriated religious symbols to solve collective action problems and rally their groups against the local state. Thus the case of Wukan illustrates how the rituals and symbols of Chinese folk religion can be exploited to strengthen state authority by showing state power in a benign light,[20] but these institutions *also* provide resources for political entrepreneurs and help bind groups together.

7.3 IMPLICATIONS FOR UNDERSTANDING THE RISE OF CHINA

In 1947, the great sociologist Fei Xiaotong began his most important work, *From the Soil*, with a simple declaration: "China is above all else a rural society."[21] Much has changed since then. The rise of China as a global economic power is fundamentally about its transformation from a rural, agrarian society to an urban, industrial country.

---

[18] There is about a 13 percent chance of this occurring three times in a row. See Hou (2013, p. 170).
[19] Hou (2013, pp. 171–172)
[20] See Yang (1961), Freedman (1979), and Eng and Lin (2002).
[21] 从基层上看去，中国社会是乡土情的。

A vital aspect of China's transformation is how it has changed property regimes, and especially land rights. The large-scale land redistribution that has taken place over the last twenty-five years represents the country's third great rural revolution of the modern era, after those launched under Mao Zedong and Deng Xiaoping. This book has shown how the CCP has used hidden tools of control to redistribute land without destabilizing rural areas.

Nor can we understand China's transformation without understanding how the last four decades have profoundly altered family life. Deng Xiaoping and his successors felt that the One Child Policy was necessary for China to grow and prosper. Even as family policies have been reversed, they have altered the relationship between families and their children, and between families and the state. This book shows how the CCP used artful forms of coercion to encourage compliance with these policies.

Nor can we understand China's transformation without understanding how the government has maintained political stability. Modernization theory would lead us to expect that as China grew richer, citizens would become more politically engaged and demand democratization. Nothing of the sort has happened to date, and the CCP continues to enjoy high levels of legitimacy and popularity. This book has shown how, in addition to hard repression, the state also relies on softer forms of informal control to discourage protest.

This book sketches a picture of China at a moment of profound transformation, and leaves at least three important questions about change over time for future research.

First, over the longer run, how has the relationship between state and rural society shifted from the imperial era to the reform era? Throughout the book, I have highlighted evidence of similarities between Imperial and contemporary China. For centuries, local elites have sought to harness the power of local communal and civic groups to strengthen state authority. Yet this dynamic has shifted over time: organizations such as lineage groups have served as allies *and* adversaries of the Imperial center. Tracing these changing dynamics would produce a more complete picture of state building throughout Chinese history.

Second, how has state management of local civil society changed during the reform era? My findings suggest that these dynamics may have changed over the course of this period. In the early stages of the reform era, rural civil society and village elections helped the state control society in a way that was stable and to some degree benefited both society and the state. Citizens traded their compliance with taxation and other policies in return for public goods provision and growth. The onset of more rapid urbanization and land development in the 2000s likely shifted this dynamic, but more research is needed to determine if this is indeed the case.

Finally, as China completes its urban and industrial transformation, what lies ahead? Modernization does not mean that these civil society groups will disappear. Some groups, like lineage organizations, seem likely to wane in importance, but other groups are likely to fill the void left by this shift. China is in the middle of an astounding religious revival, including a resurgence of attention to Buddhist, Daoist, and folk religious groups.[22] The survival of the CCP may therefore to some degree rest on whether the state can cultivate, co-opt, and infiltrate religious groups that are friendly to its authority.

7.4 IMPLICATIONS FOR GOVERNANCE IN AUTOCRACIES

How can the poor and the weak ensure that their governments respond to their needs? For the 3 billion people who live in non-democracies, and who cannot vote their leaders out of office, this question is urgent but difficult to answer.

Since power is concentrated in the hands of elites in autocracies, one way to seek accountability is from the top, through the state and formal bureaucratic channels. In China, Xi Jinping has made it clear that he believes that building systems of accountability *within* the CCP is the best way to curb local officials' rent-seeking behavior, which has generated widespread popular anger. Shortly after he took over the post of Communist Party Secretary in 2012, Xi told a gathering of the Politburo:

In recent years, the long pent-up problems in some countries have led to the venting of public outrage, to social turmoil and to the fall of governments, and corruption and graft have been an important reason ... A mass of facts tells us that if corruption becomes increasingly serious, it will inevitably doom the party and the state. We must be vigilant. In recent years, there have been cases of grave violations of disciplinary rules and laws within the party that have been extremely malign in nature and utterly destructive politically, shocking people to the core.[23]

Xi's far-reaching anti-corruption crackdown has likely discouraged officials from illegally expropriating land or abusing birth quota policies to illegally collect fines.

---

[22] Johnson (2018b).
[23] Wong (2012).

Yet top-down corruption crackdowns cannot guarantee that autocratic governments will be responsive to the interests of the weak and
poor in the long run. One problem is informational: as Ronald Wintrobe's work on the dictator's dilemma suggests, it is difficult for officials
in the central government to identify who is corrupt and who is not.[24]
This problem can be especially severe in autocracies, which lack a free
press and where officials have incentives to present a rosy picture of
conditions in their locality.[25]

However, there are deep *political* problems associated with trying to
create top-down systems of accountability in an autocracy. On some
issues, such as revenue collection, the interests of the central government are not always aligned with those of local citizens, creating weak
incentives for top-down accountability. A broad-based purge of corrupt
officials can also anger other regime elites, increasing the risks that the
ruling coalition may fracture.[26]

If top-down accountability is not enough, perhaps bottom-up feedback institutions like village elections or online complaint portals can
strengthen government responsiveness? In China, online "Mayor's Mail-
boxes" allow citizens to lodge complaints directly with officials. Research
by Gregory Distelhorst and Yue Hou shows that officials in China write
messages in response to these complaints at rates comparable to, and
sometimes higher than, those in democracies.[27]

Yet while institutions like online portals or other forms of formal
civic participation allow autocratic governments to be "responsive" in
a very literal sense – they can send messages that directly respond to citizens' grievances – it is less clear if these tools lead to meaningful *policy*
responsiveness. Policy responsiveness requires changes in the distribution of important, real-world resources like schools, residency permits,
welfare benefits, or land. Research by Iza Ding suggests that much of
this responsiveness is "performative" rather than real.[28] Future research
should continue to examine these important questions.

Nor is it clear that strengthening local democracy will improve
governance for the weak and poor. The accumulated evidence from

[24] Wintrobe (1998).
[25] To some degree, this problem can be overcome. As Lorentzen (2013, 2014) notes,
autocracies do sometimes allow limited protest and press freedoms as an information-
gathering mechanism.
[26] On the danger of insider-led coups, see Svolik (2012) and Geddes et al. (2018).
[27] Distelhorst and Hou (2017).
[28] Ding (2016).

dozens of studies suggests that the introduction of village elections in China has failed to create meaningful political accountability.[29] The re-centralization of power in townships suggests growing doubts in Beijing about the usefulness of elections as either a tool of accountability or control.

In the end, the most effective check on autocratic state power is unlikely to come from the state itself, but from an adversarial relation-ship between local civil society and the state. Independent community leaders who can mobilize their groups and threaten officials with broad-based political mobilization can help even the balance of power between the state and society, and create meaningful incentives for responsiveness.

Yet if organized resistance is the most effective path toward political accountability in autocracies, it is also the most dangerous. This book began with a brief sketch of an activist named Qingmei, whose house had been taken by the state, and who had spent time in jail because of her crusade to get compensation. When I first met Qingmei, she was wearing a t-shirt that said "Looking for Bao Gong" (找包公), a reference an upright Song Dynasty magistrate who has become a symbol of justice and un-corruptibility in China. She would have to wait a while longer for Bao Gong's reincarnation. Soon after we met, Qingmei was detained again by local authorities – this time for traveling to Beijing to petition the national government. When local officials caught her, they forced her on a train back to Sichuan.

Being an activist like Qingmei requires considerable moral and phys-ical courage. She has reached an age when many in rural China are grandmothers, but finds herself again and again in the company of young men intent on coercing her into silence. "I don't know how many times I have been in prison," she said. She told me she was not afraid of prison herself. A little while later, we were walking to a restaurant and she noticed we were being tailed by a man in his twenties whom she recog-nized – a plainclothes police officer. She waved and gave him a cheerful smile. "I just want the truth to come out."

---

[29] See O'Brien and Han (2009).

Appendix A

Additional Figures and Tables

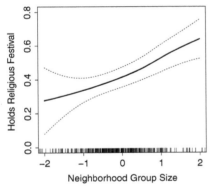

FIGURE A.1 Loess regression showing correlation between size of neighborhood groups and whether or not the village has a religious festival.

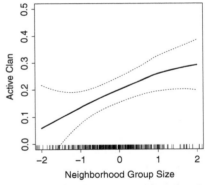

FIGURE A.2 Loess regression showing correlation between size of neighborhood groups and whether or not the village has an active lineage group.

TABLE A.1 *Descriptive statistics*

Statistic	N	Mean	St. Dev.	Min	Max
Distance to township (km)	393	5.712	5.300	0	38
Distance to county seat (km)	393	29.489	21.872	0	115
Log number of households	393	6.032	0.717	3.64	7.87

(continued)

TABLE A.1 *(continued)*

Statistic	N	Mean	St. Dev.	Min	Max
Surname fragmentation (0–1 index)	378	0.713	0.229	0.08	1
Ethnic fragmentation (0–1 index)	408	0.033	0.099	0	0.50
Ethnic minority population (percent)	408	0.080	0.240	0	1
Wealth, 1992 nighttime luminosity proxy	408	4.025	7.267	0	61
Terrain roughness (meters difference, high and low)	407	231.042	254.248	1	1,204
Agricultural suitability (1–3 index)	406	1.628	0.836	1	7
Township controls village elections (0–1 index)	408	0.159	0.209	0	1
Participation rate in elections (percent)	408	0.696	0.461	0	1
Elections have more than one candidate (percent)	408	0.616	0.305	0	1
Village has active lineage group (dummy)	408	0.279	0.449	0	1
Village lineage group has *citang* or *zupu* (dummy)	408	0.196	0.398	0	1
Lineage leader is village cadre (dummy)	408	0.154	0.362	0	1
Land seizure during leader tenure (percent)	392	0.151	0.358	0	1
Land seizures prior to tenure (percent)	392	0.048	0.215	0	1
Villagers petitioned higher levels (percent)	408	0.115	0.320	0	1
Average village income (yuan)	390	1, 899	1, 242	50	7,400
Nonagricultural employment (percent)	408	0.044	0.104	0	0.80
Average education level (years)	408	5.697	1.742	0.70	9.91
Participation in local religious festivals (percent)	408	0.119	0.195	0	1

TABLE A.2 *Variable descriptions.*

Variable	Source	Variable Description
Village coordinates	Baidu/Google Maps	Latitude and longitude.
Nighttime luminosity	DMSP	Luminosity values from 1992 DMSP stable lights raster.
Agricultural suitability	UN-FAO	1–3 scale. Nutrient availability from the Harmonized World Soil Database v1.2.
Altitude	SRTM	Meters. Mean within 10 km of village center.
Terrain roughness	SRTM	Meters. Difference between minimum and maximum altitude in 10 km radius.
Land seizure	CGSS-A: G2b	Land reallocation due to government land expropriation or confiscation for use by enterprises; limited to those occurring after current village leadership took office (from CGSS-B: C3 and C4).
Village land revenue	CGSS-B: B1f, i	Log revenue in 2004 from land sales and rental of land and other village property.
Village cultivated area	CGSS-B: A12a	Log *mu* of cultivated land in 2004 in the village.
Lineage group is active	CGSS-A: F10	Dummy variable. "Does your village have an active lineage network or organization?"
Lineage elite is cadre	CGSS-A: F11	Dummy variable. "Are the leaders or most influential members of the lineage current village cadres?" Dichotomized from Likert response scale to be 1 if response is entirely, mostly, or generally; 0 if never, or somewhat. Likert scale version shown in the appendix of Mattingly (2016).

(continued)

TABLE A.2 *(continued)*

Variable	Source	Variable Description
Distance to county	CGSS-B: A4a	Kilometers. Village cadre estimate.
Distance to township	CGSS-B: A4b	Kilometers. Village cadre estimate.
Township electoral control	CGSS-A: G14-1	Percent indicating township control over elections.
Surname fragmentation	CGSS-B: A10	0–1 index. Please see main text for formula.
Ethnic fragmentation	CGSS-A: A4	0–1 index. Please see main text for formula.
Number of households	CGSS-B: A2a	Number of households.
Public goods spending	CGSS-B: Bc, d, f	Log per capita spending on teacher salaries, welfare, and public construction.
Non-farm employment	CGSS: A7	Percent of respondents indicating non-farm employment.
Petitioning	CGSS: F8b-c	Indicator for petitioning government (*shangfang*).

Note: For descriptions of CFPS variables, please see the main text and footnotes of Chapter 4
Key: CGSS-A: Household survey; CGSS-B: Cadre survey; SRTM: Shuttle Radar Topography Mission; DMSP: Defense Meteorological Satellite Program; UN-FAO: U.N. Food & Agriculture Office

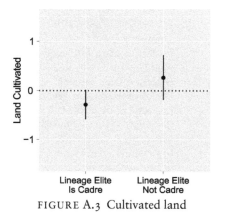

FIGURE A.3 Cultivated land

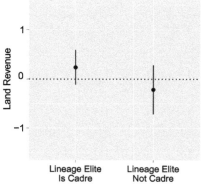

FIGURE A.4 Revenue from land

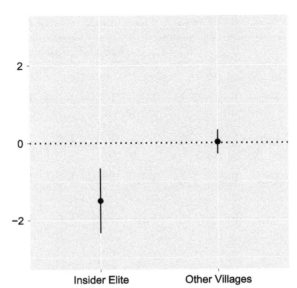

FIGURE A.5 Land expropriation correlation with net village public spending (standardized), broken down by elite type

TABLE A.3 *Chapter 4: Additional results 1*

	Dependent variable:			
	Land requisition indicator		Over birth quota	
	(1)	(2)	(3)	(4)
Active lineage hall	0.146***	0.146***	0.029**	0.029***
	(0.053)	(0.052)	(0.011)	(0.011)
Largest surname group size		−0.0004		0.0005**
		(0.001)		(0.0002)
Distance to county seat		0.00000		0.00000
		(0.00001)		(0.00000)
Ethnic minority groups		−0.035		−0.055**
		(0.110)		(0.023)
Mineral wealth		0.049		−0.043*
		(0.108)		(0.022)
Mountainous terrain		0.071		0.017
		(0.130)		(0.027)
Tourist destination		0.171		−0.049**
		(0.111)		(0.023)

(continued)

TABLE A.3 *(continued)*

	Dependent variable:			
	Land requisition indicator		Over birth quota	
	(1)	(2)	(3)	(4)
Natural disaster frequency		0.030		−0.008
		(0.057)		(0.012)
Electoral participation		0.005***		−0.001***
		(0.002)		(0.0004)
Constant	0.637***	0.198	0.140***	0.211***
	(0.037)	(0.170)	(0.008)	(0.035)
Observations	293	293	293	293

Note: *p<0.1; **p<0.05; ***p<0.01

TABLE A.4 *Chapter 4: Additional results 2*

	Dependent variable:			
	Net public spending		Protest	
	(1)	(2)	(3)	(4)
Active lineage hall	−0.002	0.070	−0.018	−0.018
	(0.276)	(0.286)	(0.023)	(0.017)
Land confiscation	−0.115	−0.077		
	(0.217)	(0.220)		
Largest surname group size		0.001		0.0001
		(0.003)		(0.0002)
Distance to county seat		0.00001		0.00000
		(0.00002)		(0.00000)
Ethnic minority groups		−0.339		−0.021
		(0.308)		(0.024)
Mineral wealth		−0.228		0.010
		(0.328)		(0.024)
Mountainous terrain		−0.246		0.029
		(0.358)		(0.029)
Tourist destination		−0.279		0.051**
		(0.306)		(0.024)
Natural disaster frequency		0.167		0.002
		(0.167)		(0.013)

(continued)

	Dependent variable:			
	Net public spending		Protest	
	(1)	(2)	(3)	(4)
Electoral participation		0.006		−0.00004
		(0.005)		(0.0004)
Active lineage hall X Land Confiscation	0.355	0.252		
	(0.328)	(0.343)		
Grievance against official			0.791***	0.821***
			(0.027)	(0.034)
Active lineage hall X Grievance against official			−0.066	−0.087*
			(0.061)	(0.047)
Constant	0.059	−0.499	−0.042***	−0.055
	(0.175)	(0.511)	(0.009)	(0.039)
Observations	271	271	288	288

Note: *p<0.1; **p<0.05; ***p<0.01

TABLE A.5 *Chapter 4: Additional results 3*

	Dependent variable:			
	Land requisition indicator		Over birth quota	
	(1)	(2)	(3)	(4)
Religious organization	0.094*	0.094*	0.019*	0.019*
	(0.052)	(0.052)	(0.011)	(0.011)
Largest surname group size		−0.001		0.0002
		(0.001)		(0.0002)
Distance to county seat		−0.00000		0.00000
		(0.00001)		(0.00000)
Ethnic minority groups		0.113		−0.033*
		(0.093)		(0.019)
Mineral wealth		0.057		−0.038
		(0.122)		(0.025)
Mountainous terrain		−0.095		0.027
		(0.166)		(0.034)
Tourist destination		−0.00002		−0.015
		(0.121)		(0.025)
Natural disaster frequency		−0.136**		0.031**
		(0.059)		(0.012)
Electoral participation		0.002		−0.001***
		(0.002)		(0.0003)
Constant	0.653***	0.581***	0.143***	0.236***
	(0.037)	(0.152)	(0.008)	(0.031)
Observations	306	306	306	306

Note: *p<0.1; **p<0.05; ***p<0.01

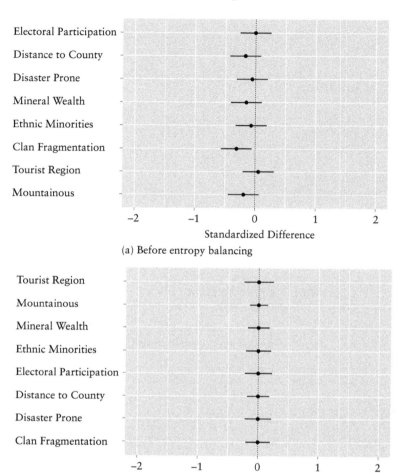

(a) Before entropy balancing

(b) After entropy balancing

FIGURE A.6 Difference between villages with and without religious organizations, before and after entropy balancing.

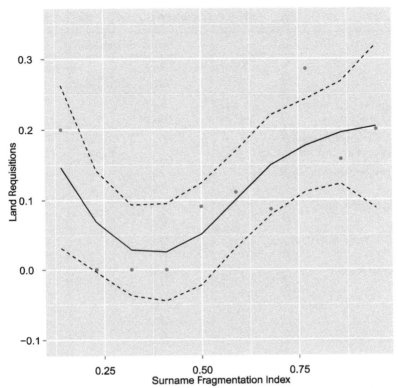

FIGURE A.7 Surname fragmentation and land expropriation. Points are binned means and the solid line is a Loess estimate using weighted least squares; the dotted lines are the 95 percent confidence intervals.

TABLE A.6 *Chapter 4: Additional results 4*

	Dependent variable:			
	Net public spending		Protest	
	(1)	(2)	(3)	(4)
Religious organization	1.135***	1.194***	−0.003	0.001
	(0.228)	(0.235)	(0.019)	(0.018)
Grievance against official			0.779***	0.776***
			(0.027)	(0.035)
Land requisition	0.134	0.162		
	(0.184)	(0.187)		

(continued)

TABLE A.6 *(continued)*

	Dependent variable:			
	Net public spending		Protest	
	(1)	(2)	(3)	(4)
Religious organization X Land requisition	−1.252*** (0.273)	−1.350*** (0.285)		
Religious organization X Grievance against official			0.013 (0.055)	0.004 (0.054)
Largest surname group size		0.004 (0.003)		−0.0004 (0.0003)
Distance to county seat		−0.00001 (0.00001)		0.00000 (0.00000)
Ethnic minority groups		−0.114 (0.231)		−0.021 (0.022)
Mineral wealth		−0.068 (0.306)		0.035 (0.028)
Mountainous terrain		−0.118 (0.382)		−0.035 (0.039)
Tourist destination		−0.471* (0.283)		0.091*** (0.029)
Natural disaster frequency		0.008 (0.146)		−0.027** (0.014)
Electoral participation		0.009** (0.004)		0.0004 (0.0004)
Constant	−0.161 (0.150)	−0.968** (0.377)	−0.045*** (0.009)	−0.059 (0.036)
Observations	279	279	301	301

Note: $^{*}p<0.1$; $^{**}p<0.05$; $^{***}p<0.01$

TABLE A.7 *Chapter 5: Additional results 1*

	Dependent variable:			
	Clan public goods		Clan helps business	
	(1)	(2)	(3)	(4)
Lineage elite is cadre	0.416** (0.209)	0.256 (0.315)	0.482** (0.211)	0.302 (0.341)
Distance to county seat		0.002 (0.007)		−0.004 (0.007)

(continued)

TABLE A.7 *(continued)*

	Clan public goods (1)	Clan public goods (2)	Clan helps business (3)	Clan helps business (4)
	Dependent variable:			
Terrain roughness		0.001* (0.001)		0.001 (0.001)
Agricultural suitability		0.043 (0.276)		0.210 (0.299)
GDP (1992 nighttime lights proxy)		0.039 (0.026)		0.050* (0.029)
Electoral manipulation index		−0.606 (0.616)		−1.057 (0.658)
Distance to township		0.029 (0.028)		0.024 (0.029)
Surname fragmentation index		−0.394 (0.618)		−0.501 (0.692)
Ethnic fragmentation index		−0.244 (1.491)		0.642 (1.534)
Number of households (log)		−0.044 (0.235)		0.289 (0.254)
Constant	1.823*** (0.153)	1.463 (1.558)	1.644*** (0.155)	−0.107 (1.688)
Observations	99	92	100	93
R^2	0.039	0.345	0.051	0.314
Adjusted R^2	0.029	0.069	0.041	0.014

Note: *$p<0.1$; **$p<0.05$; ***$p<0.01$

TABLE A.8 *Chapter 5: Additional results 2*

	Clan public goods (1)	Clan public goods (2)	Clan cultural events (3)	Clan cultural events (4)
	Dependent variable:			
Lineage elite is cadre	0.416** (0.209)	0.256 (0.315)	0.300 (0.192)	−0.034 (0.276)
Distance to county seat		0.002 (0.007)		0.003 (0.006)

(continued)

TABLE A.8 *(continued)*

	Dependent variable:			
	Clan public goods		Clan cultural events	
	(1)	(2)	(3)	(4)
Terrain roughness		0.001*		0.001**
		(0.001)		(0.001)
Agricultural suitability		0.043		−0.211
		(0.276)		(0.242)
GDP (1992 nighttime lights proxy)		0.039		0.039*
		(0.026)		(0.023)
Electoral manipulation index		−0.606		−0.964*
		(0.616)		(0.531)
Distance to township		0.029		0.036
		(0.028)		(0.026)
Surname fragmentation index		−0.394		−0.357
		(0.618)		(0.531)
Ethnic fragmentation index		−0.244		0.342
		(1.491)		(1.275)
Number of households (log)		−0.044		0.205
		(0.235)		(0.211)
Constant	1.823***	1.463	1.654***	0.562
	(0.153)	(1.558)	(0.139)	(1.418)
Observations	99	92	96	89

Note: *p<0.1; **p<0.05; ***p<0.01

TABLE A.9 *Chapter 5: Additional results 3*

	Dependent variable:			
	Clan disseminates information		Clan assists policy implementation	
	(1)	(2)	(3)	(4)
Lineage elite is cadre	0.627***	0.359	0.596**	0.212
	(0.215)	(0.331)	(0.257)	(0.394)
Distance to county seat		−0.007		−0.001
		(0.007)		(0.008)
Terrain roughness		0.0002		0.001
		(0.001)		(0.001)

(continued)

TABLE A.9 *(continued)*

	Dependent variable:			
	Clan disseminates information		Clan assists policy implementation	
	(1)	(2)	(3)	(4)
Agricultural suitability		0.212		−0.030
		(0.292)		(0.343)
GDP (1992 nighttime lights proxy)		0.038		0.047
		(0.028)		(0.032)
Electoral manipulation index		−0.752		−0.786
		(0.638)		(0.746)
Distance to township		0.041		0.037
		(0.029)		(0.034)
Surname fragmentation index		−0.711		−0.594
		(0.660)		(0.760)
Ethnic fragmentation index		−0.875		−0.555
		(1.498)		(1.735)
Number of households (log)		−0.002		−0.218
		(0.248)		(0.291)
Constant	1.697***	1.620	1.995***	3.324*
	(0.158)	(1.646)	(0.191)	(1.947)
Observations	101	94	98	91

Note: *p<0.1; **p<0.05; ***p<0.01

TABLE A.10 *Chapter 5: Additional results 4*

	Dependent variable:			
	Clan assists village committee		Clan coordinates government relations	
	(1)	(2)	(3)	(4)
Lineage elite is cadre	0.829***	0.598	0.716***	0.457
	(0.270)	(0.393)	(0.231)	(0.311)
Distance to county seat		0.003		−0.001
		(0.008)		(0.007)
Terrain roughness		0.001		0.001
		(0.001)		(0.001)

(continued)

TABLE A.10 *(continued)*

	Dependent variable:			
	Clan assists village committee		Clan coordinates government relations	
	(1)	(2)	(3)	(4)
Agricultural suitability		−0.015		0.044
		(0.343)		(0.270)
GDP (1992 nighttime lights proxy)		0.047		0.066***
		(0.032)		(0.024)
Electoral manipulation index		−0.766		−1.427**
		(0.753)		(0.590)
Distance to township		0.047		0.051*
		(0.034)		(0.027)
Surname fragmentation index		−0.712		−0.401
		(0.772)		(0.589)
Ethnic fragmentation index		0.914		−1.214
		(1.733)		(1.358)
Number of households (log)		−0.223		0.233
		(0.290)		(0.225)
Constant	1.904***	3.373*	1.823***	0.633
	(0.199)	(1.940)	(0.171)	(1.528)
Province fixed effects		✓		✓
Observations	95	88	98	91

Note: *p<0.1; **p<0.05; ***p<0.01

TABLE A.11 *Chapter 5: Additional results 5*

	Dependent variable:			
	Log taxes		Log levies	
	(1)	(2)	(3)	(4)
Lineage leader is cadre	0.776***	0.791***	0.421*	0.439*
	(0.240)	(0.256)	(0.241)	(0.265)
Active lineage	−0.083	−0.358	−0.080	−0.188
	(0.169)	(0.243)	(0.174)	(0.245)
Distance to county seat		0.002		−0.0003
		(0.003)		(0.003)

(continued)

TABLE A.11 *(continued)*

	Dependent variable:			
	Log taxes		Log levies	
	(1)	(2)	(3)	(4)
Terrain roughness		−0.0002		0.0002
		(0.0003)		(0.0003)
Agricultural suitability		−0.035		−0.012
		(0.085)		(0.088)
GDP (1992 nighttime lights proxy)		0.037***		−0.003
		(0.008)		(0.009)
Electoral manipulation index		0.478*		−0.131
		(0.281)		(0.287)
Distance to township		0.001		−0.005
		(0.011)		(0.012)
Surname fragmentation index		−0.146		0.011
		(0.261)		(0.266)
Ethnic fragmentation index		−0.335		−0.653
		(0.555)		(0.557)
Number of households (log)		0.021		−0.015
		(0.098)		(0.100)
Lineage supplies public goods		−0.046		−0.018
		(0.095)		(0.098)
Lineage dispute resolution		−0.058		0.002
		(0.097)		(0.098)
Lineage assists with business		0.204**		0.018
		(0.095)		(0.097)
Constant	−0.048	−0.494	−0.021	−0.157
	(0.057)	(0.648)	(0.057)	(0.654)
Province fixed effects		✓		✓
Observations	366	351	377	363

Note: *p<0.1; **p<0.05; ***p<0.01

TABLE A.12 *Chapter 5: Additional results 6*

	Dependent variable:			
	Birth quota difficult to enforce		Households over birth quota	
	(1)	(2)	(3)	(4)
Lineage leader is cadre	−0.369*	−0.238	−0.100	−0.060
	(0.224)	(0.240)	(0.222)	(0.238)
Active lineage	0.253	−0.022	0.430***	0.186
	(0.164)	(0.231)	(0.162)	(0.230)
Distance to county seat		0.002		0.001
		(0.003)		(0.003)
Terrain roughness		−0.0004		0.0004
		(0.0003)		(0.0003)
Agricultural suitability		−0.107		0.010
		(0.083)		(0.083)
GDP (1992 nighttime lights proxy)		−0.005		0.003
		(0.008)		(0.008)
Electoral manipulation index		0.328		0.058
		(0.268)		(0.267)
Distance to township		0.003		−0.001
		(0.011)		(0.011)
Surname fragmentation index		0.009		−0.336
		(0.248)		(0.247)
Ethnic fragmentation index		−0.606		0.423
		(0.532)		(0.529)
Number of households (log)		0.150		0.079
		(0.094)		(0.094)
Lineage supplies public goods		−0.003		−0.022
		(0.092)		(0.091)
Lineage dispute resolution		−0.019		0.135
		(0.094)		(0.093)
Lineage assists with business		0.025		−0.157*
		(0.091)		(0.090)
Constant	−0.015	−1.459**	−0.075	−0.762
	(0.055)	(0.616)	(0.055)	(0.612)
Province fixed effects		✓		✓
Observations	408	376	408	376

Note: $^{*}p<0.1$; $^{**}p<0.05$; $^{***}p<0.01$

TABLE A.13 *Chapter 5: Additional results 7*

	Dependent variable:			
	Net public spending		Petition indicator	
	(1)	(2)	(3)	(4)
Lineage leader is cadre	−0.289	−0.206	0.053	0.064
	(0.230)	(0.232)	(0.066)	(0.070)
Land confiscation	0.025	−0.057	−0.027	−0.059
	(0.158)	(0.160)	(0.048)	(0.053)
Lineage cadre X Land	−1.521***	−1.533***	0.312**	0.290**
confiscation	(0.457)	(0.465)	(0.132)	(0.140)
Distance to county seat		−0.004		−0.001
		(0.003)		(0.001)
Terrain roughness		−0.00002		0.0002**
		(0.0003)		(0.0001)
Agricultural suitability		0.176**		0.016
		(0.082)		(0.027)
GDP (1992 nighttime		−0.024***		0.002
lights proxy)		(0.008)		(0.002)
Electoral manipulation		−0.506*		0.095
index		(0.271)		(0.088)
Distance to township		−0.006		0.004
		(0.011)		(0.004)
Surname fragmentation		0.404		0.003
index		(0.262)		(0.082)
Ethnic fragmentation		−0.277		0.488***
index		(0.538)		(0.176)
Number of households		−0.143		0.078**
(log)		(0.095)		(0.031)
Constant	0.050	1.879***	0.107***	−0.470**
	(0.059)	(0.685)	(0.018)	(0.203)
Province fixed effects		✓		✓
Observations	336	325	392	376

Note: $^*p<0.1$; $^{**}p<0.05$; $^{***}p<0.01$

TABLE A.14 *Chapter 5: Additional results 8*

	Dependent variable:			
	Log income		Assets	
	(1)	(2)	(3)	(4)
Large clan	0.159***	0.133***	−0.065*	−0.035
	(0.029)	(0.031)	(0.037)	(0.037)
Land seizure	−0.062	0.010	0.084	0.006
	(0.072)	(0.077)	(0.095)	(0.092)
Large clan X Land seizure	−0.197**	−0.188*	−0.020	0.012
	(0.097)	(0.100)	(0.124)	(0.119)
Communist Youth League member		−0.071	0.149	0.033
		(0.079)	(0.094)	(0.093)
Schooling		−0.106		0.104
		(0.094)		(0.113)
Ethnic minority		−0.124		−0.227**
		(0.093)		(0.110)
Distance to city		0.001***		−0.002***
		(0.0003)		(0.0004)
Year of birth		0.003**		0.015***
		(0.001)		(0.001)
Constant	0.323***	−5.492**	−0.143***	−30.715***
	(0.022)	(2.348)	(0.029)	(2.786)
Province fixed effects		✓		✓
Observations	4,047	3,545	3,722	3,544

Note: *p<0.1; **p<0.05; ***p<0.01

TABLE A.15 *Chapter 5: Additional results 9*

	Dependent variable:		
	Log compensation for land (Standardized *yuan* per *mu*)		
	(1)	(2)	(3)
Belongs to large clan	0.226	0.190	0.237
	(0.145)	(0.160)	(0.169)
Communist Youth League member		0.743*	0.947**
		(0.385)	(0.418)
Schooling past middle school		0.348	1.254
		(0.491)	(0.712)

(continued)

TABLE A.15 *(continued)*

	(1)	(2)	(3)
	Dependent variable:		
	Log compensation for land (Standardized *yuan* per *mu*)		
Ethnic minority		−0.178	−0.142
		(0.443)	(0.461)
Distance to nearest city			−0.001
			(0.001)
Birth year			−0.002
			(0.007)
Constant	0.772	0.843	4.947
	(0.535)	(0.565)	(13.591)
Province fixed effects	Yes	Yes	Yes
Observations	198	185	176

TABLE A.16 *Chapter 5: Additional results 10*

	(1)	(2)	(3)	(4)
	Dependent variable:			
	Trust in non-lineage members			
Village holds festival	−0.119**	−0.148***	−0.155***	−0.163***
	(0.049)	(0.050)	(0.050)	(0.053)
Distance to county seat		0.002**	0.002*	0.002*
		(0.001)	(0.001)	(0.001)
Terrain roughness		−0.0002	−0.0002	−0.0002
		(0.0001)	(0.0001)	(0.0001)
Agricultural suitability		0.022	0.028	0.050
		(0.034)	(0.035)	(0.037)
GDP (1992 nighttime lights proxy)		−0.006*	−0.006*	−0.005
		(0.003)	(0.003)	(0.003)
Electoral manipulation index			−0.158	−0.125
			(0.115)	(0.121)
Distance to township			0.002	0.003
			(0.005)	(0.005)
Surname fragmentation index				−0.135
				(0.111)
Ethnic fragmentation index				0.185
				(0.241)

(continued)

TABLE A.16 *(continued)*

	(1)	(2)	(3)	(4)
	Dependent variable:			
	Trust in non-lineage members			
Number of households (log)				−0.022
				(0.042)
Constant	2.886***	2.349***	2.365***	2.526***
	(0.032)	(0.109)	(0.111)	(0.298)
Observations	408	391	391	376

Note: *p<0.1; **p<0.05; ***p<0.01

TABLE A.17 *Chapter 5: Additional results 11*

	(1)	(2)	(3)	(4)
	Dependent variable:			
	Trust in neighbors			
Village holds festival	−0.075*	−0.057	−0.057	−0.076*
	(0.039)	(0.041)	(0.041)	(0.043)
Distance to county seat		0.003***	0.002**	0.002**
		(0.001)	(0.001)	(0.001)
Terrain roughness		−0.0001	−0.0001	−0.0001
		(0.0001)	(0.0001)	(0.0001)
Agricultural suitability		−0.043	−0.039	−0.022
		(0.028)	(0.028)	(0.030)
GDP (1992 nighttime lights proxy)		−0.003	−0.003	−0.003
		(0.003)	(0.003)	(0.003)
Electoral manipulation index			−0.061	−0.039
			(0.094)	(0.097)
Distance to township			0.004	0.001
			(0.004)	(0.004)
Surname fragmentation index				0.047
				(0.090)
Ethnic fragmentation index				−0.021
				(0.194)
Number of households (log)				−0.013
				(0.034)
Constant	3.295***	3.163***	3.156***	3.186***
	(0.025)	(0.088)	(0.090)	(0.240)
Observations	408	391	391	376

Note: *p<0.1; **p<0.05; ***p<0.01

TABLE A.18 *Chapter 6: Additional results 1*

	Ordinary least squares			
	Land requisitions			
	(1)	(2)	(3)	(4)
Number of people per cell	−0.043**	−0.055***	−0.057***	−0.046*
(standardized log population)	(0.018)	(0.019)	(0.019)	(0.025)
Active lineage group		−0.096	−0.094	−0.058
		(0.061)	(0.060)	(0.064)
Lineage leader is cadre		0.216***	0.206**	0.205**
		(0.083)	(0.082)	(0.086)
Religious festival		0.069*	0.068*	0.087**
		(0.038)	(0.038)	(0.043)
Distance to county seat		−0.001	0.00004	0.0002
		(0.001)	(0.001)	(0.001)
Terrain roughness		−0.0001	−0.0001	0.00005
		(0.0001)	(0.0001)	(0.0001)
Agricultural suitability index		0.033	0.029	0.038
		(0.022)	(0.022)	(0.030)
Wealth (1992 nighttime		0.001	0.001	0.002
lights proxy)		(0.003)	(0.003)	(0.003)
Township control over elections			0.144*	0.145
			(0.087)	(0.099)
Distance to township			−0.011***	−0.009**
			(0.004)	(0.004)
Surname fragmentation index				0.136
				(0.090)
Ethnic fragmentation index				−0.170
				(0.196)
Number of households (log)				0.056
				(0.037)
Constant	0.153***	0.116**	0.130**	−0.234
	(0.018)	(0.053)	(0.056)	(0.257)
Province fixed effects	No	No	No	Yes
Observations	387	385	385	371

Note: $^{*}p<0.1$; $^{**}p<0.05$; $^{***}p<0.01$

TABLE A.19 *Chapter 6: Additional results 2*

	Ordinary least squares			
	Cadres report enforcement difficult			
	(1)	(2)	(3)	(4)
Number of cell leaders per village	−0.069*** (0.027)	−0.078*** (0.026)	−0.082*** (0.026)	−0.081*** (0.029)
Birth quota		−0.296** (0.115)	−0.326*** (0.116)	−0.547 (0.399)
Over quota fines		−0.015 (0.054)	−0.053 (0.054)	−0.237 (0.170)
Ethnic minority percent		−0.462* (0.271)	−0.244 (0.271)	−0.372 (0.283)
Number of households (log)			0.170*** (0.038)	0.121** (0.049)
Distance to county seat			0.002 (0.001)	0.001 (0.001)
Terrain roughness			0.011 (0.028)	−0.056 (0.038)
Agricultural suitability index			−0.033 (0.031)	−0.086** (0.043)
Wealth (1992 nighttime lights proxy)			−0.006 (0.004)	0.0003 (0.004)
Township control over elections				0.105 (0.135)
Distance to township				−0.0002 (0.006)
Surname fragmentation index				−0.008 (0.127)
Constant	0.457*** (0.027)	0.920*** (0.190)	0.016 (0.284)	1.068** (0.527)
Observations	348	348	346	333

Note: *p<0.1; **p<0.05; ***p<0.01

TABLE A.20 *Chapter 6: Additional results 3*

	Ordinary least squares			
	Time spent enforcing birth quota			
	(1)	(2)	(3)	(4)
Number of cell leaders per village	−0.171*** (0.062)	−0.189*** (0.062)	−0.203*** (0.061)	−0.155** (0.064)
Birth quota		−0.136 (0.269)	−0.158 (0.268)	−1.123 (0.874)
Over quota fines		−0.062 (0.126)	−0.138 (0.126)	−0.435 (0.371)
Ethnic minority percent		−1.447** (0.656)	−0.912 (0.648)	−0.962 (0.639)
Number of households (log)			0.396*** (0.088)	0.324*** (0.106)
Distance to county seat			0.007** (0.003)	0.001 (0.003)
Terrain roughness			0.031 (0.065)	−0.096 (0.084)
Agricultural suitability index			−0.087 (0.073)	−0.064 (0.093)
Wealth (1992 nighttime lights proxy)			−0.014* (0.009)	−0.005 (0.009)
Township control over elections				−0.215 (0.295)
Distance to township				−0.002 (0.012)
Surname fragmentation index				−0.205 (0.280)
Constant	2.344*** (0.062)	2.681*** (0.446)	0.417 (0.659)	3.322*** (1.153)
Observations	344	344	342	330

Note: *p<0.1; **p<0.05; ***p<0.01

Appendix B

Survey Design

In July 2013, I conducted a face-to-face survey in a major city in Guangdong with a research partner from a local university and a team of student enumerators. The survey sites ranged from villages where many residents remained farmers to "villages-in-the-city" (*chengzhong-cun*) that had effectively become part of the city's urban fabric. Even in these highly urbanized villages, villagers still retained rights to vote for their village leadership.

We sampled twenty-two villages using a multi-stage procedure. The sample was stratified by district and then by whether or not the village was on a list of urban villages the municipality planned to redevelop. Initial research had suggested that redevelopment might influence the strength of lineage and other communal ties. However, whether or not a village was being redeveloped does not influence the results presented here.

Within each randomly selected village, the enumeration team canvassed door-to-door and in public spaces. The sampling strategy did not produce a random draw of households, but the sample nevertheless approximates some of the demographic characteristics of these urban villages. The sample was 50 percent male, with a lower middle-school education, and a mean age of 54. While I traveled with the team to each village, I did not participate in interviews because I was concerned that my presence as a foreigner might influence the results. Each team of enumerators contained one woman and one man.

Table B.1 presents descriptive statistics for the survey sample.

TABLE B.1 *Descriptive statistics of sample population. Sample size is 433.*

Variable	Mean	St. Dev.
Female	0.505	0.501
Currently employed	0.339	0.474
Currently retired	0.446	0.498
Has greater than primary school education	0.446	0.498
Age	54.2	15.1
Participates in temple activities	0.245	0.430
Participates in lineage hall activities	0.300	0.497
Lineage group member is the village Party Secretary	0.187	0.390
Lineage group member is the village chief	0.236	0.425
Is renting out (a) room(s) for additional income	0.538	0.499

Appendix C

Qualitative Research Design

The qualitative research was central to understanding the dynamics of political control in China. This research helped inform initial hypothesis and, through a combination of process tracing and paired comparison, helped me understand the causal processes at work.

Interviews and case selection proceeded in two waves. During the first wave, from July 2012 to December 2012, I conducted preliminary research in Beijing, Guangdong, Henan, Hong Kong, Hunan, and Sichuan. I conducted the most intensive research in Guangdong, where I visited several research sites (marked with †) nearly every day over the course of three months. This wave of research helped inform initial hypotheses. I conducted follow-up research in these sites (marked with †) more intermittently across three months in the Summer of 2013 and during brief visits through January 2018.

During a second wave of qualitative research, during the spring and summer of 2013, I built paired comparisons of villages in Henan, Hunan, Guangdong, and Jiangsu (marked with ∧). These structured comparisons involved less sustained engagement with field sites than the initial quasi-ethnographic research, spending on average a little over a week in each site. I also continued engaging with the initial field sites after this period. See the main text for a discussion of the advantages and drawbacks of paired comparison.

I selected the four provinces with two main considerations in mind. The first was access. Based on prior contacts, I planned to visit Henan and Hunan Provinces. The second consideration was an attempt to select regions that, while not necessarily representative of China as a whole, at least showed some of its variety in terms of wealth and local culture.

Guangdong and Jiangsu are among the ten wealthiest provinces. Henan and Hunan are less wealthy. Guangdong and Jiangsu tend to have civil society groups with strong formal organizations. (In the case of Guangdong, lineage associations with ancestral halls; in the case of Jiangsu, well-organized temple fairs.) The regions of Henan and Henan I visited tend to lack formal civil society organizations.

To construct as balanced a picture as possible, I triangulated among different sources. Overall, I conducted formal interviews with 103 individuals in addition to dozens of informal conversations. These included seventy-eight village residents (including current lineage heads, business leaders, ex-village committee members, and local rights activists), twelve current local officials (ten township or village cadres and two members of village security teams), four NGO workers, five academics (in addition to many other informal conversations), and four land developers. In cases where local development projects had divided a community among supporters and opponents, I attempted to interview citizens from both sides.

I supplemented these interviews by gathering relevant government documents. Wherever possible, I visited a local municipal archive or library to acquire publicly available material. At the archives, I presented a letter of introduction with my official research affiliation in China and asked for relevant material on local history and development, such as local gazetteers and yearbooks. Where possible, I also went to public spaces to read and photograph public message boards that included official government notices.

Below I describe in more detail the fieldwork conducted in each field site. Initial field sites marked with a †, second-wave field sites are marked with a ∧.

Yang Village, Guangdong Province†: I gained access to Yang Village through a local academic who introduced me to one of the village's major rights activists. The rights activist introduced me to individuals in the village. I also conducted additional interviews on my own over the course of visits spread over several months. For some interviews, I hired students to translate from Cantonese into Mandarin. I was unable to directly interview members of the village government. However, material in the municipal archives and newspaper coverage of the case helped fill out the government's perspective. I visited the village between Summer 2012 and Winter 2018.

Longjing and Meilong Villages, Guangdong Province†: I visited these villages numerous times between Summer 2012 and Winter 2018. I began by interviewing individuals active in the local lineage and retiree associations, including former and current cadres, about the village's history and politics. I conducted additional interviews through a combination of snowball referrals and further cold interview attempts. I also discussed the cases with consultants to the government's urban planning officials.

Headwater and Peng Village, Guangdong Province∧: I selected these villages based on data in the CGSS. (See Chapter 5 for further explanation.) I visited these villages in Spring 2013, and hired a local to translate from the Chaozhou dialect into Mandarin. I gathered material from the municipal archive, and gathered additional material from news reports and online petitions from 2013 to 2018.

Kaijia and Chalong Villages, Jiangsu Province∧: Similar to the Headwater and Peng Village sites, I had initially planned to choose a pair of villages based on CGSS data. However, one of the field sites was too politically sensitive, so I decided in the field to switch sites to two nearby villages. I visited them over the course of a week in Spring 2013, and hired a local to translate from the Xuzhou dialect into Mandarin. I gathered additional material from news reports and online petitions from 2013 to 2018.

Wujia, Taiping, Beiyan, and Xiaogang, Henan Province∧: I visited Henan in 2012–2013. For the anonymity and security of the individuals who helped me access a politically sensitive research site, additional details are omitted. I am extremely grateful for their help.

Rivertown and Wucun, Hunan Province∧: I visited Hunan in 2012–2013. For the anonymity and security of the individuals who helped me access the research sites, additional details are omitted. I am extremely grateful for their help.

Wukan Village, Guangdong Province: The protest movement over land rights in Wukan made it one of the most famous villages in China. I traveled to Wukan Village in Summer 2013 and conducted interviews with local cadres, protest organizers, and regular citizens. Elsewhere in southern China, I conducted interviews with academics and activists involved in the implementation of village elections and land reclamation.

Bibliography

Abramowitz, M. and Chertoff, M. (2018). The global threat of China's digital authoritarianism. *The Washington Post*.

Acemoglu, D., Reed, T., and Robinson, J. A. (2014). Chiefs: Economic development and elite control of civil society in Sierra Leone. *Journal of Political Economy*, 122(2):319–368.

Acemoglu, D. and Robinson, J. A. (2017). The emergence of weak, despotic and inclusive states. *NBER Working Paper No. 23657*. www.nber.org/papers/w23657.pdf. Last accessed July 30, 2019.

Achebe, C. (1992). *Things Fall Apart*. Everyman's Library.

Albertus, M. (2015). *Autocracy and Redistribution: The Politics of Land Reform*. Cambridge University Press.

Albertus, M. and Menaldo, V. (2012). Coercive capacity and the prospects for democratization. *Comparative Politics*, 44(2):151–169.

Alpermann, B. (2001). The post-election administration of Chinese villages. *The China Journal*, (46):45–67.

Arendt, H. (1961). *Between Past and Future: Eight Exercises in Political Thought*. The Viking Press.

Aytaç, S. E., Schiumerini, L., and Stokes, S. (2017a). Protests and repression in new democracies. *Perspectives on Politics*, 15(1):62–82.

Aytaç, S. E., Schiumerini, L., and Stokes, S. (2017b). Why do people join backlash protests? Lessons from Turkey. *Journal of Conflict Resolution*, 62(6): 1205–1228.

Bai, Y. and Kung, J. K. (2014). The shaping of an institutional choice: Weather shocks, the great leap famine, and agricultural decollectivization in China. *Explorations in Economic History*, 54:1–26.

Baldwin, K. (2013). Why vote with the chief? Political connections and public goods provision in Zambia. *American Journal of Political Science*, 57(4):794–809.

Baldwin, K. (2014). When politicians cede control of resources: Land, chiefs, and coalition-building in Africa. *Comparative Politics*, 46(3):253–271.

Baldwin, K. (2016). *The Paradox of Traditional Chiefs in Democratic Africa*. Cambridge University Press.

Berman, S. (1997). Civil society and the collapse of the Weimar Republic. *World Politics*, 49(3):401–429.

Bhavnani, R. R. and Lee, A. (2018). Local embeddedness and bureaucratic performance: Evidence from India. *The Journal of Politics*, 80(1):71–87.

Birney, M. (2014). Decentralization and veiled corruption under China's "rule of mandates." *World Development*, 53:55–67.

Blaydes, L. (2010). *Elections and Distributive Politics in Mubarak's Egypt*. Cambridge University Press.

Blaydes, L. (2018). *State of Repression: Iraq under Saddam Hussein*. Princeton University Press.

Boone, C. (2003). *Political Topographies of the African State: Territorial Authority and Institutional Choice*. Cambridge University Press.

Boone, C. (2013). *Property and Political Order in Africa: Land Rights and the Structure of Politics*. Cambridge University Press.

Brady, H. E. and Collier, D. (2010). *Rethinking Social Inquiry: Diverse Tools, Shared Standards*. Rowman & Littlefield Publishers.

Brown, M. and Xie, Y. (2015). Between heaven and earth: Dual accountability in Han China. *Chinese Journal of Sociology*, 1(1):56–87.

Bush, S. S. (2015). *The Taming of Democracy Assistance*. Cambridge University Press.

Cahill, S. E. (1993). *Transcendence and Divine Passion: The Queen Mother of the West in Medieval China*. Stanford University Press.

Cai, M. (2016). Land for welfare in China. *Land Use Policy*, 55:1–12.

Cai, Y. (2003). Collective ownership or cadres' ownership? The non-agricultural use of farmland in China. *The China Quarterly*, 175:662–680.

Cai, Y. (2008). Local governments and the suppression of popular resistance in China. *The China Quarterly*, 193:24–42.

Cai, Y. (2010). China's below-replacement fertility: Government policy or socioeconomic development? *Population and Development Review*, 36(3):419–440.

Cai, Y. and Sheng, Z. (2013). Homeowners' activism in Beijing: Leaders with mixed motivations. *The China Quarterly*, 215:513–532.

Cantor, M. (1992). Radicalism, religion and the American workingclass. *Irish Journal of American Studies*, 1:17–33.

Cathcart, A. (2006). *Kinship and Clientage: Highland Clanship 1451–1609*. Brill.

Central Party School Editorial Office (2017). *Xi Jinping's Seven Years as a Sent-Down Youth (Xi Jinping de Qi Nian Zhiqing Suiyue)*. Central Party School Publishing House.

Chakravarty, A. (2015). *Investing in Authoritarian Rule: Punishment and Patronage in Rwanda's Gacaca Courts for Genocide Crimes*. Cambridge Studies in Law and Society. Cambridge University Press.

Chambers, S. and Kopstein, J. (2001). Bad civil society. *Political Theory*, 29(6):837–865.

Chan, A., Madsen, R., and Unger, J. (1984). *Chen Village: The Recent History of a Peasant Community in Mao's China*. University of California Press.

Chan, A., Madsen, R., and Unger, J. (2009). *Chen Village: Revolution to Globalization*. University of California Press.

Chau, A. Y. (2008). *Miraculous Response: Doing Popular Religion in Contemporary China.* Stanford University Press.

Chen, C.-s. (2001). The symbolic and historical significance of popular cults in Chaozhou. *Journal of Historical Science*, 1:121–133.

Chen, F. and Kang, Y. (2016). Disorganized popular contention and local institutional building in China: A case study in Guangdong. *Journal of Contemporary China*, 25(100):596–612.

Chen, J., Retherford, R. D., Choe, M. K., Xiru, L., and Ying, H. (2009). Province-level variation in the achievement of below-replacement fertility in China. *Asian Population Studies*, 5(3):309–328.

Chen, T. and Kung, J. K. (2016). Do land revenue windfalls create a political resource curse? Evidence from China. *Journal of Development Economics*, 123: 86–106.

Chen, T. and Kung, J. K. (2018). Busting the "princelings": The campaign against corruption in China's primary land market. *The Quarterly Journal of Economics*, 134(1):185–226.

Chen, X. (2017). Origins of informal coercion in china. *Politics & Society*, 45(1):67–89.

Chengdu Government (2016). Secretary Liu Renyuan investigates land requisitions, demolition, and illegal construction in Cuiwei Lake, Xindu District *Liu renyuan shuji diaoyan xin du jiedao cuiwei hu pianqu zhengdi chaiqian yu wei jian zhili gongzuo.*

Chhibber, P., Kumar, T., and Sekhon, J.S. (2018). Preferences for Descriptive Representation: Asymmetries between Hindus and Muslims in India. Working paper, Department of Political Science, University of California, Berkeley. sekhon.berkeley.edu/papers/cks_public.pdf. Last accessed July 30, 2019.

China Renmin University, Michigan State University, and Landesa (2011). Landesa China survey. Technical report. www.landesa.org/wp-content/uploads/Landesa_China_Survey_Report_2011.pdf. Last accessed July 30, 2019."

Chuang, J. (2014). China's rural land politics: Bureaucratic absorption and the muting of rightful resistance. *The China Quarterly*, 219:649–669.

Collier, R. B. and Collier, D. (1991). *Shaping the Political Arena: Critical Junctures, the Labor Movement, and Regime Dynamics in Latin America.* Princeton University Press.

Collins, K. (2004). The logic of clan politics: Evidence from the Central Asian trajectories. *World Politics*, 56(02):224–261.

Collins, K. (2006). *Clan Politics and Regime Transition in Central Asia.* Cambridge University Press.

Collinson, P. (1994). *Elizabethan Essays.* A&C Black.

Corbin, D. A. (2015). *Life, Work, and Rebellion in the Coal Fields: The Southern West Virginia Miners, 1880–1922.* 2nd Edition. West Virginia University Press.

Corrales, J. (2015). Autocratic legalism in Venezuela. *Journal of Democracy*, 26(2):37–51.

Corrales, J. and Hidalgo, M. (2017). The quality of the Venezuelan democracy under Hugo Chavez (1999–2013). *Partecipazione e Conflitto*, 10(1):89–118.

Cumming-Bruce, N. (2018). UN panel confronts China over reports that it holds a million Uighurs in camps. *The New York Times.* www.nytimes.com/2018/08/10/world/asia/China-xinjiang-un-uighurs.html. Last accessed February 9, 2019.

Dahl, R. A. (2005). *Who Governs?: Democracy and Power in an American City.* Yale University Press.

Davenport, C. (2007a). State repression and political order. *Annual Review of Political Science,* 10:1–23.

Davenport, C. (2007b). *State Repression and the Domestic Democratic Peace.* Cambridge University Press.

Davenport, C. (2015). *How Social Movements Die: Repression and Demobilization of the Republic of New Africa.* Cambridge University Press.

De Bary, W. T. and Lufrano, R. (2010). *Sources of Chinese Tradition: From 1600 through the Twentieth Century,* volume 2. Columbia University Press.

DeBernardi, J. E. (2006). *The Way That Lives in the Heart: Chinese Popular Religion and Spirit Mediums in Penang, Malaysia.* Stanford University Press.

Deininger, K. and Jin, S. (2009). Securing property rights in transition: Lessons from implementation of China's rural land contracting law. *Journal of Economic Behavior & Organization,* 70(1):22–38.

Deng, Y. (2017). "Autonomous redevelopment": Moving the masses to remove nail households. *Modern China,* 43(5):494–522.

Deng, Y. and O'Brien, K. J. (2013). Relational repression in China: Using social ties to demobilize protesters. *The China Quarterly,* 215:533–552.

Devine, T. M. (1994). *Clanship to Crofter's War: The Social Transformation of the Scottish Highlands.* Manchester University Press.

Ding, I. (2016). *Invisible Sky, Visible State: Environmental Governance and Political Support in China.* PhD thesis, Department of Government, Harvard University.

Distelhorst, G. (2013). *Publicity-Driven Accountability in China.* PhD thesis, Massachusetts Institute of Technology.

Distelhorst, G. and Hou, Y. (2017). Constituency service under nondemocratic rule: Evidence from China. *The Journal of Politics,* 79(3):1024–1040.

Dodgshon, R. A. (1998). *From Chiefs to Landlords: Social and Economic Change in the Western Highlands and Islands, c. 1493–1820.* Edinburgh University Press.

Duara, P. (1988). *Culture, Power, and the State: Rural North China, 1900–1942.* Stanford University Press.

Earl, J. (2011). Political repression: Iron fists, velvet gloves, and diffuse control. *Annual Review of Sociology,* 37:261–284.

Economist Staff (2018). China has turned Xinjiang into a police state like no other. *The Economist.* www.economist.com/briefing/2018/05/31/China-has-turned-xinjiang-into-a-police-state-like-no-other. Last accessed January 13, 2019.

Edin, M. (2003). State capacity and local agent control in China: CCP cadre management from a township perspective. *The China Quarterly,* 173:35–52.

Eng, I. and Lin, Y.-M. (2002). Religious festivities, communal rivalry, and restructuring of authority relations in rural Chaozhou, southeast China. *The Journal of Asian Studies*, 61(04):1259–1285.

Evans-Pritchard, E. E. (1940). *The Nuer*. Oxford Clarendon.

Fagen, R. R. (1969). *The Transformation of Political Culture in Cuba*. Stanford University Press.

Faure, D. (1986). *The Structure of Chinese Rural Society: Lineage and Village in the Eastern New Territories, Hong Kong*. Oxford University Press.

Faure, D. (2007). *Emperor and Ancestor: State and Lineage in South China*. Stanford University Press.

Feeney, G. and Feng, W. (1993). Parity progression and birth intervals in China: The influence of policy in hastening fertility decline. *Population and Development Review*, pages 61–101.

Fei, X. (1992). *From the Soil: The Foundations of Chinese Society*. University of California Press.

Feuchtwang, S. (2003). *Popular Religion in China: The Imperial Metaphor*. Routledge.

Fox, R. G. (1971). *Kin, Clan, Raja, and Rule: State-hinterland Relations in Preindustrial India*. University of California Press.

Freedman, M. (1965). *Lineage Organization in Southeastern China*. University of London, Athlone Press.

Freedman, M. (1979). *The Study of Chinese Society: Essays*. Stanford University Press.

Frye, T. (2000). *Brokers and Bureaucrats: Building Market Institutions in Russia*. University of Michigan Press.

Frye, T. (2004). Credible commitment and property rights: Evidence from Russia. *American Political Science Review*, 98(03):453–466.

Frye, T. (2017). *Property Rights and Property Wrongs: How Power, Institutions, and Norms Shape Economic Conflict in Russia*. Cambridge University Press.

Frye, T., Reuter, O. J., and Szakonyi, D. (2014). Political machines at work: Voter mobilization and electoral subversion in the workplace. *World Politics*, 66(2):195–228.

Frye, T., Reuter, O. J., and Szakonyi, D. (2017). Vote brokers, clientelist appeals, and voter turnout: Evidence from Russia and Venezuela. Working paper, Social Science Research Network. papers.ssrn.com/sol3/papers.cfm?abstract_id=2901586. Last accessed July 30, 2019.

Fu, D. (2017a). Disguised collective action in China. *Comparative Political Studies*, 50(4):499–527.

Fu, D. (2017b). Fragmented control: Governing contentious labor organizations in china. *Governance*, 30(3):445–462.

Fu, D. (2017c). *Mobilizing without the Masses: Control and Contention in China*. Cambridge University Press.

Gallagher, M. (2004). The limits of civil society in a late Leninist state. In Alagappa, M., ed., *Civil Society and Political Change in Asia: Expanding and Contracting Democratic Space*, pages 419–52. Stanford University Press.

Gallagher, M. and Miller, B. (2018). The progression of repression: When does online censorship move to real world repression? Working Paper, Department of Political Science, University of Michigan.

Gandhi, J. and Przeworski, A. (2007). Authoritarian institutions and the survival of autocrats. *Comparative Political Studies*, 40(11):1279–1301.

Gans-Morse, J. (2017). *Property Rights in Post-Soviet Russia: Violence, Corruption, and the Demand for Law*. Cambridge University Press.

Geddes, B., Wright, J., and Frantz, E. (2018). *How Dictatorships Work: Power, Personalization, and Collapse*. Cambridge University Press.

Gehlbach, S. and Keefer, P. (2011). Investment without democracy: Ruling-party institutionalization and credible commitment in autocracies. *Journal of Comparative Economics*, 39(2):123–139.

Graham, B. (1967). Billy Graham on Social Injustice. https://billygraham.org/story/billy-graham-on-social-injustice/. Accessed May 21, 2018.

Gramsci, A. (1971). *Selections from the Prison Notebooks*. Lawrence and Wishart London. Translated by Quintin Hoare and Geoffrey Nowell Smith.

Grant, B. and Idema, W. L. (2011). *Escape from Blood Pond Hell: The Tales of Mulian and Woman Huang*. University of Washington Press.

Greenhalgh, S. (2008). *Just One Child: Science and Policy in Deng's China*. University of California Press.

Greenhalgh, S. and Winckler, E. A. (2005). *Governing China's Population: From Leninist to Neoliberal Biopolitics*. Stanford University Press.

Greitens, S. C. (2016). *Dictators and Their Secret Police: Coercive Institutions and State Violence*. Cambridge University Press.

Greitens, S. C. (2017). Rethinking China's coercive capacity: An examination of PRC domestic security spending, 1992–2012. *The China Quarterly*, 232:1002–1025.

Greskovits, B. (2017). Rebuilding the Hungarian right through civil organization and contention: The Civic Circles movement. Working Paper, Robert Schuman Centre for Advanced Studies, European University Institute.

Greskovits, B. and Wittenberg, J. (2013). Civil society and democratic consolidation in Hungary in the 1990s and 2000s. Council for European Studies. Twentieth International Conference of Europeanists, Amsterdam.

Grossman, S. (2019). The politics of order in informal markets: Evidence from Lagos. *World Politics*, forthcoming.

Grzymala-Busse, A. (2015). *Nations under God: How Churches Use Moral Authority to Influence Policy*. Princeton University Press.

Grzymala-Busse, A. (2016). Weapons of the meek: How churches influence public policy. *World Politics*, 68(01):1–36.

Hainmueller, J. (2012). Entropy balancing for causal effects: A multivariate reweighting method to produce balanced samples in observational studies. *Political Analysis*, 20(1):25–46.

Hainmueller, J., Hopkins, D., and Yamamoto, T. (2014). Causal inference in conjoint analysis: Understanding multidimensional choices via stated preference experiments. *Political Analysis*, 22(1):1–30.

Hainmueller, J. and Xu, Y. (2011). Ebalance: A Stata package for entropy balancing.

Han, R. (2018). *Contesting Cyberspace in China: Online Expression and Authoritarian Resilience*. Columbia University Press.

Handlin, S. (2016). State-mobilized contention in Bolivarian Venezuela: Threats, arenas, and evolution of state-mobilized organizations. Paper Prepared for Workshop "State Mobilized Contention: The State-Protest Movement Nexus," Harvard University.

Harari, Y. N. (2014). *Sapiens: A Brief History of Humankind*. Random House.

Hassan, M. (2017). The strategic shuffle: Ethnic geography, the internal security apparatus, and elections in Kenya. *American Journal of Political Science*, 61(2):382–395.

Havel, V. (1978). The Power of the Powerless. *East European Politics and Societies*, 32(2), 353–408.

He, S. and Xue, D. (2014). Identity building and communal resistance against landgrabs in Wukan village, China. *Current Anthropology*, 55(S9):S126–S137.

He, X. and Tong, Z. (2002). A three-level analysis on the structure of village power: Also on the post-election legitimacy of village power. *Social Sciences in China*, 1:014.

Hegel, G. W. F. (1991). *Hegel: Elements of the Philosophy of Right*. Cambridge University Press.

Helmke, G. and Levitsky, S. (2004). Informal institutions and comparative politics: A research agenda. *Perspectives on Politics*, 2(04):725–740.

Henley, J. (2018). Putin takes icy plunge to mark Russian Orthodox Epiphany. *The Guardian*. www.theguardian.com/world/2018/jan/19/vladimir-putin-takes-icy-plunge-to-mark-orthodox-epiphany. Last accessed January 13, 2019.

Herbst, J. (2000). *States and Power in Africa: Comparative Lessons in Authority and Control*. Princeton University Press.

Hesketh, T., Lu, L., and Xing, Z. W. (2005). The effect of China's one-child family policy after 25 years. *New England Journal of Medicine*, 353(11):1171–1176.

Hesketh, T. and Zhu, W. X. (1997). Health in China: The one child family policy: The good, the bad, and the ugly. *BMJ: British Medical Journal*, 314(7095):1685.

Heurlin, C. (2016). *Responsive Authoritarianism in China: Land, Protests and Policymaking*. Cambridge University Press.

Holland, A. C. (2014). The distributive politics of enforcement. *American Journal of Political Science*, 59(2):357–371.

Holland, A. C. (2016). Forbearance. *American Political Science Review*, 110(02):232–246.

Honig, L. (2015). Land, state-building, and political authority in Senegal. Working paper, Cornell University Department of Government.

Honig, L. (2017). Selecting the state or choosing the chief? The political determinants of smallholder land titling. *World Development*, 100:94–107.

Horsley, J. (2018). China's Orwellian social credit score isn't real. *Foreign Policy*. https://foreignpolicy.com/2018/11/16/Chinas-orwellian-social-credit-score-isnt-real/. Last accessed February 13, 2019.

Hou, Y. (2013). The role of religious force in the Wukan incident. *The China Nonprofit Review*, 5(1):155–175.

Hou, Y. (2019). *The Private Sector in Public Office: Selective Property Rights in China*. Cambridge University Press.

Hsiao, K.-c. (1960). *Rural China: Imperial Control in the Nineteenth Century*. University of Washington.

Hsing, Y.-t. (2010). *The Great Urban Transformation: Politics of Land and Property in China*. Oxford University Press.

Hu, J., Wu, T., and Fei, J. (2018). Flexible governance in China: Affective care, petition social workers, and multi-pronged means of dispute resolution. *Asian Survey*, 58(4):679–703.

Huang, P. C. (2008). Centralized minimalism: Semiformal governance by quasi officials and dispute resolution in China. *Modern China*, 34(1):9–35.

Huntington, S. P. (1968). *Political Order in Changing Societies*. Yale University Press.

Huntington, S. P. (1993). *The Third Wave: Democratization in the Late Twentieth Century*, volume 4. University of Oklahoma Press.

Jamal, A. A. (2009). *Barriers to Democracy: The Other Side of Social Capital in Palestine and the Arab World*. Princeton University Press.

Jameson, E. C. (1922). Billy Sunday keeps his promise and "fixes" bird who plans to destroy American institutions. *The Charleston Daily Mail (West Virginia)*.

Jiang, J. and Yang, D. L. (2016). Lying or believing? Measuring preference falsification from a political purge in China. *Comparative Political Studies*, 49(5):600–634.

Jing, J. (1998). *The Temple of Memories: History, Power, and Morality in a Chinese Village*. Stanford University Press.

Johnson, I. (2018a). Pastor charged with "inciting subversion" as China cracks down on churches. *The New York Times*. www.nytimes.com/2018/12/13/world/asia/China-religion-crackdown.html. Last accessed January 13, 2019.

Johnson, I. (2018b). *The Souls of China: The Return of Religion after Mao*. Vintage.

Johnson, I. (2019). How the state is co-opting religion in China. *Foreign Affairs*. www.foreignaffairs.com/articles/China/2019-01-07/how-state-co-opting-religion-China. Last accessed January 13, 2019.

Kasara, K. (2007). Tax me if you can: Ethnic geography, democracy, and the taxation of agriculture in Africa. *American Political Science Review*, 101(1):159–172.

Kelliher, D. (1992). *Peasant Power in China: The Era of Rural Reform, 1979–1989*. Yale University Press.

Kelliher, D. (1997). The Chinese debate over village self-government. *China Journal*, (37):63.

Kennedy, J. J. (2013). Finance and rural governance: Centralization and local challenges. *Journal of Peasant Studies*, 40(6):1009–1026.

Kennedy, S. (2009). *The Business of Lobbying in China*. Harvard University Press.

Kingsley, P. (2018). How Viktor Orban bends Hungarian society to his will. *The New York Times*. www.nytimes.com/2018/03/27/world/europe/viktor-orban-hungary.html. Last accessed February 9, 2019.

Kong, S. T. and Unger, J. (2013). Egalitarian redistributions of agricultural land in China through community consensus: Findings from two surveys. *China Journal*, (69):1–19.

Kopecký, P. and Mudde, C. (2003). Rethinking civil society. *Democratization*, 10(3):1–14.

Kosfeld, M. and Rustagi, D. (2015). Leader punishment and cooperation in groups: Experimental field evidence from commons management in Ethiopia. *American Economic Review*, 105(2):747–783.

Koss, D. (2018). *Where the Party Rules: The Rank and File of China's Communist State*. Cambridge University Press.

Koss, D. and Sato, H. (2016). A micro-geography of state extractive power: The case of rural China. *Studies in Comparative International Development*, 51(4):389–410.

Kuo, L. (2018). UK confirms reports of Chinese mass internment camps for Uighur Muslims. *The Guardian*. www.theguardian.com/world/2018/oct/31/uk-believes-china-has-interned-about-1-million-uighur-muslims. Last accessed February 9, 2019.

Kuran, T. (1991). Now out of never: The element of surprise in the East European revolution of 1989. *World Politics*, 44(01):7–48.

Landry, P. F. (2008). *Decentralized Authoritarianism in China: The Communist Party's Control of Local Elites in the Post-Mao Era*. New York: Cambridge University Press.

Landry, P. F., Davis, D., and Wang, S. (2010). Elections in rural China: Competition without parties. *Comparative Political Studies*, 43(6):763–790.

Lee, A., Schultz, K. A., et al. (2012). Comparing British and French colonial legacies: A discontinuity analysis of Cameroon. *Quarterly Journal of Political Science*, 7(4):365–410.

Lee, C. K. (2007). *Against the Law: Labor Protests in China's Rustbelt and Sunbelt*. University of California Press.

Levi, M. (1989). *Of Rule and Revenue*. University of California Press.

Li, J. and Zhao, X. (2018). Promoting villager small group autonomy and innovating grassroots social governance (*Tuixing cunmin xiaozu zizhi chuangxin jiceng shehui zhili*). Nanjing Municipal Committee for Agriculture and Industry. http://nc.nanjing.gov.cn/qyjj/201805/t20180518_5401003.html. Last accessed February 7, 2017.

Li, L. and O'Brien, K. J. (2008). Protest leadership in rural China. *The China Quarterly*, 193:1–23.

Lieberman, E. S. (2003). *Race and Regionalism in the Politics of Taxation in Brazil and South Africa*. Cambridge University Press.

Lin, J. Y. (1988). The household responsibility system in China's agricultural reform: A theoretical and empirical study. *Economic Development and Cultural Change*, 36(S3):S199–S224.

Linz, J. J. (1996). *Crisis, Breakdown, and Reequilibration*. Johns Hopkins University Press.

Linz, J. J. and Stepan, A. (1996). *Problems of Democratic Transition and Consolidation: Southern Europe, South America, and Post-Communist Europe*. Johns Hopkins University Press.

Liu, H. (2017). Five concepts for doing good religious work under new circumstances (Zuo hao xin xingshi xia zongjiao gongzuo yao shuli wu zhong
guannian). *China United Front Magazine (Zhongguo Tongyizhanxian)*.

Liu, X., Li, Z., and Chang, B. (2018). Grassroots party building
leads rural revitalization (*Jiceng dangjian yinling xiangcun zhenxing*).
Guangxi Daily (Guangxi Ribao). www.zytzb.gov.cn/tzb2010/S1824/201804/
4df46758ca5d4e4e90ddfd6439d099e2.shtml. Last accessed February 13,
2019.

Lorentzen, P. (2013). Regularizing rioting: Permitting public protest in
an authoritarian regime. *Quarterly Journal of Political Science*, 8(2):
127–158.

Lorentzen, P. (2014). China's strategic censorship. *American Journal of Political
Science*, 58(2):402–414.

Lorentzen, P. (2017). *China's Controlled Burn: Information Management and
State-Society Relations under Authoritarianism*. Unpublished Manuscript,
Department of Economics, University of San Francisco.

Lü, X. and Landry, P. F. (2014). Show me the money: Interjurisdiction political
competition and fiscal extraction in China. *American Political Science Review*,
108(03):706–722.

Luo, Q. and Andreas, J. (2016). Using religion to resist rural dispossession: A case
study of a Hui Muslim community in north-west China. *The China Quarterly*,
226: 477–498.

Luo, R., Zhang, L., Huang, J., and Rozelle, S. (2007). Elections, fiscal reform
and public goods provision in rural China. *Journal of Comparative Economics*,
35(3):583–611.

Lust-Okar, E. (2006). Elections under authoritarianism: Preliminary lessons from
Jordan. *Democratization*, 13(3):456–471.

Lynch, M. (2011). After Egypt: The limits and promise of online challenges to
the authoritarian Arab state. *Perspectives on Politics*, 9(2):301–310.

Macinnes, A. I. (1988). Scottish Gaeldom: The first phase of clearance. In Devine,
T. and Mitchison, R., editors, *People and Society in Scotland, Volume 1, 1760–
1830*, pp. 70–90. John Donald Publishers.

Madsen, R. (1984). *Morality and Power in a Chinese Village*. University of
California Press.

Malesky, E. and Schuler, P. (2010). Nodding or needling: Analyzing delegate
responsiveness in an authoritarian parliament. *American Political Science
Review*, 104(03):482–502.

Malesky, E. and Schuler, P. (2011). The single-party dictator's dilemma: Information in elections without opposition. *Legislative Studies Quarterly*, 36(4):491–
530.

Manion, M. (2006). Democracy, community, trust: The impact of elections in
rural China. *Comparative Political Studies*, 39(3):301–324.

Manion, M. (2014). "Good types" in authoritarian elections: The selectoral connection in Chinese local congresses. *Comparative Political Studies*, 50(3):362–
394.

Mann, M. (1984). The autonomous power of the state: Its origins, mechanisms
and results. *European Journal of Sociology*, 25(02):185–213.

Mann, M. (2012). *The Sources of Social Power: Global Empires and Revolution, 1890–1945*, volume 3. Cambridge University Press.

Mares, I. and Zhu, B. (2015). The production of electoral intimidation: Economic and political incentives. *Comparative Politics*, 48(1):23–43.

Markus, S. (2015). *Property, Predation, and Protection: Piranha Capitalism in Russia and Ukraine*. Cambridge University Press.

Martinez-Bravo, M., Padro-i Miquel, G., Qian, N., and Yao, Y. (2011). Political reform in China: Elections, public goods and income distribution. Presented at the CEPR/AMID/BREAD Conference, Paris.

Matsuzaki, R. (2019a). State building amid resistance: Administrative intermediaries and the making of colonial Taiwan. *Polity*, 51(2):231–260.

Matsuzaki, R. (2019b). *Statebuilding by Imposition: Resistance and Control in Colonial Taiwan and the Philippines*. Cornell University Press.

Mattingly, D. C. (2017). Colonial legacies and state institutions in China: Evidence from a natural experiment. *Comparative Political Studies*, 50(4): 434–463.

Mattingly, D. C. (2016). Elite capture: How decentralization and informal institutions weaken property rights in China. *World Politics*, 68(03):383–412.

Mattingly, D. C. (2020). Responsive or repressive? How frontline bureaucrats enforce the One Child Policy in China. *Comparative Politics*, 52(2).

McElroy, M. and Yang, D. T. (2000). Carrots and sticks: Fertility effects of China's population policies. *The American Economic Review*, 90(2):389–392.

Meek, J. (1999). Russian Patriarch "was KGB spy." *Forbes*. www.theguardian .com/world/1999/feb/12/1. Last accessed February 9, 2019.

Mertha, A. C. (2008). *China's Water Warriors: Citizen Action and Policy Change*. Cornell University Press.

Migdal, J. S. (1988). *Strong Societies and Weak States: State-Society Relations and State Capabilities in the Third World*. Princeton University Press.

Ministry of Land and Resources. (2014). *Chinese Land Resources Report 2013 (Zhongguo Guotu Ziyuan Gongbao)*. www.mnr.gov.cn/sj/tjgb/201807/ P020180704391899436702.pdf. Last accessed July 30, 2019.

Montgomery, J. M., Nyhan, B., and Torres, M. (2016). How conditioning on post-treatment variables can ruin your experiment and what to do about it. Annual meeting of the Midwest Political Science Association, Chicago, IL, April.

Murtazashvili, J. B. (2016). *Informal Order and the State in Afghanistan*. Cambridge University Press.

National Bureau of Statistics of the People's Republic of China (2004–2016). 中国国土资源统计年鉴. *China Land and Natural Resources Statistical Yearbooks, 2004–2016*.

National Bureau of Statistics of the People's Republic of China (1983). *Statistical Yearbook of China, 1983* (中国统计年鉴 1983).

National Bureau of Statistics of the People's Republic of China (2009). *Statistical Yearbook of China, 2008* (中国统计年鉴 2008). www.stats.gov.cn/tjsj/ndsj/ 2009/indexch.htm, Last accessed July 23, 2019.

Newland, S. A. (2016). Which public? Whose goods? What we know (and what we don't) about public goods in rural China. *The China Quarterly*, 228:881.

Nugent, E. R. and Berman, C. E. (2017). Ctrl-alt-revolt? *Middle East Law and Governance*, 10(1):59–90.

Nylan, M., editor. (2014). *The Analects* (Norton Critical Editions). WW Norton & Company.

Oates, R. (2012). Puritans and the "Monarchical Republic": Conformity and conflict in the Elizabethan church. *The English Historical Review*, 127(527):819–843.

O'Brien, K. J. (1994). Implementing political reform in China's villages. *The Australian Journal of Chinese Affairs*, pages 33–59.

O'Brien, K. J. and Deng, Y. (2015a). The reach of the state: Work units, family ties and "harmonious demolition." *The China Journal*, 74:1–17.

O'Brien, K. J. and Deng, Y. (2015b). Repression backfires: Tactical radicalization and protest spectacle in rural China. *Journal of Contemporary China*, 24(93):457–470.

O'Brien, K. J. and Han, R. (2009). Path to democracy? Assessing village elections in China. *Journal of Contemporary China*, 18(60):359–378.

O'Brien, K. J. and Li, L. (1995). The politics of lodging complaints in rural China. *The China Quarterly*, 143:756–783.

O'Brien, K. J. and Li, L. (1999). Selective policy implementation in rural China. *Comparative Politics*, 31(2):167–186.

O'Brien, K. J. and Li, L. (2000). Accommodating "democracy" in a one-party state: Introducing village elections in China. *The China Quarterly*, 162:465–489.

O'Brien, K. J. and Li, L. (2006). *Rightful Resistance in Rural China*. Cambridge University Press.

Oi, J. C. (1991). *State and Peasant in Contemporary China: The Political Economy of Village Government*. University of California Press.

Oi, J. C., Babiarz, K. S., Zhang, L., Luo, R., and Rozelle, S. (2012). Shifting fiscal control to limit cadre power in China's townships and villages. *The China Quarterly*, 211:649–675.

Oi, J. C. and Rozelle, S. (2000). Elections and power: The locus of decision-making in Chinese villages. *The China Quarterly*, 162:513–539.

Ong, L. (2014). State-led urbanization in China: Skyscrapers, land revenue and "concentrated villages." *The China Quarterly*.

Ong, L. (2018). Thugs and outsourcing of state repression in China. *The China Journal*, 80(1):94–110.

Osnos, E. (2015). Born red. *The New Yorker*, 91(7):42–55.

Ostrom, E. (1990). *Governing the Commons: The Evolution of Institutions for Collective Action*. Cambridge University Press.

Padró i Miquel, G., Qian, N., Xu, Y., and Yao, Y. (2015). Making democracy work: Culture, social capital and elections in China. Working paper, Social Science Research Network. papers.ssrn.com/sol3/papers.cfm?abstract_id=2590221. Last accessed July 30, 2019.

Paik, W. and Lee, K. (2012). I want to be expropriated!: The politics of *xiaochanquanfang* land development in suburban China. *Journal of Contemporary China*, 21(74):261–279.

Pan, J. (2018). *Hush Money: How China's Use of Welfare and Surveillance to Prevent Collective Action Backfires.* Unpublished manuscript.

Parish, W. L. (1985). *Chinese Rural Development: The Great Transformation.* ME Sharpe.

Pastor, R. A. and Tan, Q. (2000). The meaning of China's village elections. *The China Quarterly,* 162:490–512.

Pearson, M. M. (1994). The Janus face of business associations in China: Socialist corporatism in foreign enterprises. *The Australian Journal of Chinese Affairs,* (31):25–46.

Pearson, M. M. (2000). *China's New Business Elite: The Political Consequences of Economic Reform.* University of California Press.

Pepinsky, T. B., Pierskalla, J., and Sacks, A. (2017). Bureaucracy in the developing world. *Annual Review of Political Science,* 20(1):249–268.

Perry, E. J. (1980). *Rebels and Revolutionaries in North China, 1845–1945.* Stanford University Press.

Perry, E. J. (2002). *Challenging the Mandate of Heaven: Social Protest and State Power in China.* ME Sharpe.

Pertsev, A. (2017). President and Patriarch: What Putin wants from the Orthodox Church. Carnegie Moscow Center. https://carnegie.ru/commentary/75058. Last accessed January 13, 2019.

Pierskalla, J. H. (2010). Protest, deterrence, and escalation: The strategic calculus of government repression. *Journal of Conflict Resolution,* 54(1):117–145.

Popkin, S. L. (1979). *The Rational Peasant: The Political Economy of Rural Society in Vietnam.* University of California Press.

Portes, A. (1998). Social capital: Its origins and applications in modern sociology. *Annual Review of Sociology,* 24(1):1–24.

Posner, D. N. (2005). *Institutions and Ethnic Politics in Africa.* Cambridge University Press.

Potter, S. H. and Potter, J. M. (1990). *China's Peasants: The Anthropology of a Revolution.* Cambridge University Press.

Przeworski, A. and Teune, H. (1970). *The Logic of Comparative Social Inquiry.* Wiley-Interscience.

Putnam, R. D. (1994). *Making Democracy Work: Civic Traditions in Modern Italy.* Princeton University Press.

Putnam, R. D. (2000). *Bowling Alone: The Collapse and Revival of American Community.* Simon & Schuster, New York.

Rae, D. W. (2008). *City: Urbanism and Its End.* Yale University Press.

Read, B. L. (2000). Revitalizing the state's urban "nerve tips." *The China Quarterly,* 163:806–820.

Read, B. L. (2003). Democratizing the neighbourhood? New private housing and home-owner self-organization in urban China. *The China Journal,* (49):31–59.

Read, B. L. (2007). Assessing variation in civil society organizations: China's homeowner associations in comparative perspective. *Comparative Political Studies,* 41(9):1240–1265.

Read, B. L. (2012). *Roots of the State: Neighborhood Organization and Social Networks in Beijing and Taipei.* Stanford University Press.

Richards, J. F. (1996). *The Mughal Empire.* Cambridge University Press.

Rithmire, M. (2015). *Land Bargains and Chinese Capitalism: The Politics of Property Rights under Reform*. Cambridge University Press.

Ritter, E. H. and Conrad, C. R. (2016). Preventing and responding to dissent: The observational challenges of explaining strategic repression. *American Political Science Review*, 110(1):85–99.

Roberts, M. E. (2018). *Censored: Distraction and Diversion Inside China's Great Firewall*. Princeton University Press.

Robles, F. (2018). "We are Nicaragua": Students revolt, but now face a more daunting task. *The New York Times*. www.nytimes.com/2018/04/27/world/americas/nicaragua-students-protest.html. Last accessed July 30, 2019.

Satter, D. (2009). Putin runs the Russian state – and the Russian church too. *Forbes*. www.forbes.com/2009/02/20/putin-solzhenitsyn-kirill-russia-opinions-contributors_orthodox_church.html. Last accessed on February 9, 2019.

Satyanath, S., Voigtländer, N., and Voth, H.-J. (2017). Bowling for fascism: Social capital and the rise of the Nazi Party. *Journal of Political Economy*, 125(2):478–526.

Schurmann, F. (1966). *Ideology and Organization in Communist China*. University of California Press.

Scoggins, S. E. and O'Brien, K. J. (2016). China's unhappy police. *Asian Survey*, 56(2):225–242.

Scott, J. C. (1977). *The Moral Economy of the Peasant: Rebellion and Subsistence in Southeast Asia*. Yale University Press.

Scott, J. C. (1998). *Seeing like a State: How Certain Schemes to Improve the Human Condition Have Failed*. Yale University Press.

Shaanxi People's Publishing House. (2018). *Liangjiahe*. Excerpt of chapter "*Yongyuan de Caifu*" www.thepaper.cn/newsDetail_forward_2805832. Last accessed February 6, 2019.

Shih, V., Adolph, C., and Liu, M. (2012). Getting ahead in the Communist Party: Explaining the advancement of Central Committee members in China. *American Political Science Review*, 106(01):166–187.

Shue, V. (1988). *The Reach of the State: Sketches of the Chinese Body Politic*. Stanford University Press.

Singh, P. (2015). *How Solidarity Works for Welfare: Subnationalism and Social Development in India*. Cambridge University Press.

Siu, H. F. (1989). *Agents and Victims in South China: Accomplices in Rural Revolution*. Yale University Press.

Slater, D. (2009). Revolutions, crackdowns, and quiescence: Communal elites and democratic mobilization in Southeast Asia. *American Journal of Sociology*, 115(1):203–254.

Slater, D. (2010). *Ordering Power: Contentious Politics and Authoritarian Leviathans in Southeast Asia*. Cambridge University Press.

Smith, A. H. (2004). *Village Life in China: A Study in Sociology*. FH Revell Company.

Snow, E. (1961). *Red Star over China*. Grove Press.

Starr, C. (2016). Wang Yi and the 95 theses of the Chinese reformed church. *Religions*, 7(12):142.

Stepan, A. C. (1978). *The State and Society: Peru in Comparative Perspective*. Princeton University Press.

Stone, C. N. (1989). *Regime Politics: Governing Atlanta, 1946–1988*. University Press of Kansas.

Straus, S. (2013). *The Order of Genocide: Race, Power, and War in Rwanda*. Cornell University Press.

Sun, X. (2014). Autocrats' dilemma: The dual impacts of village elections on public opinion in China. *China Journal*, (71):109–131.

Sun, X. (2015). Selective enforcement of land regulations: Why large-scale violators succeed. *China Journal*, (74):66–90.

Sun, X., Warner, T. J., Yang, D. L., and Liu, M. (2013). Patterns of authority and governance in rural China: Who's in charge? Why? *Journal of Contemporary China*, 22(83):733–754.

Svolik, M. W. (2012). *The Politics of Authoritarian Rule*. Cambridge University Press.

Szonyi, M. (2017). *The Art of Being Governed: Everyday Politics in Late Imperial China*. Princeton University Press.

Tang, J. (1996). Contemporary rural China's clan revival (*dangdai zhongguo jiazu fuxing de Beijingg*). *Social Science Research (Shehuixue Yanjiu)*, 2:24.

Tarrow, S. (2010). The strategy of paired comparison: Toward a theory of practice. *Comparative Political Studies*, 43(2):230–259.

Teets, J. C. (2014). *Civil Society under Authoritarianism: The China Model*. Cambridge University Press.

Tendler, J. and Freedheim, S. (1994). Trust in a rent-seeking world: Health and government transformed in northeast brazil. *World Development*, 22(12):1771–1791.

Tilly, C. (1990). *Coercion, Capital, and European States, AD 990–1992*. Wiley-Blackwell.

Tilly, C. (2003). *The Politics of Collective Violence*. Cambridge University Press.

Tomba, L. (2014). *The Government Next Door: Neighborhood Politics in Urban China*. Cornell University Press.

Torres, P. and Casey, N. (2017). Armed civilian bands in Venezuela prop up unpopular president. *The New York Times*. www.nytimes.com/2017/04/22/world/americas/armed-civilian-bands-in-venezuela-prop-up-unpopular-president.html. Last accessed May 29, 2018.

Truex, R. (2016). *Making Autocracy Work: Representation and Responsiveness in Modern China*. Cambridge University Press.

Truex, R. (2018). Focal points, dissident calendars, and preemptive repression. *Journal of Conflict Resolution*, 63(4):1032–1052.

Tsai, L. L. (2002). Cadres, temple and lineage institutions, and governance in rural China. *The China Journal*, (48):1–27.

Tsai, L. L. (2007a). *Accountability without Democracy: Solidarity Groups and Public Goods Provision in Rural China*. Cambridge University Press.

Tsai, L. L. (2007b). Solidary groups, informal accountability, and local public goods provision in rural China. *American Political Science Review*, 101(02):355–372.

Tyler, T. R. (1998). Trust and democratic governance. In Braithwaite, V. and Levi, M., editors, *Trust and Governance*, pages 269–294. Russell Sage Foundation.

Tyler, T. R. (2006). *Why People Obey the Law*. Princeton University Press.

Tyler, T. R. and Degoey, P. (1996). Trust in organizational authorities. In Tyler, T. R. and Kramer, R. M., editors, *Trust in Organizations: Frontiers of Theory and Research*, pages 331–356. Sage Publications.

Unger, J. (1989). State and peasant in post-revolution China. *The Journal of Peasant Studies*, 17(1):114–136.

Unger, J. (1998). Cultural revolution conflict in the villages. *The China Quarterly*, 153:82–106.

Unger, J. (2012). Continuity and change in rural China's organization. In Bislev, A. and Thøgersen, S., editors, *Organizing Rural China*, pages 15–34. Lexington Books.

United Front Work Department and Xinhua News Agency (2011). The best region for governance and clan management (*Zhengquan yu zongzu guanli de zui jia quyu*). www.zytzb.gov.cn/tzb2010/S18210/201105/261ca2e5219949ce91da7e3bef1322c1.shtml. Last accessed February 6, 2019.

United Front Work Department of Yunnan Province (2018). Builds a grassroots united front network system in Longyang district (*Longyangqu jiji goujian jiceng tongzhan gongzuo wangluo tixi*). Technical report. www.zytzb.gov.cn/tzdkt/294183.jhtml. Last accessed February 13, 2019.

Vermeer, E. B. (1982). Income differentials in rural China. *The China Quarterly*, 89:1–33.

Wagner, T. E. and Obermiller, P. J. (2011). A double-edged sword: Social control in Appalachian company towns. In Brunn, S. D., editor, *Engineering Earth*, pages 1917–1935. Springer.

Walder, A. G. (1988). *Communist Neo-traditionalism: Work and Authority in Chinese Industry*. University of California Press.

Wang, H. (1991). Lineage Culture in Contemporary China. (*Dangdai Zhongguo Cunluo Jiazu Wenhua*). Shanghai People's Publishers (*Shanghai Renmin Chubanshe*).

Wang, Y. (2014). *Tying the Autocrat's Hands: The Rise of the Rule of Law in China*. Cambridge University Press.

Wang, Y. (2018). A single spark can ignite the fight against poverty in Hunan: Research on the democratic supervision work of poverty alleviation (*Zhuran hunan tuopin gongjian de "xingxing zhi huo" – min jin zhongyang kaizhan tuopin gongjian minzhu jiandu gongzuo diaoyan ceji*). *Newspaper of the Chinese People's Political Consultative Conference Renmin Zhengxie Bao*. www.zytzb.gov.cn/tzb2010/lzjz/201711/8f63ed8e5cb34cf1a3625fd34f6f8c48.shtml. Last accessed February 13, 2019.

Wang, Y. and Minzner, C. (2015). The rise of the Chinese security state. *The China Quarterly*, 222:339–359.

Watson, J. L. (1982). Chinese kinship reconsidered: Anthropological perspectives on historical research. *The China Quarterly*, 92(2):589–622.

White, T. (2006). *China's Longest Campaign: Birth Planning in the People's Republic, 1949–2005.* Cornell University Press.

Whiting, S. (2004). The cadre evaluation system at the grass roots: The paradox of party rule. In Naughton, B. and Yang D. L., editors, *Holding China Together: Diversity and National Integration in the Post-Deng Era*, pages 101–119. Cambridge University Press.

Whiting, S. (2006). *Power and Wealth in Rural China: The Political Economy of Institutional Change.* Cambridge University Press.

Whiting, S. (2011). Values in land: Fiscal pressures, land disputes and justice claims in rural and peri-urban China. *Urban Studies*, 48(3):569–587.

Whyte, M. K., Feng, W., and Cai, Y. (2015). Challenging myths about China's One-Child Policy. *China Journal*, (74):144–159.

Wibbels, E., Krishna, A., and Sriram, M. (2016). Satellites, slums and social networks: Evidence on the origins and consequences of property rights from 157 slums in Bangalore. Working Paper, Department of Political Science, Duke University. pdfs.semanticscholar.org/4b13/48642af21a0da57db9cc9de8e4cc110f8f85.pdf. Last accessed July 30, 2019.

Wilfahrt, M. (2018a). The politics of local government performance: Elite cohesion and cross-village constraints in decentralized Senegal. *World Development*, 103:149–161.

Wilfahrt, M. (2018b). Precolonial legacies and institutional congruence in public goods delivery: Evidence from decentralized West Africa. *World Politics*, 70(2):239–274.

Wintrobe, R. (1998). *The Political Economy of Dictatorship.* Cambridge University Press.

Wolbrecht, C. and Campbell, D. E. (2007). Leading by example: Female members of parliament as political role models. *American Journal of Political Science*, 51(4):921–939.

Wong, E. (2012). New Communist Party chief in China denounces corruption in speech. *The New York Times.* www.nytimes.com/2012/11/20/world/asia/new-communist-party-chief-in-China-denounces-corruption.html. Last accessed February 13, 2019.

Xie, R. (2015). Recommendations for striking hard against unlawful clan activity (*Guanyu Yanzhong Daji Weifa Zongzu Huodong de Jianyi*). Technical report, United Front Work Department of the CPC Central Committee and China National Democratic Construction Association. www.zytzb.gov.cn/jcjyxd/272956.jhtml. Last accessed February 6, 2019.

Xie, Y. and Hu, J. (2014). An introduction to the China Family Panel Studies (CFPS). *Chinese Sociological Review*, 47(1):3–29.

Xie, Y. and Zhou, X. (2014). Income inequality in today's China. *Proceedings of the National Academy of Sciences*, 111(19):6928–6933.

Xu, B. (2017). *The Politics of Compassion: The Sichuan Earthquake and Civic Engagement in China.* Stanford University Press.

Xu, Y. and Yao, Y. (2015). Informal institutions, collective action, and public investment in rural China. *American Political Science Review*, 109(02): 371–391.

Yan, X. (2012). "To get rich is not only glorious": Economic reform and the new entrepreneurial Party Secretaries. *The China Quarterly*, 210:335–354.

Yang, C. K. (1961). *Religion in Chinese Society: A Study of Contemporary Social Functions of Religion and Some of their Historical Factors*. University of California Press.

Yang, D. L. (1998). *Calamity and Reform in China: State, Rural Society, and Institutional Change since the Great Leap Famine*. Stanford University Press.

Yang, S. and Liu, X. (2000). Some theoretical issues with recent research on rural China's lineage groups (Jinqi zhongguo nongcun jiazu yanjiu de ruogan lilun wenti). *China Social Science (Zhongguo Shehui Kexue)*, 5:83–90.

Zhang, W. (1999). Implementation of state family planning programmes in a northern Chinese village. *The China Quarterly*, 157:202–230.

Zhao, D. (2009). The Mandate of Heaven and performance legitimation in historical and contemporary China. *American Behavioral Scientist*, 53(3):416–433.

Zhenglin, G. and Bernstein, T. P. (2004). The impact of elections on the village structure of power: The relations between the village committees and the party branches. *Journal of Contemporary China*, 13(39):257–275.

Zhou, H. (2018). Igniting the "two types of village" growth engine. (jizhi chuangxin dianran "liang xing xiangcun" fazhan yinqing). Chenzhou Reform and Development Commission. http://fgw.czs.gov.cn/fzggdt/lxsh/content_777632.html. Last accessed February 14, 2019.

Zhou, K. X. et al. (1996). *How the Farmers Changed China: Power of the People*. Westview Press.

Zhu, J. (2005). A transitional institution for the emerging land market in urban China. *Urban Studies*, 42(8):1369–1390.

Index

Other Books in the Series (*continued from page ii*)

Laia Balcells, *Rivalry and Revenge: The Politics of Violence during Civil War*
Lisa Baldez, *Why Women Protest? Women's Movements in Chile*
Kate Baldwin, *The Paradox of Traditional Chiefs in Democratic Africa*
Stefano Bartolini, *The Political Mobilization of the European Left, 1860–1980: The Class Cleavage*
Robert Bates, *When Things Fell Apart: State Failure in Late-Century Africa*
Mark Beissinger, *Nationalist Mobilization and the Collapse of the Soviet State*
Pablo Beramendi, *The Political Geography of Inequality: Regions and Redistribution*
Nancy Bermeo, ed., *Unemployment in the New Europe*
Carles Boix, *Democracy and Redistribution*
Carles Boix, *Political Order and Inequality: Their Foundations and their Consequences for Human Welfare*
Carles Boix, *Political Parties, Growth, and Equality: Conservative and Social Democratic Economic Strategies in the World Economy*
Catherine Boone, *Merchant Capital and the Roots of State Power in Senegal, 1930–1985*
Catherine Boone, *Political Topographies of the African State: Territorial Authority and Institutional Change*
Catherine Boone, *Property and Political Order in Africa: Land Rights and the Structure of Politics*
Michael Bratton and Nicolas van de Walle, *Democratic Experiments in Africa: Regime Transitions in Comparative Perspective*
Michael Bratton, Robert Mattes, and E. Gyimah-Boadi, *Public Opinion, Democracy, and Market Reform in Africa*
Valerie Bunce, *Leaving Socialism and Leaving the State: The End of Yugoslavia, the Soviet Union, and Czechoslovakia*
Daniele Caramani, *The Nationalization of Politics: The Formation of National Electorates and Party Systems in Europe*
John M. Carey, *Legislative Voting and Accountability*
Kanchan Chandra, *Why Ethnic Parties Succeed: Patronage and Ethnic Headcounts in India*
Eric C. C. Chang, Mark Andreas Kayser, Drew A. Linzer, and Ronald Rogowski, *Electoral Systems and the Balance of Consumer-Producer Power*
José Antonio Cheibub, *Presidentialism, Parliamentarism, and Democracy*
Ruth Berins Collier, *Paths toward Democracy: The Working Class and Elites in Western Europe and South America*
Daniel Corstange, *The Price of a Vote in the Middle East: Clientelism and Communal Politics in Lebanon and Yemen*
Pepper D. Culpepper, *Quiet Politics and Business Power: Corporate Control in Europe and Japan*
Sarah Zukerman Daly, *Organized Violence after Civil War: The Geography of Recruitment in Latin America*
Christian Davenport, *State Repression and the Domestic Democratic Peace*
Donatella della Porta, *Social Movements, Political Violence, and the State*